NEW BROADWAYS

NEW BROADWAYS

THEATRE ACROSS AMERICA:
APPROACHING A NEW MILLENNIUM

REVISED EDITION

GERALD M. BERKOWITZ

APPLAUSE
NEW YORK • LONDON

New Broadways
Theatre Across America: Approaching a New Millennium
by Gerald M. Berkowitz
Copyright © 1997 by Gerald M. Berkowitz

Library of Congress Cataloging-in-Publication Data

Berkowitz, Gerald M.
    New Broadways : theatre across America as the millennium
approaches / by Gerald Berkowitz.
        p.   cm.
    ISBN 1-55783-257-9 (pbk.)
    1. Theater--United States--History--20th century.
[PN2266.B49 1997]
792' . 0973'0904--dc21   97-37922
                                                              CIP

British Library Cataloging-in-Publication Data

    A catalog record for this book is available from the British Library

APPLAUSE BOOKS   A&C BLACK

211 West 71st Street   Howard Road, Eaton Socon
New York, NY 10023   Huntington, Cambs PE19 3EZ
Phone (212) 496-7511   Phone 0171-242 0946
Fax: (212) 721-2856   Fax 0171-831 8478

Distributed in the U.K. and European Union by A&C Black

Printed in Canada

CONTENTS

To My Parents

PREFACE

This is a wholly revised and expanded second edition of a book first published in 1982. The first edition covered only the years 1950–1980, and I have taken this opportunity not only to bring it up to date, but also to fill in some of the backstory and to make extensive changes in the judgments and analyses of the main body of the work, with the benefits of an additional fifteen years' perspective and the invaluable assistance of more than two dozen theatre professionals. The result is almost twice the length of the original, and I doubt whether there are two consecutive paragraphs anywhere in the book that remain unchanged.

Still, the focus of the book remains on the second half of the twentieth century, since that period saw revolutionary changes in the breadth, shape, and corporate and financial structure of the American theatre. As I said in the preface to the first edition, "This history, unlike many, has a plot — one of growth and change and liberation. If it doesn't have a happy ending, that's because the story isn't over; certainly things are happier when it stops than they were when it began."

The second half of the twentieth century saw two amazing changes in the face of the American theatre: its expansion to truly national proportions and its evolution from a purely commercial enterprise to, in many cases, an institutional status approaching those of museums and symphony orchestras. As is not always the case with such expansion and evolution, the process was accompanied by a flowering of creativity and vitality; on almost every possible scale the American theatre was healthier, more creative, and more appreciated as the millennium approached than it was in 1950. How, why, and with whom that happened is the subject of this book.

Any general survey must be selective, and my mode has been to focus on outstanding or representative illustrations of each development or stage in the history of the American theatre. To those whom I have omitted, and particularly to those whom I may inadvertently have misrepresented in attempting to fit them into the general picture, my apologies. For those readers looking for details and insights beyond the scope of this study, I have appended a bibliography and suggestions for further research.

I must thank the writers of all the books and articles I used in my research. I thank Northern Illinois University for granting me released time for research and writing. My gratitude to Jim Feather of Rowman and Littlefield, publisher of the first edition, and to Glenn Young and Len Fleischer of Applause Theatre Books, publisher of this wholly revised version, is based in equal parts on their faith in the project, their editorial counsel, and their wise taskmastering.

I am especially grateful to the many theatre and funding professionals quoted in the pages that follow for donating their time and wisdom to this volume. They include such current or former artistic directors of non-profit theatres as Andre Bishop (Lincoln Center Theatre), Gregory Boyd (Alley Theatre), Arvin Brown (Long Wharf Theatre), Bill Bushnell (Los Angeles Theatre Center), Robert Falls (Goodman Theatre), Jon Jory (Actors Theatre of Louisville), Woodie King (New Federal Theatre), Judith Malina (Living Theatre), Theodore Mann (Circle-in-the-Square), Julia Miles (The Women's Project), Gregory Mosher (Circle-in-the-Square, formerly Lincoln Center Theatre and the Goodman Theatre), Lloyd Richards (Yale Repertory Theatre and the Eugene O'Neill Theatre Center), Tim Sanford (Playwrights Horizons), and George White (Eugene O'Neill Theatre Center); from the managerial side of the non-profit theatre community: Bernard Gersten (Lincoln Center Theatre) and Barry Grove (Manhattan Theatre Club; commercial producers and theatre owners: Alexander H. Cohen, Eric Krebs, David Richenthal, and Ben Sprecher; from the funding community: Gigi Bolt (National Endowment for the Arts), Ben Cameron (Dayton Hudson Foundation), Ruth Mayleas (Ford Foundation and the National Endowment for the Arts), and Suzanne Sato (AT&T Foundation and The Rockefeller Foundation). Other theatre professionals include critic, playwright, and translator Michael Feingold, Arthur Gelb of *The New York Times*, Scott Steele (Executive Director, University Resident Theatre Association), theatre educator Howard Stein, and John Sullivan (Executive Director, Theatre Communications Group).

And I close with the same inadequate note as in the first edition: Alfred Weiss, my uncle, colleague, and friend, who has shared his love of theatre with me all my life, shared his knowledge and editorial skills just as unselfishly while I worked on this project. The book would be dedicated to him were there not two people with a prior claim.

Times Square

1

THE BACKSTORY:
THE AMERICAN THEATRE TO 1950

The city of New York has five subdivisions called boroughs, of which the most famous is Manhattan, an island near the mouth of the Hudson River, about fourteen miles long and two miles across. Except for the southern tip, which is old New Amsterdam and has the winding streets of a European city, Manhattan is laid out on a grid, with numbered streets going east and west, and numbered avenues north and south. The notable exception is Broadway, which cuts across the grid on a rough diagonal from southeast to northwest. Broadway crosses Seventh Avenue at Forty-fifth Street, and the lopsided-hourglass-shaped plaza thus formed, extending from Forty-third to Forty-seventh, is Times Square. On the streets off Times Square are about thirty theatres, most built in the first quarter of the twentieth century, with conventional proscenium stages and an average capacity of about twelve hundred.

And that, for half of the twentieth century, was the American theatre.

☆

That is an oversimplification, of course, but not a misleading one. For almost fifty years, theatre outside New York — indeed, outside that square mile of Manhattan — consisted essentially of amateur and student groups, road companies, summer stock revivals of Broadway hits, and, in a narrow corridor of northeastern cities, pre-Broadway tryouts. The vital center of the American theatre, the source of its dramatic literature and its acting and production styles, and the home (or goal) of its most talented actors, directors, composers, and designers was Broadway.

It had not always been thus. This extreme centralization was in fact a fairly recent development in the history of a broadly national American theatre. The first record of European-style theatre on the American continent is in Mexico in 1538, a series of religious plays performed on Corpus Christi Day. Spanish missionaries in Florida put on a religious play in 1567, and there were other Spanish plays performed in what is now Texas before the end of the sixteenth century. In the British colonies there is record of a play being produced in Virginia in 1665, and of theatres being built in several cities in the early years of the next century. A professional British actor appeared in South Carolina in 1703, and by 1749 an American company began performing Shakespeare and other plays in Philadelphia, Annapolis, and other cities.

Generally, the Cavalier South was more receptive to the theatre than Puritan New England or Quaker Pennsylvania, and the first sustained theatre company, a British group led by Lewis Hallam in 1752, made the southern colonies the base of their tours and later their residencies.

> By 1774 they had built or renovated playhouses in New York, Philadelphia, Williamsburg, Annapolis, and Charleston; they had developed and presented a diverse and popular repertory, comparable to what would have been presented in the best English provincial houses, and they had established an audience capable of sustaining them. It remained for the next generation to develop native talent. [Mahard 9]

The first play written by an American may have been Thomas Godfrey's *The Prince of Parthia*, a verse tragedy written around 1760 and first staged in Philadelphia, by an American company, in 1767. Professional theatrical activity was interrupted by the Revolutionary War, when the Continental Congress forbade theatricals and other frivolity, though amateur productions by soldiers and officers on both sides helped fill idle hours; there were even plays performed by Washington's men during the winter at Valley Forge. Professional activity returned after Independence; and by the 1790s theatres had been built in Boston, Washington, Philadelphia, Providence, Baltimore, Annapolis, and Charleston. Acting companies led by Thomas Wignell (Philadelphia), Thomas Wade West and John Bignall (Charleston), John Hodgkinson (Boston), William Dunlop (New York), and others were quickly established.

Having overcome its Quaker scruples, Philadelphia soon became the artistic capital of the country (as it would remain until New York seized the title late in the nineteenth century). But, in addition to the theatrical centers already mentioned, secondary companies operated in or regularly visited New Orleans, Cincinnati, Pittsburgh, and almost every other big or medium-sized city. By the 1820s America was a sufficiently large theatrical market to attract such British stars as Edmund Kean, Junius Brutus Booth, and Laura Keene to profitable tours, and to create its own stars: Edwin Forrest and later Edwin Booth, Charlotte Cushman, Joseph Jefferson III, James O'Neill, and others.

With growth came popularization, as Mahard notes: "Where the colonial theatre had been enjoyed primarily by an elite group of prosperous, well-connected citizens, after the Revolution the theatre was embraced by a broad cross section of the American public" [Mahard 9]. The geographical expansion of the country in the nineteenth century brought an expansion of the American theatre, with the "opera house" ranking just behind the schoolhouse, church, jail, and saloon as a construction priority in every new western town with any pretension to culture. By the middle of the century every large city and many smaller ones had resident professional stock companies, and new plays were as likely to be produced in, say, San Francisco, Chicago, or St. Louis as in New York. Big stars, British and American, could tour the entire country, performing with local companies which had rehearsed around them. By the 1890s there were as many as five thousand theatres in the United States, spread out over almost that many cities, and about two thousand resident acting companies.

But with popularization also came a change in literary content. The Colonial dramatic repertoire was at first dominated by the classics, with Shakespeare almost inevitably the most-produced playwright. Some of the earliest American plays were written in clear imitation of Shakespeare, large- or small-scale blank verse tragedies like Godfrey's *The Prince of Parthia* and George Henry Boker's *Francesca da Rimini* (1855). Many of these represented conscious attempts to give legitimacy and majesty to the experience of the new country by translating history — John Daly Burk's *Bunker Hill* (1797), William Dunlop's *André* (1798) — and myth — George Washington Parke Custis' *Pocahontas* (1830) — into the materials of pseudo-Shakespearean tragedy.

As Witham notes, however, "the American theatre was created and sustained by a tension between what was perceived as 'commerce' and what was 'art'" [2]. David Rinear adds,

> But the business of the American theatre impeded the development of a significant and uniquely American dramatic literature. As was the case in England, serious persons of letters wrote for the page, not for the stage ... The business of dramatic writing fell to professional theatre folk. [69–70]

These critics are a bit unfair in their criticism of nineteenth-century American drama; as Rinear acknowledges, Britain was also living through a fallow period for dramatic literature of high literary quality, and a variety of historical and sociological forces were at work, not just the questionable taste of the broad American public.

The vitality of the popular theatre in the first fifty years after independence can be seen in stage comedy, which quickly found its natural subject in Royall Tyler's *The Contrast* (1787), which told with delighted irony of the triumph of the seemingly unsophisticated Yankee (replaced by later writers with the farmer, backwoodsman, etc.) over the disdainful but ultimately outfoxed British (Bostonians, city slickers, etc.). The many successful variants on the theme include Samuel Wentworth's *The Forest Rose* (1825) and J. K. Paulding's *The Lion of the West* (1830); and the synergy of page and stage is evidenced by the fact that many of these comedies were written by or for actors who specialized in stock comic figures: the Yankee characters of James Hackett and George Handel Hill, the frontiersmen of Hackett and Danforth Marble, the street-smart Bowery boy of Frank S. Chanfrau.

Still, it is true that it is difficult for a broadly popular entertainment form to retain very high artistic ambitions; and the expansive growth and success of the American theatre during the nineteenth century almost inevitably led to a coarsening of product. Few of the plays mentioned, or of the hundreds of others written during the century, had much purely literary merit, though many were technically adept theatre pieces and audience-pleasers. As *Contrast*-type comedies and pseudo-Shakespearean tragedies continued to be written and produced, two other broad strands developed.

One was the large-scale swashbuckling costume drama like Steele MacKaye's *Paul Kauver* (1887) and Charles Fechter's *Count of Monte Cristo* (1868), which was so popular that James O'Neill later toured continuously with it, playing no other role for more than twenty years. The other was the more domestic melodrama with clearly defined heroes, villains, and damsels-in-distress. The genre is probably best known in its somewhat degenerated form in early silent movies, but it had an undeniable theatrical vitality; George Aiken's dramatization of *Uncle Tom's Cabin* (1852) held the stage for fifty years, with as many as four hundred simultaneous productions around the country. Only at the very end of the nineteenth century would there be the first signs of renewed artistic and literary ambition in the American drama.

While some of the thousands of theatres across America by the end of the nineteenth century may have been modest structures, and some of the local acting companies barely professional, many were elaborate constructions that were home to artists doing ambitious work. The second half of the nineteenth century was the golden age of the proscenium theatre, as producers and designers in Europe as well as America strove to create awe-inspiringly realistic stage tableaux and effects. Playwright-director Steele MacKaye and producer David Belasco, among others, put real trees, real animals and casts of hundreds on their stages, and actors like Edwin Booth, Joseph Jefferson, Ada Rehan, and James O'Neill helped create an American style of acting.

No single event caused the collapse of all these theatres, but the growing importance of New York as a producing center was an important factor. Many companies depended on the occasional visits of touring stars for income, which meant that repertoires began to be determined by the plays those actors were willing to perform. Typically, a star such as Edwin Booth would book a tour to act in the same one or two plays everywhere; local companies would rehearse each play with a hole in the middle for the visitor; and then he would have a quick run-through before the performance to make sure they did it his way. To the extent that stars wanted to tour in a play they had been successful with in New York, the New York repertoire began to dominate the road, or at least to be perceived as carrying a certain glamour.

As the practice of repertory booking — that is, a different play each night — gradually gave way during the nineteenth century to long runs of single plays, the phenomenon of the Broadway hit was created, and plays bearing the glory of New York success became more attractive to regional audiences than locally-produced new works. With the spread of the railroads in the last quarter of the century, New York-based entrepreneurs discovered that it cost very little more — and was much more profitable — to send a complete cast on tour, rather than just one or two leading actors, and the local companies, deprived of their guest stars, had trouble competing. Indeed, for many producers a New York run was merely a tryout for the far more lucrative tour, the brief prerequisite for being able to advertise a show as "Direct from Broadway."

The late nineteenth century was the era of monopolies and trusts in American business, and in 1896 the biggest New York and Philadelphia producers, led by Charles Frohman, Marc Klaw, and Abraham Erlanger, combined forces to buy or build theatres across the country and to force exclusive contracts on other theatre-owners, so they could produce their own shows and then organize the tours and play in their own houses. (Similar combinations around the same time monopolized control of vaudeville and burlesque, and helped to hasten the death of those entertainment forms.) The primary purpose of The Syndicate, as it was commonly called, was to block out competing producers and booking agents. But in the process the monopolists also effectively stole the audiences of many local resident companies and drove them out of business. So, even though The Syndicate's monopolistic hold did not last long, its effects were extensive.

What damage was left undone by The Syndicate's success was continued by its collapse; its hold was broken by a competing New York-based tour-producing firm, the Shubert Brothers, who then spent the first third of the twentieth century buying or building theatres in every large city to house Shubert productions, and thus ironically continued the process of destroying local competition. (A federal antitrust suit in the 1950s forced the Shubert Organization to sell most of its theatres outside New York and to concentrate on Broadway ownership and producing.) The advent of motion pictures struck the final blow to the local stock companies, as it did to vaudeville. Increasingly in the new century, and by 1920 at the latest, American theatre meant New York theatre, and New York theatre meant Broadway.

Broadway itself had changed and grown during this period. The history of New York City is the story of slow expansion northward from the southern tip of Manhattan; as late as the mid-nineteenth century it hadn't gotten much beyond Fourteenth Street, and it did not reach anything resembling its present extent until the end of the century. At any given stage the outskirts of town were the most desirable areas, where the rich built their mansions, and so the social and artistic center of the city generally moved with the leading edge of expansion.

The earliest New York theatres, built in the 1730s, were at the edge of New Amsterdam, in what is now the Wall Street area; George Washington attended performances at the John Street Theatre in 1789. By the turn of the century the Bowery (the beginning of the main road to Boston) was the most fashionable street in the city; and the construction of the Park Theatre in 1798 helped move New York's theatrical center northward. In 1849 competing productions of *Macbeth* by the American star Edwin Forrest at the Bowery Theatre and the British William Charles Macready at the nearby Astor Place Opera House led to an infamous riot as patriotic Forrest supporters attacked the Astor Place, resulting in twenty-two deaths. But fashion and the city were already moving on, and the Bowery area was soon left behind. (By the early twentieth century, the former artistic and social center had become New York's Skid Row.)

In part simply because it was an important north-south thorough-fare, Broadway became the spine of the northward expansion of the city, and the rest of the nineteenth century watched theatres being built along Broadway, used for a few years, and then abandoned as replacements were built a half-mile or a mile further north. The fact that Broadway's diagonal path produced plazas every ten blocks or so created convenient focal points for the new social and artistic centers: Union Square, just north of Fourteenth Street; Madison Square, in the Twenties; Herald Square, in the Thirties.

Producer Oscar Hammerstein (father of the lyricist) finally crossed Forty-second Street in 1895, building the Olympia Theatre at Broadway and Forty-fourth Street on what was then called Longacre Square. Within the next twenty years new headquarters for *The New York Times* (with the resulting change in the name of the Square) and the construction of the nearby New York Public Library and Grand Central Station would help establish Forty-second Street and Times Square as the new cultural center. More than eighty theatres were built in the area in the first thirty years of the twentieth century; and Forty-second Street was host to such performers as George M. Cohan, Houdini, Fred Astaire, the Marx Brothers, and the many stars of the *Ziegfeld Follies*.

Movement continued at a slower pace in the twentieth century. The somewhat overbuilt theatre district gradually contracted, with most of the outlying theatres being abandoned to film, broadcasting, or new construction, leaving a core of about thirty theatres within a block or two of Times Square. One last lurch northward left Forty-second Street, the original center of the area, behind; Forty-second's theatres converted to movie houses and the street became the city's new Skid Row. (The construction in the 1960s of Lincoln Center for the Performing Arts twenty blocks further north can be seen as the natural next step in the northward progression, except that "Broadway" hasn't followed it, and seems anchored in the Times Square area.)

So professional, new-play-producing theatres across the continent died out or were forced out of business; and the professional, new-play-producing theatre of New York City was concentrated in a single cluster of buildings and a small artistic community. Unlike the similar centralization of the motion picture industry in Hollywood, the Broadway monopoly severely limited the opportunity for audiences around the country to see first-class theatrical productions. A film could play simultaneously in hundreds of theatres, with every audience getting essentially the same experience and the same quality entertainment. But when even major cities such as Chicago and Los Angeles had to rely on the brief visits of New York-based road companies and the modest offerings of local amateur groups, the experience of seeing the best theatre America had to offer was limited for decades to those lucky enough to live in or visit New York City.

And the theatre itself suffered. Talented and ambitious actors, directors, and designers were drawn to Broadway, where the inevitably fierce competition meant that many would never get their chance; and there was no alternative arena, particularly for those wishing to do experimental or innovative work. The odds were even worse for young dramatists, since Broadway was the source of virtually all the new plays produced in the country. (I must repeat my *caveat* that the situation was not as absolutely bleak as these generalizations suggest, but the few exceptions, such as the active semi-professional community theatres in Cleveland and Pasadena, did not significantly affect the overall picture.)

On the other hand, the concentration of theatrical activity in New York for five decades had some salutary effects. It allowed the twentieth-century American theatre and drama to develop a unity and identity that could not otherwise have appeared. By choice, inertia, inbreeding, or historical accident, there developed by 1950 a distinctly American style in drama, acting, and production.

The artistically serious American drama was really born along with Broadway — that is to say, around the turn of the twentieth century. Drama historians frequently cite James A. Herne's *Margaret Fleming* (1890) as the first serious twentieth-century-style drama, though it is for the most part a rather conventional nineteenth-century melodrama with only a few notably "modern" touches: like several other plays of the period it uses its sensationalistic story as a vehicle for at least touching on contemporary social issues (in this case, the double standard and the moral obligations of the rich); unlike most other plays of the period it does not find easy solutions to its problems, and is thus likely to leave its audience troubled rather than placated. Some of the early plays of Rachel Crothers, such as *A Man's World* (1910), also about gender roles and the double standard, have the same quality of striving to be About Something and not just idle entertainments.

But the real birth (or rebirth) of serious, artistically ambitious drama in America came a little later, when the plays of Ibsen, Chekhov, and Shaw finally reached America and inspired a generation of young writers to consider the theatre as a vehicle for serious art. To the extent that they were breaking with the American theatrical past these new writers found themselves exploring new forms as well as new subjects; and from the 1910s to the 1930s, American plays were marked by a variety of experiments in style.

Leader of this movement, both in precedence and in quality, was Eugene O'Neill, America's first truly great playwright. Unlike some of his predecessors, theatrical writers who discovered along the way that they might have something to say, O'Neill clearly was driven primarily by his artistic vision and ambition. Despite a lifelong suspicion of the theatre's capacity for depth and seriousness — O'Neill's father had been a star of the late nineteenth-century theatre, leaving the son with little respect for the inherited melodramatic forms — he turned to the drama to express an essentially tragic view of the limitations built into the human condition, a set of dark insights into individual psychology and marital and family relationships, and a complex and overlapping array of metaphysical explanations for his insights, drawn from a mix of Nietzsche, Freud, and Catholicism.

Determined to make the theatre capable of carrying the new weight of his artistic vision and philosophical concerns, O'Neill constantly stretched its boundaries and tested his audience's capacity; it is only a slight exaggeration to say that for the first twenty years of his career he never wrote two plays in the same style: expressionism (*The Emperor Jones*, 1920), naturalism (*Desire Under the Elms*, 1924), myth (*The Fountain*, 1925), masks (*The Great God Brown*, 1926), spoken thoughts (*Strange Interlude*, 1928), epic (*Marco Millions*, 1928), Greek-style tragedy (*Mourning Becomes Electra*, 1931), and various permutations and combinations of these and other modes.

The recurring theme of O'Neill's plays throughout this period is limitation. In *The Emperor Jones* the central figure cannot escape his personal and racial memories; in *The Hairy Ape* (1922) a laborer learns how irrelevant he is to the world at large. *Desire Under the Elms* shows three people fighting for possession of a barren New England farm but destroyed by their own obsessions; *Lazarus Laughed* (1928) calls for epic length and a cast of hundreds to dramatize humanity's inability to accept a gospel of life and joy. In *Strange Interlude* a determined woman uses all her energies to control the men and the world around her, only to admit defeat in the end; and *Mourning Becomes Electra* transforms Aeschylus' *Oresteia* into the saga of a curse-haunted American family. While some of these plays have become staples of the classroom (if not always of the stage), O'Neill's own frustration is evident in the rejection of each mode as quickly as he adopted it.

Other dramatists of the 1920s and 1930s also experimented with nontraditional forms: Elmer Rice (*The Adding Machine*, 1923) and Sophie Treadwell (*Machinal*, 1928) with expressionism, Maxwell Anderson (*Elizabeth the Queen*, 1930, and others) with Shakespearean-style verse tragedy, Thornton Wilder (*Our Town*, 1938) with bare staging and violations of space and time. Some of the key plays of the American repertoire came out of these explorations — *Our Town* in particular, with its deceptively simple story of life and death in rural America and its insistence that the audience contribute its imaginative powers to the creation of its reality, is that rare thing: a great work that is also broadly accessible. But none of the alternative styles proved sustainable beyond one or two works. Though experiments continued, American drama in the first few decades of the century was still searching for its true voice.

This is certainly one area in which the Broadway monopoly directly affected the nature of the drama. The fact that these experiments were taking place within a small and localized artistic community (O'Neill actually began his career in one of the amateur Little Theatres of the late 1910s, but quickly moved to Broadway) meant that every active American dramatist in the first half of the century was very much aware of the work of his or her contemporaries, and able to learn from their successes and failures. There were no self-styled "schools" or "movements" in American drama, as there were in some European cultures. There were individual playwrights trying to write effective plays and occasionally stumbling on something that worked, in a context that allowed other writers to become instantly aware of the new discoveries and to build on them.

It was this informal trial-and-error process that led to the appearance, in the 1930s and 1940s, of what was to be the dominant twentieth-century American dramatic form. A trigger for that development was the Great Depression of the 1930s. Attempting to explain the American experience to Americans, social dramatists experimented with plays of epic scope, such as Elmer Rice's *We, the People* (1933). But they quickly found that they could best express their analyses of economic and political forces indirectly, by dramatizing the effects of such forces on the day-to-day lives of ordinary people. Sidney Kingsley's *Dead End* (1935) shows a cross-section of a city neighborhood and quietly watches every facet of life — childhood, young love, ambition, crime and death —

affected by the Depression. Clifford Odets' *Awake and Sing!* (1935) shows the day-to-day domestic events within an ordinary family and, hardly mentioning larger economic and social forces, makes their presence felt.

The important discovery in these and other plays of the period was not just that the broader national experience could be dramatized through a domestic story, but that the true story *was* the domestic one. The story that audiences could respond to, the story that they wanted to be told, was how larger issues affected their everyday lives. And the American drama found its natural voice in the mode that could tell this story: realistic, domestic, contemporary, middle-class melodrama — plays about home, work, love and marriage, family relations, and the like, that reflected the world outside that setting or the psychological, philosophical, or metaphysical truths underlying that setting, without ever straying far from the intimate domestic stories at their core.

The process of discovery is encapsulated in microcosm in the career of Eugene O'Neill: after trying virtually every imaginable dramatic style, O'Neill returned in his great final masterpieces to the domestic setting and realistic mode, finding metaphors for his deepest metaphysical and psychological explorations in family quarrels and barroom dreams. And two writers who appeared in the 1940s, by exploring and developing the potential of this style to its fullest, dominated and defined the serious American drama at mid-century.

Arthur Miller and Tennessee Williams had strikingly parallel early careers. Both were of the generation that came of age in the Depression, an experience that shook the security of their middle-class families. Both began writing in college, experimenting with fiction and poetry as well as drama. After a false start — Miller's first Broadway play (*The Man Who Had All the Luck*, 1944) closed after four performances and Williams's (*Battle of Angels*, 1940) withered in its pre-Broadway tryout — each entered the scene with an award-winning play and followed up with a truly major work, unquestionably the best play of his entire career. And though both toyed with elements of expressionism, their plays were rooted in realistic domestic drama. The differences between the two mark the bounds of the mainstream American drama of mid-century.

Philosophically, Arthur Miller was the artistic heir of Ibsen and, more directly, of Odets and the socialist writers of the 1930s; he shared with them the impulse toward social criticism and the need to write plays that were overtly About Something, with his characters clearly representatives of larger forces or issues. But, as Harold Clurman notes, "while many dramatists of that period were bent on recording the shock of opposing forces — capital and labor, democracy and fascism, etc. — Miller examines the individual in his moral behavior under specific social pressures" [xiv]. His criticism was always personal and specific, not theoretical; his recurring subject was the manner in which individual crises and tragedies pointed up injustices in the state, the society or even the universe.

In Miller's first success, *All My Sons* (1947), an ordinary American is faced with a moral issue that would not have been out of place in a Shakespearean tragedy, the conflict between his personal values and his larger social responsibility. A munitions manufacturer sold the military some defective airplane parts because withholding them would mean failing in what he has been taught is his primary obligation, supporting his family. The events of the play force him to recognize the conflicting moral imperative implied by the title: the fliers who died in his planes were also his responsibility.

If the larger themes of *All My Sons* are sometimes awkwardly grafted onto the personal domestic situation — the actual plot centers on a romance between the manufacturer's son and the daughter of a man he ruined — the play illustrates the three assumptions that characterize all of Miller's work: that the values or roles taught by society can be actively harmful in practice, that large moral issues are reflected in the lives of ordinary people, and that therefore the Common Man (Miller's phrase) can be shown dramatically to experience crises of heroic and even tragic proportions.

Death of a Salesman (1949), considered by many to be the archetypal American play, is written in the same mold. Its plot is deceptively ordinary: Willy Loman, an aging salesman, loses his job and, he thinks, the respect of his family. Unable to bear the sense of failure and committed to the faith that his sons can still succeed, he kills himself to give them his insurance money. While guiding the audience to a sympathetic identification with Willy's pain and despair, Miller also generates moral outrage through the realization that Willy's failure comes from too simple and blind a faith in the American Dream. Convinced by his culture that financial success is available to everyone, Willy is confused and condemned by failure and reduced to thinking himself worth more dead than alive.

Miller makes us see, and allows Willy's elder son to sense, that there are other definitions of success by which Willy might have defined himself — self-fulfillment, the love of family and friends — and that the

Photo: Inge Morath/Magnum

Photo: I

Arthur Miller   **Tennessee Williams**

great evil lurking in the American Dream is not just that it does not always deliver what it promises, but that it controls its adherents' perceptions so they must blame themselves for its failures. Typically, Miller points an accusing finger at a social or cultural force that dooms an honorable man, while celebrating the majesty of the Common Man by showing that the largest issues and emotions are within the scope of his experience.

If Miller belonged to a dramatic school extending at least as far back as Ibsen, Tennessee Williams had less in common with any previous playwrights than with that school of southern gothic novelists that found in extreme and even bizarre circumstances some insights into the mysteries of ordinary human emotions. He also brought a poet's sensibility to the theatre more fully and successfully than any other American writer, combining a mastery of lush and expressive language with a delight in overt and evocative symbolism. While Miller's attention was drawn outward to social issues, Williams looked inward to understand the psychological and emotional burdens of his characters. And while Miller celebrated the unappreciated nobility of the common man, Williams sought to expand our definition of humanity by showing how much we shared with the cripples and freaks of the world; as Harold Clurman realized, this is "the essential trait of his work: identification with and compassion for victims of our society . . . He doubts that they will ever achieve a state of grace [but] there is the abiding hope of understanding" [xvii-xviii].

Williams's first success, *The Glass Menagerie* (1944), is the story of an emotionally crippled family inhabiting a private world set in but apart from the realities of Depression America. The mother hides from the present in memories of her past as a southern coquette; the daughter uses extreme shyness and a limp as excuses to retreat from the world into her collection of glass animals; and the son dreams of poetry and adventure while straining to escape both the sterility of the home and the drudgery of a factory job. The plot, centering on an attempt to recruit a gentleman caller for the daughter, is just an excuse for an exploration and appreciation of the beautiful fragility of these characters, ill-equipped to deal with harsh reality but fortunate enough to inhabit a safe private world of their own.

Any list of the greatest American plays would have the same three at the very top, in some order: Eugene O'Neill's *Long Day's Journey into Night*, Miller's *Death of a Salesman* and Williams's *A Streetcar Named Desire* (1947). Far more violent and passion-filled than the elegiac *Glass Menagerie*, *Streetcar* traces the mental and emotional destruction of the faded beauty Blanche Dubois in a world ruled by the crude sexual energy and practicality represented by Stanley Kowalski. Committed to values of culture and idealism but unable to live up to their demands herself, Blanche searches for allies and protectors.

It is a mark of Williams's courage and honesty that, although his sympathies are obviously with Blanche, he not only accepts her destruction at the hands of her brother-in-law but justifies it, by showing that the demands of her beautiful culture are ultimately life-denying while Stanley's uncouth sexuality is life-giving and supportive. In a world as insecure and uncertain as the one we inhabit, says the play, anything that weakens, however beautiful it is, must be regretfully rejected; anything that offers strength, however un-beautiful, must be embraced with gratitude. Through Williams's mastery of language and symbol the clash between the two (which in plot terms amounts to little more than the antagonism of in-laws) achieves mythic scope, the confrontation of a beautiful and noble but enervated civilization and the raw energy of the survival instinct. Not incidentally, it also provides two of the most vibrant characters and challenging acting roles in all of world drama.

Towering over Williams and Miller is Eugene O'Neill, but his position in the mid-century American drama is a strange one. Although his final plays are now recognized as his masterpieces, they were either unknown or unappreciated then. Sick and embittered, O'Neill had withdrawn from the world, and his two plays produced during the 1940s, *The Iceman Cometh* (1946) and *A Moon for the Misbegotten* (1947), were both critically and commercially unsuccessful. It would take another ten years, and his death, for him to be rediscovered, making the posthumous O'Neill more a playwright of the 1950s and 1960s. It was Williams and Miller who defined the serious American drama at mid-century; the pamphleteer of social issues and the poet of loneliness and fear were poles of a continuum on which most other dramatists of the late 1940s lay.

Among the already established writers, Lillian Hellman continued her practice of translating public issues into matters of private morality, begun with such plays as *The Children's Hour* (1934) and *The Little Foxes* (1939), with *Another Part of the Forest* (1946) and an adaptation of Robles's *Montserrat* (1949). Sidney Kingsley's *Detective Story* (1949) presented a frightened man trying to cope with a world that wasn't as ordered as he thought, while Clifford Odets's *The Country Girl* (1950) dissected the psychology and power politics of an apparently doomed marriage.

Few younger writers of the postwar period suggested major status. Arthur Laurents's *Home of the Brave* (1945) was a study of the psychological effects of anti-Semitism that put him alongside Miller in the socially conscious tradition of Odets and Kingsley, while William Inge's *Come Back, Little Sheba* (1950), like his later plays, presented little people who achieved some sort of happiness only by accepting their limitations; though considerably more sentimental than Williams, he shared his commitment to offering hope for emotional survival in a frightening world.

American comedy, always a staple of the Broadway theatre, shared the serious drama's interest in the present and familiar, but needed no period of experiment to find that focus. While eighteenth and nineteenth-century comedies rarely strayed far from the unsophisticated-Yankee-outwits-the-city-slicker model, twentieth-century Broadway comedy found its voice as early as Langdon Mitchell's *The New York Idea* (1906), about the romantic adventures of a sophisticated couple. There would be little beyond topical references to identify the date of most stage comedies for the next fifty years: the plays of Philip Barry might be a little more sophisticated than most, those of S. N. Behrman a little deeper, those of Booth Tarkington a little more folksy, but the spectrum was not a wide one.

The setting of a Broadway comedy was generally contemporary America, more often than not the upper middle-class New York of the majority of the audience; the subject was generally romance; the humor was generally that of situation and jokes, rather than physical farce or pure wit; and the plays were generally forgettable. The most successful Broadway comedy of the 1940s was actually a holdover from the previous decade: Howard Lindsay and Russel Crouse's adaptation of Clarence Day's *Life With Father* (1939), the adventures of an unusual nineteenth-century family. Mary Ellen Chase's *Harvey* (1944), Garson Kanin's *Born Yesterday* (1946), and Norman Krasna's *John Loves Mary* (1947) were popular, and Joshua Logan and Thomas Heggen's *Mister Roberts* (1948) held enough sincere affection for its characters to give its string of wartime hi-jinks an emotional core.

There was also a third branch of the American drama. The Broadway musical ranks close behind jazz and modern dance as one of America's original contributions to world culture, and it was approaching its zenith at mid-century. Theatre historians can trace the form back to *The Black Crook*, an 1866 melodrama by Charles M. Barras with songs and dances added by producer William Wheatley to make use of a dance troupe he had under contract. But the modern musical comedy is really a twentieth-century development. Its immediate ancestor was the lavish, waltz-filled, Viennese costume operetta of the late nineteenth century, and many in the first generation of twentieth-century Broadway composers were European born (Rudolf Friml, Victor Herbert, Sigmund Romberg) or trained (Jerome Kern). The special American flavor came from the theatre's lively and vulgar cousin, vaudeville, particularly as filtered through the talent and sensibility of writer-composer-performer-producer George M. Cohan in the first decade of the century. As Cecil Smith explains,

> Cohan's musical comedies introduced a wholly new conception of delivery, tempo, and subject matter into a form of entertainment that was rapidly dying for want of new ideas of any kind. Brushing aside the artificial elegances and the formal developments of the musical comedies based on English and German models, he reproduced successfully the hardness, the compensating sentimentality, the impulsive vulgarity, and the swift movement of New York life, which, except for surface sophistications, has not changed much between then and now. [151]

The third significant ingredient in the development of the musical was the instinct for spectacle of producer Florenz Ziegfeld, Jr., whose annual editions of the *Follies* between 1909 and 1927 developed an audience taste for big stars, pretty girls, and lavish productions. Between 1900 and 1920 these elements blended into something new — a light and spirited entertainment built on a flimsy, usually romantic plot and interrupted as often as possible by songs ranging from ballads to elaborate production numbers. Cecil Smith quotes an unsigned 1907 *Dramatic Mirror* review whose cynical appraisal could just as easily have been written twenty or even thirty years later:

> *Fascinating Flora* is just another musical comedy built along the same lines as scores of its predecessors. Nothing but the expected happens: choruses sing, dance, stand in line, smile, wear colored clothes; principals get into trouble and out of it, burst into song at intervals commensurate with their importance, make jokes about New York, do specialties of more or less cleverness; the curtain falls to divide the evening into two parts; the orchestra plays the air that the promoter hopes will be popular. The whole thing is done according to formula as accurately as a prescription is compounded in a drug store. And the audience . . . is pleased. [129]

The relative importance of story and songs in these shows is reflected in the convention, still prevalent, of crediting a musical to its songwriters even when the "book" is strong; one thinks of Leonard Bernstein's *West Side Story*, not Arthur Laurents' (or Shakespeare's), Rodgers and Hammerstein's *The Sound of Music*, not Lindsay and Crouse's. The importance of the music makes it extraordinarily fortunate that the most talented composers and lyricists were drawn to this form, and a list of Broadway musical collaborators from 1920 to 1950 is a pantheon of American popular music: Irving Berlin, Jerome Kern, George and Ira Gershwin, Cole Porter, Richard Rodgers, Lorenz Hart, Oscar Hammerstein, and so on.

The development of the musical was another positive product of the Broadway monopoly. It required a pool of talented performers and experienced producers, and the cross-fertilization of writers who could learn from and be challenged by each other. Moreover, as Smith suggested in his comment on George M. Cohan, in some only vaguely explainable way the musical seemed to be the product of the New York City sensibility; despite some notable exceptions (e.g., Cole Porter from Indiana) the majority of significant Broadway composers and lyricists after 1920 were born and raised in New York. (Another curious fact, that the overwhelming majority — again with occasional exceptions such as Porter — were Jewish, can be explained in part by the fact that, for various reasons, New York's Jewish population made up a disproportionately large part of the Broadway audience, so that Broadway was a significant part of its culture.) Until an unprecedentedly successful British invasion late in the century, attempts at the musical form by artists from other parts of the country or other countries generally lacked the special spark of the Broadway product.

Fortunately the Broadway product was exportable, and not only became a popular representative of American theatre abroad, but also was the most accessible theatre to the majority of Americans. A hit musical might have two or three touring companies crossing the country during or after its Broadway run, making it the only experience of live professional theatre available in many places. Because of the talented composers and lyricists, and the glamour popularly associated with Broadway, theatre songs dominated American popular music until the advent of rock and roll, with show tunes becoming national hits even though the majority of radio listeners or record buyers would never get a chance to see the play itself. As late as 1956, songs from *My Fair Lady* were recorded by dozens of popular singers, and more than twice as many people bought the original cast recording in the first year than could possibly have seen the show.

Photo: Rodgers and Hammerstein Collection

Richard Rodgers and Oscar Hammerstein

Oklahoma

The history of the musical from the 1920s to the 1950s is one of a gradual maturity in form and content, marked by an increasing inclination to break away from the formulas and conventions described in the 1907 *Fascinating Flora* review, and by attempts to deal with more serious subjects and complex characterizations. Kern and Hammerstein's *Show Boat* (1927), Rodgers and Hart's *Pal Joey* (1940), and Weill and Gershwin's *Lady in the Dark* (1941) were significant steps in this progress, but Rodgers and Hammerstein's *Oklahoma!* (1943) is generally considered the key landmark in the development of the genre. More than any of their predecessors Rodgers and Hammerstein succeeded in integrating the musical and nonmusical parts of the play, particularly through the use of "book songs" that took the place of spoken dialogue rather than just interrupting it, and through the introduction of dance sequences (choreographed by Agnes De Mille) that helped to develop plot or establish character rather than being self-justifying spectacle. Combined with a story that was a little darker than most and that had no place for some of the stultifying conventions of earlier musicals (the obligatory opening production number, the chorus line, etc.), these innovations produced something recognizably different from what had come before; and critics began to reach for new labels—the mature musical, the integrated musical, the musical play—to describe the new genre.

The success of *Oklahoma!* led to many imitations in the next decade, some of them purely mechanical—for a period in the mid-1940s the insertion of a dream ballet in a musical comedy became as arbitrary and conventional a device as anything in *Fascinating Flora*—and some of them honorable attempts to explore and develop the possibilities of this new type of musical. Thus, just as Williams and Miller defined between them the serious American drama of 1950, Richard Rodgers and Oscar Hammerstein II dominated the American musical theatre. After their first collaboration on *Oklahoma!* the two produced *Carousel* (1945), the unsuccessful *Allegro* (1947), and *South Pacific* (1949); in the process they not only set very high standards for their competition to match, but also firmly established their style of musical—fully integrated in form, romantic but solidly dramatic in plot, entertaining but also inspirational in tone—as the norm.

Other successful musicals in the same spirit were Burton Lane and E. Y. Harburg's *Finian's Rainbow* (1947), in which an Irish leprechaun battled racial prejudice in the American South, and Alan Jay Lerner and Frederick Loewe's *Brigadoon* (1947), about an enchanted Scottish village that offered refuge to a man torn by the pressures of modern America. Cole Porter's characteristic mask of world-weary cynicism may have been more in tune with the 1930s than with the postwar years, but his *Kiss Me, Kate* (1948) employed musical integration with a vengeance, with songs appropriate both to Shakespeare's *The Taming of the Shrew* and the backstage adventures of its actors. And if Irving Berlin's *Annie Get Your Gun* (1946) and Frank Loesser's *Guys and Dolls* (1950) were more elementary and old-fashioned in their construction, they just proved that the conventional musical comedy was still a vital genre, especially when a score included "There's No Business Like Show Business" or "Sit Down, You're Rocking the Boat."

☆

As the American drama found its natural voice in realistic domestic melodrama, the American theatre found its natural style in a distinctively realistic mode of acting and production. The American style of acting, which has had a profound effect on world theatre and which symbiotically reinforced the native drama in its growth, is a special offshoot of the revolution begun by the Russian director Konstantin

Stanislavski at the end of the nineteenth century. Stanislavski's ideas were brought to America and transmuted into their American forms through several parallel channels. The Yiddish theatre movement in New York City, which flourished in the first twenty years of the century, was patterned after and strongly influenced by Stanislavski's Moscow Art Theatre, and it in turn influenced many American actors and directors. Stanislavski veterans Maria Ouspenskaya and Richard Boleslavsky taught his methods at the American Laboratory Theatre in New York in the 1920s. The Moscow Art Theatre itself first played in New York in 1923, and Stanislavski's *An Actor Prepares* was translated into English in 1936.

The Group Theatre, one of the strongest "alternative" companies of the 1930s, was committed to Stanislavski; and when it disbanded in the mid-1940s, several of its members formed the Actor's Studio, which quickly became the most influential acting school in America. Other acting teachers of the 1940s — notably Stella Adler (also a former Group member), Sanford Meisner, and Aristide D'Angelo — were offering similar approaches to actor training. But it is with the Actor's Studio and its director Lee Strasberg that America's popular perception of "Method Acting," the American version of Stanislavski, is most closely associated.

The American Method is an extension of Stanislavski's suggestions to an actor preparing for a role. Much of nineteenth-century acting had been conventional: performers were trained in a repertoire of artificial gestures, poses and inflections, which audiences were trained through exposure to decode as expressions of emotion; the last remnants of that style can be seen in early silent-film acting, which now seems to be merely broad overacting. To oversimplify, Stanislavski taught that an actress faced with playing, say, Masha in Chekhov's *Three Sisters*, a woman torn between an unhappy marriage and an unavailable lover, should recall occasions when she herself had felt love or unhappiness and borrow attitudes, gestures, and intonations from those experiences. The idea, readily apparent now but revolutionary then, was that imitation of actual behavior would be more realistic than any stylized or invented mannerisms.

The American Method, again to oversimplify, would have the actress hunt out the passionate or frustrated sides of her own personality, bring them to the fore so that in a controlled way she actually felt the emotions, and then behave naturally, as the emotions moved her; the idea was that actual behavior was even more true than the imitation of behavior. As the essentially unsympathetic critic Richard Hornby puts it,

> Theatre imitates life, the more closely and directly the better. The good actor therefore repeats on stage what he does in everyday life, drawing on his personal experiences, but, more important, reliving his emotional traumas. Strasberg specifically maintained that an actor, through an interesting process called affective memory, should learn to stimulate in himself a dozen or so real-life emotions, which he could then call up singly or in combination. [6]

David Garfield put it more positively in a history of the Actor's Studio: Strasberg's "concept of acting [was] the creation of real experience in response to imaginary stimuli," and the results could transcend the limits of conscious acting, just as an effectively recreated memory of a lemon's taste can create actual salivation [175].

Method acting at its best could be devastatingly real and powerful, with actor and role blending into a totally believable performance. There was, inevitably, a price to be paid for this stress on psychological realism; as even Garfield admits,

> Despite Strasberg's doctrinaire theorizing about the illimitable applicability of the Method approach, the truth is that the American Method simply does not have a record of accomplishment in the production of noncontemporary plays. Elia Kazan stated it quite directly in the early seventies when he said, "We have not solved the classical acting problem. I failed with it." [181–82]

Hornby is more specific in both his praise and criticism:

> The Actors Studio itself had turned out many actors who were stunning in their ability to play Williams, Miller, Inge. They were also wonderful in film, primarily a realistic form. But the same actors were obviously incapable of playing Shakespeare, Moliere, or Shaw, not to mention Brecht, O'Casey, or Pinter. [238]

In a modern realistic play an American-trained actor will almost certainly outshine a British actor of equal talent, but in Shakespeare, Restoration comedy, or even Ibsen the British actor can rely on purely technical training that the American has not had. (Of course this has been noticed by acting schools on both sides of the Atlantic, who have adjusted their curricula accordingly, but the imbalance remains.)

At mid-century, however, the limitations of Method Acting had yet to be discovered, and its powers, particularly in the kinds of plays being written for the American theatre at that time, were a revelation. The archetypal Method performance—and, to many who witnessed greatest—was Marlon Brando's Stanley Kowalski in Willia. *Streetcar Named Desire*. Brando had previously appeared on Broad.. ay in such varied roles as a homicidal soldier in Maxwell Anderson's *Truckline Cafe* (1946) and the sentimental poet Marchbanks in Shaw's *Candida* (1946). But audiences were not prepared for the intense sexuality and the ability to communicate the passions and pains of an almost inarticulate character that he brought to the Williams play. Except for a brief summer stock appearance in 1953 Brando never acted on a stage again, but the legendary stature of his Stanley, along with his film performances, fixed the new acting style—its faults and excesses as well as its virtues—in the public consciousness.

Other Method-type actors of the period (not all of whom studied at the Actor's Studio) include Lee J. Cobb, Julie Harris, Geraldine Page, and Kim Stanley; Garfield lists hundreds of Life Members of the Studio, crossing the generations from Franchot Tone to Al Pacino. Of course Broadway at mid-century also had established stars of earlier generations: Katharine Cornell, Helen Hayes, Alfred Lunt and Lynn Fontanne, Frederic March, and Florence Eldridge; and in musicals Ethel Merman, Mary Martin, Alfred Drake, and Ray Bolger.

Two directors earlier associated with the Group Theatre helped bring its methods (and The Method) to Broadway. Harold Clurman, who had directed many of the Group's most successful plays, was able to create a similar realism and ensemble playing in such Broadway productions as Carson McCullers' *The Member of the Wedding* (1950). Clurman also had a particularly acute visual sense, and constructed stage pictures and tableaux that embodied a play's meanings and remained in the audience's mind long afterward. Elia Kazan, director of both *Death of a Salesman* and *A Streetcar Named Desire*, was more dynamic. His method was to seek out the emotional core of a play and shape the staging and characterizations to its expression rather than to the surface plot; in *Streetcar*, for example, he saw that the strongest emotional line of the play was Blanche's decline and fall, and built each scene around her experience of the moment. The result was a passionate intensity in the acting and a fluidity of action that carried audiences to the play's deeper emotional levels. Clurman's and Kazan's focus on a play's inner meanings and instinct for how they could be communicated on a stage helped the realistic American drama flourish in its maturity, and when Clurman withdrew partially from directing to become an influential critic, Kazan became the most significant Broadway director of the 1950s. Two other successful directors were Joshua Logan, equally adept at drama, comedy, and musicals, and frequently a collaborator in the writing of plays he directed; and George Abbott, who specialized in giving musicals and light comedies a rapid pace and inventive staging that enhanced good shows and disguised the weaknesses of poor ones.

Realistic plays and realistic acting on proscenium stages imply realistic production styles, and once the experiments of the 1920s and 1930s had passed, a theatregoer attending a new Broadway play could confidently expect the curtain to go up on a solid, real-looking set. For the most part Broadway sets, lighting and costumes were merely functional, though there were occasional attempts to reflect a play's emotional and psychological truth more than external verisimilitude for its own sake. Designer Jo Mielziner was particularly skilled at creating this sort of setting; the house in *Death of a Salesman*, for example, was solid enough but placed and lit so that it faded into the shadows for the play's memory and fantasy sequences, when the real location of the action was the inside of the main character's head.

Producing a Broadway play was an *ad hoc* operation. A producer got a likely script from an author or agent and contracted to put it on. He or she then raised the necessary money; hired a director, actors, and staff (designers, press agent, etc.); rented a theatre; and oversaw the preparations. The director and actors rehearsed in rented halls while the set was built by a carpentry firm and the costumes were created or supplied by a costume company. When the show was ready it went on an out-of-town tour, on a circuit that usually included Philadelphia, Boston, and New Haven, to be tested in front of audiences and revised if necessary. Then it opened in New York, was reviewed, and ran as long as it made money. The weekly operating surplus — the amount by which ticket sales exceeded running costs (rent, salaries, etc.) — was returned to the investors until they were repaid, and then was split between investors and producer. When a show stopped making a weekly profit it closed and everyone involved went their separate ways.

A *New York Times* article of 1925 breaks down the pre-opening costs of an unnamed but unusually expensive play this way: $7700 for sets, props and other equipment; $4500 for costumes; $2000 for rehearsal-period salaries; and $12,000 for a money-losing out-of-town tryout tour ["What it Costs" 1]. By 1950 the preliminary costs for a simple one-set play might total $60,000; for an elaborate musical, over $200,000. (In 1995, according to producer David Richenthal, a three-character, one-set Off-Broadway play was capitalized at $416,000 — $50,000 for the physical

Marlon Brando and Jessica Tandy in *A Streetcar Named Desire*

Photo: The Elia Kazan Collection

Elia Kazan

production; $150,000 in rehearsal costs, salary guarantees, and the like; $100,000 for advertising and marketing; and, since the play did not have the large advance ticket sales big musicals could sometimes command, $100,000 in reserve to cover anticipated money-losing weeks until it caught on. The producer estimated that on Broadway all those figures would have been at least doubled.)

Unless producers could put up their own money, producing meant finding "angels," investors who would supply the funds needed to meet the production's original expenses. Angeldom was not an activity likely to attract a conservative banker; only one show in five made enough and ran long enough to recoup its initial investment before it closed, and the biggest hit might pay back three or four times its cost over a period of years — not bad, certainly, but given the odds, not the most prudent investment. So the Broadway investor was almost always someone with an emotional motive and not just a financial one — a commitment to the particular script or company, a love of theatre in general, or a desire to bask in the reflected glory of the Broadway world.

Anyone with a script and the ability to raise money could be a Broadway producer, and in fact as many as 40 percent of each season's new shows were the work of new producers. In practice, though, most successful shows were produced by full-time professionals who maintained permanent offices and might have several projects at various stages of development simultaneously. The most active producing organization in the 1940s was the Theatre Guild, which offered several plays a year and raised much of its working capital by selling season subscriptions in advance. Other prolific producers during this decade were John C. Wilson, Max Gordon, and Michael Todd.

While the producer's job was primarily a managerial one, some took an active artistic role as well. Critic Michael Feingold speaks with admiration of the "money men" who helped create and maintain Broadway's dominance in the first half of the century:

> The point is that the people who built Broadway were producers who had some artistic input — Ziegfeld and Oliver Morosco and John Golden and Henry Miller, and Lawrence Langner and Theresa Helburn of the Theatre Guild. These people made artistic decisions, and they didn't make them from a position of ignorance.
> [Interview]

Alexander H. Cohen, himself a Broadway producer in the 1960s and after, credits the creative producer with having "a mind of his own, which can develop a story idea from reading the newspaper or from living and breathing in the country...It's a matter of erudite taste and inherent showmanship, and those are rare commodities" [Interview].

It was the Theatre Guild, for example, that proposed that Rodgers and Hammerstein collaborate in adapting a play that the Guild had previously produced into a musical, and thus created *Oklahoma!* After their early successes, Rodgers and Hammerstein formed their own producing organization to stage their musicals as well as other shows. The Playwrights' Company was a consortium of dramatists who produced their own plays; and directors (Kazan, Clurman, Abbott), performers (Jose Ferrer, Sonia Henie), and even theatre owners (the Shuberts) sometimes doubled as producers. However it was created, every Broadway show was an independent project involving dozens or even hundreds of unrelated entrepreneurs, artists and investors brought together solely for that occasion and disbanded when it closed.

☆

It is not absolutely true that there was no theatre outside New York for the first half of the twentieth century. The years before the First World War saw a proliferation of nonprofessional "Little Theatres" around the country. Some, like Chicago's Hull House Players, were offshoots of community centers, with agendas more in the area of social service than art; one function of the Hull House Players was to help immigrants learn English. Some, like the Provincetown Players, grew out of the political movements of the period, as young radicals attempted to revolutionize art as well as society. Most, like the Pasadena Playhouse and Cleveland Play House, existed primarily to provide self-expression for their amateur actors and entertainment for theatre-starved audiences. But, while some of these Little Theatres served as training grounds for future professionals (designer Robert Edmund Jones, producer Lawrence Langner, playwright Eugene O'Neill), most were ephemeral, products of the enthusiasms of their amateur founders and unable to create new work or sustain an audience.

Still, nonprofessional theatres, either amateur community groups or university student programs, existed across the country in the hundreds, and it would be wrong to ignore them entirely. They satisfied the hunger for live theatre in communities far removed from Broadway and even from the routes of road companies. But there was no real connection or continuity between the amateur and the professional theatre. With isolated exceptions, university theatre departments were structured to produce university theatre professors or high school "speech" teachers, not professional actors, playwrights, and directors, while participants in community theatres were shopkeepers, dentists, and housewives not likely to leave home and search for new careers on Broadway.

Repertoires were made up almost entirely of recent Broadway hits, with an occasional classic at the universities, and even within that framework the amateur groups inevitably found light comedies and thrillers more attractive and more within their range than serious drama. Licensing of nonprofessional productions was dominated by two firms, Samuel French (founded in 1830) and Dramatists Play Service (organized by a group of playwrights in 1936 to fight the French monopoly). Each not only collected authors' royalties but sold acting scripts with all the staging and acting directions written in, virtually eliminating any need for imagination or talent in the amateur directors. Meanwhile, as W. McNeil Lowry pointed out in a 1961 speech to university deans, "the man who is trained to teach theatre history is not necessarily qualified to direct a play" [109].

So production and acting in university and community theatres could range from nearly professional to awful, but the difference rarely mattered to participants or audiences. The motivation was as much social (the fun of putting on a show or raising money for a worthy cause) or, in the colleges, educational as artistic, so the "success" of such ventures frequently had little to do with theatrical quality. Thus, while the community and academic theatres provided entertainment and a chance for self-expression for thousands of Americans, their real value was atheatrical, and they were a peripheral and generally sterile part of the American theatre.

There were some companies whose age, accomplishments, or ambitions made them stand out. Two mentioned earlier, the Cleveland Play House (founded 1916) and the Pasadena Community Playhouse (1917), were amateur groups with sufficient community support and commitment to permanence to employ professional directors and management. Both began as part of the Little Theatre movement, devoted to producing classics and uncommercial plays, but through the years their repertoires became safer and more conventional. Still, the Cleveland Play House had premiered some plays that went on to Broadway runs; and the Pasadena group had one of the most ambitious schedules of any community theatre and was also the home of a drama school, a branch of the University of California, that was the training ground of hundreds of New York and Hollywood actors. Two younger amateur companies — the Alley Theatre in Houston, founded in 1947, and the Arena Stage in Washington, D.C., founded in 1950 — would become successful and respected enough to turn professional a few years later, signaling the birth of a new kind of regional theatre.

There were also some professional theatres outside New York, almost all summer stock companies providing unpretentious fare to undiscriminating vacationers; the Barter Theatre in Virginia, founded in 1932 and named the official State Theatre in 1941, represented this genre at its best. In Dallas, Margo Jones's Theatre '50 was the first and only not-for-profit resident repertory theatre in the country; it had opened (as Theatre '47) with the world premiere of Tennessee Williams's *Summer and Smoke*, but generally offered classics and revivals in two- or three-week runs.

Back in New York City, there was a theatrical alternative to Broadway, though the interested theatregoer might have to hunt to find it. There were about 150 non-Broadway productions in New York in the 1948–1949 season, but most were very short-lived and virtually all were amateur, in fact or name, since Actors' Equity, the actors' union, set regulations and minimum salaries that the small companies could not meet. Equity occasionally looked the other way, especially for theatres that operated in the slow summer months; and in the summer of 1949 Equity negotiated an agreement with a group of Off-Broadway theatres that relaxed its requirements and encouraged professional Off-Broadway activ-

most of the almost 300 productions of the 1949–1950 season ...ited to two or three performances, and many were little more ...ditions hoping to attract Broadway producers. Off-Broadway as a significant alternative was on the verge of appearing, but in 1950 it was still a fringe curiosity.

☆

In the first week of January 1950 there were twenty-seven shows on Broadway: eight dramas, six comedies, eight musicals, three revues, one ballet, and an ice show. Among the plays were *Death of a Salesman, Detective Story, Mister Roberts, The Member of the Wedding,* Lunt and Fontanne in *I Know My Love,* and Katharine Cornell in *That Lady.* Musicals included *South Pacific, Kiss Me, Kate, Where's Charley?,* and *Gentlemen Prefer Blondes. A Streetcar Named Desire* and *Born Yesterday* had just closed; and *As You Like It* with Katharine Hepburn, *The Corn is Green* with Eva LeGallienne, and Eliot's *The Cocktail Party* were about to open. The dedicated theatregoer might know of some Off-Broadway plays; the only one that could afford to advertise was a production of Strindberg's *Creditors.* And a production of Sartre's *Respectful Prostitute,* which had begun Off-Broadway two seasons back and then had a Broadway run, was playing five times a day between showings of a movie in a Forty-second Street "grind house."

During the same week there were five productions in Philadelphia and five in Boston, either pre-Broadway tryouts or post-Broadway road companies, while Chicago had six road companies. *Mister Roberts* was playing in Kansas City, and *Oklahoma!* was in San Francisco. Tallulah Bankhead was touring Texas in *Private Lives,* playing two nights each in Houston, San Antonio, and Fort Worth. Most of the rest of the country had no live theatre at all.

☆

That was about to change.

2

OFF-BROADWAY

Off-Broadway was not wholly an invention of the 1950s. There had been an alternative theatre of some sort in New York through most of the twentieth century. The same art theatre movement that gave birth to the amateur theatres in Cleveland and Pasadena before the First World War produced two notable New York companies that had brief professional lives. The Washington Square Players grew out of a play-reading group in the Liberal Club in 1914 and produced their first season of new American and European plays in 1915. They premiered such works as Eugene O'Neill's early *In The Zone* before the war brought a halt to their activities in 1918. An offshoot of the Washington Square Players, the Provincetown Playhouse began as a summer theatre in Massachusetts and produced intermittently in New York from 1916 to 1925. The 1920s saw the flourishing of Eva LeGallienne's Civic Repertory Theatre, and the 1930s produced left-leaning, socially conscious companies such as the Worker's Drama League and the Theatre Collective, as well as the several units of the government-sponsored Federal Theatre.

Two theatrical traditions that are not normally thought of as part of Off-Broadway are worth mentioning here. The Yiddish Theatre was a vital force in the lives of New York's immigrant Jewish population for almost fifty years. Such actor-managers as Maurice Schwartz, Jacob Ben-Ami, and Boris Thomashevsky led repertory companies that offered quality productions of Shakespeare (with the perhaps apocryphal program note "translated and improved by Maurice Schwartz"), Gogol, Strindberg, and other European masters as well as the plays of Jewish writers. And the short-lived "Harlem Renaissance" that peaked in the 1920s was reflected in a flourishing theatre district in New York's African-American community, where the Alhambra, Lafayette, Lincoln, and Crescent Theatres produced plays, many since lost, written by black authors for black audiences.

But none of these companies was able to create a lasting and fruitful alternative to the Broadway monopoly. Some, like the black theatres of the 1920s and the workers' theatres of the 1930s, were products of their time and died when their era was over. The others all fed into Broadway instead of growing apart from it. The Washington Square Players and the Provincetown Playhouse are historical footnotes whose greatest importance lies in the fact that the first evolved after 1920 into the Theatre Guild, one of the most active Broadway producing organizations of the next forty years, while the second produced most of the earliest plays of Eugene O'Neill. The Yiddish Theatre died out as its audience became Americanized, but it had served as a bridge between the European theatre — particularly the Moscow Art Theatre, on which several Yiddish companies were modeled — and the American. It also played an important role in nurturing the love of theatre in New York City's Jewish population, which has subsequently made up a disproportionately large segment of the Broadway audience.

The most influential alternative company of the 1930s was the Group Theatre, which actually operated on Broadway. It spoke more effectively than any other theatre for the disaffected, left-leaning generation of the Depression, and introduced the plays of Clifford Odets and Sidney Kingsley. But even its real importance lies in its contribution to Broadway, in the professionalism, social awareness, and commitment to Stanislavski that its members brought to their later work. Director and critic Harold Clurman, director Elia Kazan, producer Cheryl Crawford, and teachers Lee Strasberg and Stella Adler, all Group alumni, played important roles in shaping the mainstream (i.e., Broadway) theatre of the postwar years.

The Off-Broadway movement of the 1950s was different in that its influence rippled outward. Although its first significant period lasted only about fifteen years, it directly and indirectly spawned other alternative movements throughout the country. Off-Broadway broke the Broadway monopoly in the public perception and created room for other possibilities. The generation of young actors who got their start Off-Broadway in the 1950s — George C. Scott, Jason Robards, James Earl Jones, and dozens of others — produced the film and theatre stars of the next decades; and younger actors, seeing that Broadway was not the only place to make a career, found growth and challenges in regional theatres.

Audiences across America heard the recording of the Off-Broadway *Threepenny Opera* or saw touring companies of *The Fantasticks*, discovered that they were as entertaining and approachable as any Broadway musical, and were more receptive to the next play carrying the Off-

Broadway label. Producers and civic leaders around the country sensed this increased theatrical interest and fed it by establishing theatres and companies to match the excitement of Off-Broadway. And even as Off-Broadway's innovative fervor began to wane in the 1960s, another generation of ambitious and experimental theatre artists followed its lead and created Off Off-Broadway as an alternative to the alternative.

All this activity encouraged young writers, particularly those interested in exploring styles and ideas that did not fit into the Broadway mainstream; and essentially all of the best dramatic writing in America from the late 1960s on was first staged someplace other than Broadway. Off-Broadway itself produced plays, styles, and individual artists of importance, but its greatest significance lies in the alternative sensibility it created and the other alternatives it inspired.

The history of this Off-Broadway movement can be divided into four periods. The first, covering most of the decade of the 1950s, saw the birth of the alternative theatre in the formation of several key companies whose successes attracted audiences and began the careers of a generation of actors. Noticeably missing in this period were new American playwrights, since the repertoire was dominated by classics, revivals, and American premieres of modern European plays. The second period, roughly the 1960s, redressed this imbalance as a generation of young American dramatists were discovered and their plays produced. Although this renaissance proved somewhat abortive, with many of the writers unable to live up to the promise of their first works, the period of excitement led New York and regional theatres to seek out and encourage other young writers of their own, expanding the ripple effect of Off-Broadway.

From the late 1960s through the next decade, Off-Broadway's revolutionary significance waned and it evolved into a valid alternative in the expanded mainstream, the home of plays and productions which might not be inherently different in form and content from those on Broadway but which were more appropriate to smaller theatres, more modest budgets, and more sophisticated audiences. Finally, as the theatrical revolutions occurring elsewhere in the country definitively shifted the artistic center-of-gravity away from Broadway, Off-Broadway became the regional theatre's base in New York City, dominated, as the outside-New York theatre was, by permanent, subsidized, not-for-profit companies.

☆

Most of the hundreds of non-Broadway productions in New York in the years immediately following the Second World War were not really part of Off-Broadway. Many were amateur or student efforts, and some were vanity exercises subsidized by the stage-struck participants or their loving families. A large number were one- or two-performance show-cases for authors or actors hoping to attract the attention of Broadway producers. The growth of a professional alternative theatre was ham-pered by the fact that Actors' Equity, the performers' union, forbade its members to work alongside nonmembers and demanded minimum salaries which, however modest, were beyond the shoestring budgets of most non-Broadway companies.

Still, actors want to act, and acting for carfare and coffee seemed better to many young performers than not acting at all. Increasingly to-ward the end of the 1940s Equity was forced to look the other way as its members violated its regulations to appear in Off-Broadway produc-tions. In 1949 five professional companies — Interplayers, Off-Broadway Incorporated, People's Drama, Studio Seven, and We Present — united to form the Off-Broadway Theatre League and nego-tiated an agreement with Equity that allowed union actors to appear with nonmembers as long as a token salary was paid. The Off-Broadway movement of the 1950s was born.

Nothing happened overnight, of course. There was no proven audi-ence for Off-Broadway, and thus little to attract experienced Broadway producers and investors. (The first established Broadway producer to venture Off-Broadway, Kermit Bloomgarden, waited until 1961 to do so.) The young actors and directors who wanted to work Off-Broadway had to become producers as well, and it was typical of this Off-Broadway generation that its members did not come together to put on single plays but to form what were meant to be continuing companies, com-plete in many cases with artistic manifestos declaring their commitment (in the case of the Phoenix Theatre) "to release actors, directors, play-wrights and designers from the pressures forced on them by the hit-or-flop pattern of Broadway [and] to provide for the public a playhouse within the means of everyone" [Hambleton 29]; or (New York Shakespeare Festival) "to create a style of acting not too internal, not too bombastic, so that poetic plays could be done on the stage in a highly realistic way, without sacrificing the poetry and the style" [Papp 11]; or (Living Theatre) "to explore untried methods and techniques for the extension of the boundaries of theatrical expression" [Beck and Malina].

Economics and tradition lured most of these young artists to Green-wich Village, the bohemian district in the southern part of Manhattan, roughly where old New Amsterdam ends and the numbered streets begin. Some operated in theatres left from the Little Theatre period earlier in the century, such as the Cherry Lane and the Provincetown Playhouse, while others created playing spaces in vacant lofts, nightclubs, and movie houses. Budgets ranged from zero to a few thousand dollars for an entire season, at a time when a single Broadway play cost $60,000 or more. They supported themselves with nontheatrical jobs, scrounged materials and props from friends and trash piles, and maneuvered their way through or around fire and zoning regulations. Many of their histories resemble the plots of the Mickey Rooney-Judy Garland movies of the 1940s, and there is no doubt that youthful innocence and exuberance led them to successes that wiser heads would have considered impossible.

Four especially significant companies were born at this time: the Circle in the Square, the Living Theatre, the Phoenix Theatre, and the New York Shakespeare Festival. Only part of their importance lies in the work they produced in their early years; much of it is in the patterns they set for other groups in New York and elsewhere. Each of the four had a different beginning, style, and philosophy; and each evolved through several stages as they matured. Their similarities and differences mark the general outlines of the Off-Broadway movement in its first period, outlines that they helped form through their influence on others.

The roots of the Circle in the Square are very much in the "Hey, kids, let's put on a show!" tradition. In the late 1940s a group of young actors took over an old theatre in Woodstock, New York, for several summer seasons. By 1950 their number included Panamanian-born director Jose Quintero and business manager Theodore Mann, who were among the core group determined to form a permanent theatre in New York City. As Mann recalls,

> At the end of that summer we had paid all the debts, and everybody in Woodstock was elated about it because we were the first theatre company that went away without owing money. And so we decided that, with that affirmation from the community, we would like to go on and try to start a theatre in New York. [Interview]

With financial help from their Woodstock supporters and Mann's family, they rented a former nightclub in Greenwich Village's Sheridan Square, converted its circular dance floor into a three-sided arena stage, and named it the Circle in the Square. Unable to meet the stringent city regulations for licensing as a theatre, they found convenient loopholes, first by giving performances that were technically free —

> Jose would get up and make a speech, and we had the bread baskets from the old nightclub, and we would pass them around in the audience to get some money.

— and then by meeting the letter, if not the spirit, of the law —

> The definition of a cabaret was a place of entertainment that served food and/or drink. It didn't say anything about alcohol. So I went back to the police department and said we were entertainment and we served cookies and orange drink. And they gave us a cabaret license. [Mann interview]

They lived commune-style in rooms above the theatre and, starting in 1951, put on a season of modern European and American plays, including Jean Anouilh's *Antigone* and John Steinbeck's *Burning Bright*. "Many times we played and there were more people onstage than in the audience," recalls Mann. "It was a very hard struggle to get recognition from the critics, because the critics were ignoring Off-Broadway at the time."

By their second season some of the youthful idealism had worn off, and many of the original company left, bringing an end to thoughts of a repertory company. Now casting individual shows, with Mann as producer and Quintero as director of almost every play, they were able to draw from the large pool of young actors in New York. In April 1952 they revived Tennessee Williams's *Summer and Smoke*, which had failed on Broadway in 1948, featuring a young actress Quintero knew from drama school, Geraldine Page. Brooks Atkinson of *The New York Times* came, and wrote "Nothing has happened in the theatre for quite a long time as admirable as this production." The Circle in the Square, and Off-Broadway, had its first smash hit.

> The next day I came in to work the box office, which was a little table sitting in the lobby. Before the review the phone would ring maybe three times a day. After the review, as I came to the theatre, there was a line up to Seventh Avenue and the phone just never stopped ringing. [Mann interview]

Much of the credit for the Circle's early success must go to its director. Jose Quintero was not a methodical analyst and theoretician as Harold Clurman and Elia Kazan were, or a master of pure technique, as George Abbott was. He operated through instinct and through a total emotional commitment to his work that freed his imagination and sensitivity. In his memoirs he recalled his first visit to the garishly painted nightclub that would become his theatre:

> Looking at one of the walls, I saw a painted leopard. I permitted him to become real for a few seconds.... He began to circle the center pole where I was standing, then proceeded in a series of curves until he reached the farthest poles of the arena.... The leopard never walked a straight line. He curved himself around as he walked, almost in the shape of an S. At that moment I began to understand the kind of movement that the three-quarter arena demanded. [79]

There had been experiments in non-proscenium staging before, but Quintero was one of the first directors to sense that arena staging was not just a matter of audience placement but required a wholly new kind of blocking and movement, that the straight crossings and diagonals of the proscenium stage must be replaced by wide arcs and more circular motions, to reflect the audience's sense of the room they were in. Quintero also saw that the company's poverty freed it from the solid sets and realistic props of the commercial theatre, and that an almost bare stage would challenge and liberate the imagination of actors and audience. Certainly one of the direct legacies of Off-Broadway was the discovery that theatre could happen in unconventional spaces, and Quintero's insights into how such spaces could reshape acting and production styles were seminal.

Quintero demanded the same sort of complete freedom of the imagination from his actors, using a childhood memory of a circus clown kissing a member of the audience as a model of the kind of emotional openness he wanted. Directing was a matter of guiding the performers toward the confidence and identification with their roles that would allow them to take such emotional risks. Quintero's account of the rehearsals for Eugene O'Neill's *Long Day's Journey into Night* (1956) is filled with extended discussions and arguments with and between the actors *in character*, and with almost confessional statements and anecdotes by the director, designed both to communicate a particular mood and to encourage the actors toward similar self-exposure [215-64]. There was little attention to mechanics in Quintero rehearsals; if the actors found the truth of their roles and the ability to express it honestly, he was sure line readings and movements would follow naturally.

Quintero was thus more dependent on his actors than a more doctrinaire director would be, and he was fortunate in having a pool of young, determined, and talented performers to work with. *Summer and*

Smoke was Geraldine Page's first big New York role after several years in summer stock. Jason Robards got the starring role in the Circle's second great success, O'Neill's *The Iceman Cometh* (1956), by demanding it and by auditioning with a dynamic reading that convinced Quintero that the tall, thin young actor could make the audience see O'Neill's fat and aging protagonist. "Jason desperately wanted to play this part," says Mann.

> He had read for it and been turned down, and begged for a chance to read for it again. By this time Jason had gone away and had a couple of drinks and come back, and he read for Jose. And Jose came in with starry eyes and said he's found his Hickey. [Interview]

Peter Falk played a small role in *Iceman*; Colleen Dewhurst, Salome Jens, George C. Scott, and George Segal were also among the Circle's alumni in its first decade.

The Circle's *Iceman Cometh*, which ran from 1956 to 1958, was important for another reason: it was the direct and immediate cause of America's rediscovery of its greatest dramatic genius. Eugene O'Neill's reputation was made in the 1920s with such experimental and non-naturalistic plays as *The Hairy Ape* and *Strange Interlude*, which seemed dated and unplayable thirty years later. Although O'Neill had returned to realism in his later plays, he had not released most of them for pro-

Photo: Martha Swope

Jose Quintero

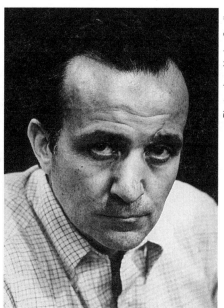

Photo: Jos. Abeles Studio

Ted Mann

Photo: Billy Rose Theatre Collection,
New York Public Library at Lincoln Center

Eugene O'Neill

duction, and his two plays produced in the 1940s, *The Iceman Cometh* and *A Moon for the Misbegotten*, had been failures.

The Circle's *Iceman*, thanks to Quintero's direction and Robards' bravura performance, proved that O'Neill was not a dated experimenter but a great naturalistic writer with a vision that was evidently particularly meaningful to the Cold War generation. The message of *Iceman* — that self-delusion, however crippling or degrading it may be, is nonetheless absolutely essential to survival, since humanity is simply unequipped to deal with the naked horrors of reality — had seemed nihilistic in 1946, but was welcomed as a key to self-acceptance and self-forgiveness ten years later, as audiences responded to O'Neill's argument that we must not feel guilty about a need as basic and inescapable as those for food and shelter.

O'Neill's widow and literary executor, Carlotta Monterey, had taken a liking to Mann and Quintero and was so impressed by their production of *Iceman* that she offered them an extraordinary opportunity.

> Shortly thereafter we got a call from Mrs. O'Neill wanting to see Jose and me. When we got there she bolted up from her chair, before we even sat down, and said "Do you want to produce *Long Day's Journey into Night* on Broadway next season?" [Mann interview]

Quintero directed *Long Day's Journey* on Broadway in November 1956. O'Neill had intended to keep the play secret until twenty-five years after

Florence Eldridge, Bradford Dillman, Jason Robards Jr., and
Frederick March in *Long Day's Journey into Night*

his death, so it is directly to the Circle in the Square that we owe the availability of what is almost certainly the greatest of all American plays.

Even more purely than *Iceman*, *Long Day's Journey* is a play of forgiveness and reassurance, facing humanity's inherent limitations and finding comfort in the realization that our failure to be perfect is not our fault. That the play is undisguisedly autobiographical, using O'Neill's own tormented family as its metaphor, only makes the courage of his search for truth and the charity of his sharing his discovery that much more overwhelming. *Long Day's Journey into Night* was followed in turn by other posthumous plays and revivals, confirming the discovery that O'Neill's return to realism in his later career produced his and the American drama's true masterpieces.

The Circle in the Square was born out of the desire of young and talented people to work. Its choice of plays was determined by available performers and personal enthusiasms rather than by a particular social or artistic position. Although the talent of its director and of the actors who appeared regularly helped it develop an identity and style, that result was unpremeditated. In their own ways the other three seminal Off-Broadway companies were generated by specific literary, theatrical, or philosophical ideals. As a result each was somewhat more a direct reflection of its founders' personalities, strengths, and obsessions.

The roots of the Living Theatre go back to 1946 when artist Julian Beck and his wife, actress Judith Malina, began to theorize about a new kind of theatre. Their early statements and manifestos show that they were not really sure what form this new production style would take, except that it should break with the conventions of the commercial theatre and somehow reflect the vitality and evocative power of modern art. As late as 1959 Julian Beck expressed himself in terms more theoretical than practical, showing that they hadn't gone far beyond being sure what they *didn't* want to do, and incidentally proving that the very mystical turn their later work took was not an accident:

> With obstinate devotion we believe in the theatre as a place of intense experience, half-dream half-ritual, in which the spectator approaches something of a vision of self-understanding, going past the conscious to the unconscious, to an understanding of the nature of all things.... That is why at The Living Theatre we are trying to work beyond the limitations of realistic techniques of staging and of acting. [Beck 3]

In their search for material of high literary quality that would also help them explore the boundaries of the theatrical experience, the Becks were drawn at first to poetic and nonlinear drama; and their early repertoire was dominated by such nontraditional writers as Gertrude Stein, Paul Goodman, T. S. Eliot, Pablo Picasso, and Jean Cocteau.

Chronically impoverished, the Becks offered their first brief season in 1951 in their own living room, and subsequently in cellars, lofts, and theatres all over Manhattan; they were subject to long silent periods when they had no money and no theatre. Their choice of plays and playing spaces led to frequent brushes with authorities, which the Becks interpreted (or promoted) as attempts at censorship, as playwright Jack Gelber later recalled:

> I think the role of embattled revolutionaries, misunderstood artists, and disturbing theatre people was . . . cultivated by Julian as a tool of survival. Every revolutionary movement needs its mythology. [11]

The image of Off-Broadway as a place where bohemian mystics performed strange plays in curious settings was an almost immediate caricature in the public perception, but like all caricatures it reflected a part of reality. And the reality or the caricature was an inspiration and model to other young dreamers who began to realize that they too might be able to explore their theatrical ideas outside the Broadway mainstream.

All the Living Theatre's productions from 1951 to 1960 totaled only one thousand performances, and more than half of those were in the 1959–1960 season. Obviously the Living Theatre was much slower in achieving popular success than the Circle in the Square, and its real contributions began in the second period of Off-Broadway's history. But even during the 1950s the close identification of the Living Theatre's work with the passions and personalities of the Becks, along with its conscious dedication to the expansion of the theatrical repertoire and vocabulary, helped shape the identity and power of Off-Broadway. Once the Living Theatre achieved success and then notoriety, its influence would be even greater and more direct.

If the Becks were visionaries, the founders of the Phoenix Theatre were solid professionals. Norris Houghton and T. Edward Hambleton each had had twenty years' experience in various aspects of commercial theatre when they combined forces to form an alternative art theatre that could produce uncommercial plays. Their inspiration, Houghton later wrote, was the Lyric Hammersmith Theatre in London, a fringe venue where established stars frequently appeared in limited runs of plays not commercial enough for the West End. "I wasn't interested in

The Living Theatre, 1961

Front: playwright Jack Gelber, directors Julian Beck and Judith Malina

Rear: choreographer Merce Cunningham,
stage manager Peter Feldman, administrator James Spicer

creating a showcase for young talent; my sights were set on the Peggy Ashcrofts and Pamela Browns" [219].

They drew on their Broadway contacts for their initial financial support, with "partners" including Oscar Hammerstein, Arthur Miller, Roger L. Stevens, Howard Lindsay, and Russel Crouse, and in 1953 opened the Phoenix in a twelve hundred seat theatre at the edge of Greenwich Village, originally the home of the New Yiddish Art Theatre and more recently a Spanish movie house. "If we could produce and break even at one fourth of Broadway's cost, we could offer our partners four properties for the price of one and hope to repay their investment—not a bad deal at all" [Houghton 222].

As Houghton's language suggests, the Phoenix was an alternative to Broadway only in its location and budgets. The first season was made up almost entirely of star vehicles, in most cases packages that had been looking for Broadway producers: Hume Cronyn and Jessica Tandy in Sidney Howard's *Madam, Will You Walk?*, Robert Ryan in *Coriolanus*, John LaTouche and Jerome Moross's new musical *The Golden Apple*, and Montgomery Clift in *The Seagull*. Given such casts and the commercial experience of the two producers, they were perhaps a bit disingenuous when they said, "The Phoenix was by no means founded as a proving ground for possible Broadway hits. But if one of our productions is judged worthy of moving to Broadway, ... we see nothing wrong with

Photo: Phoenix Theatre Collection

The Phoenix Theatre: T. Edward Hambleton and Norris Houghton with director-choreographer Jerome Robbins

that" [Hambleton 94]. Houghton admitted as much when he wrote, almost forty years later, "whether or not we recognized our aim at the time — we wanted to create a microcosm of Broadway under one roof" [253].

Despite individual critical successes, the Phoenix's early seasons lost thousands of dollars, and any plan of supporting the theatre by Broadway transfers never worked out. Still, the absolute dedication of Houghton and Hambleton kept it alive even if, true to its name, it had to be reborn in a new form every few years. Houghton had previously operated a theatregoer's club called Theatre Incorporated, and in 1957 the moribund but still legally extant operation was merged into the Phoenix, giving the Phoenix its subscription list and not-for-profit status. For two seasons (1959–1961) they established and maintained a resident repertory company, and in 1961 moved to a smaller and more economical theatre.

After 1959 Houghton gradually withdrew from active involvement while beginning a new career as Professor of Drama at Vassar and later at SUNY Purchase. He officially resigned in 1964, the same year that Hambleton combined forces with the Association of Producing Artists, a Michigan-based touring repertory company, and offered several Broadway seasons, the Phoenix providing the organization and the APA the plays. While this partnership led to some striking productions and the brief return of rotating repertory to Broadway, its awkwardness (who was in charge of what?) and the differing personal and corporate styles of Phoenix director Hambleton and APA director Ellis Rabb led to increasing difficulties and deficits, and the partnership was dissolved in 1969.

The APA soon broke up, while the Phoenix returned to producing, first on Broadway, then as a touring company with a repertory of classics, then as an Off-Broadway theatre devoted to new plays, dying and rising in a new manifestation at regular intervals before its final dissolution in 1982. As Stuart W. Little noted,

> Throughout its history the Phoenix . . . occupied an anomalous position somewhere between Broadway and off-Broadway in size, somewhere between New York and regional theatre in sophistication, somewhere between the commercial and the art theater in audience appeal, . . . somewhere between the contemporary theater and the classic in the thrust of its programming . . . . By adaptation and structural change the Phoenix repeatedly found the means of survival. [*Off* 153]

Delacorte Theatre, Central Park

And in every manifestation the Phoenix maintained high standards of professionalism that counterbalanced the inexperience of many Off-Broadway companies. If the Phoenix never had the groundbreaking hits or the myth-inspiring colorfulness of some other theatres, its continuity and relative orthodoxy helped give Off-Broadway legitimacy in the eyes of more conservative audiences.

The guiding spirit of the New York Shakespeare Festival was Joseph Papp, a unique figure combining in his own way the theatrical instincts of Quintero, the vision of the Becks, and the practical expertise of Houghton and Hambleton. Papp was the American theatre's nearest approach to a Diaghilev, a workaholic totally dedicated to his theatre and as skilled in raising money and manipulating civic authorities as he was in spotting and supporting artistic talent in others.

As a young and undistinguished theatre and television director in the early 1950s he had the vision of a new American style of Shakespearean production that would give classical acting the naturalness and vitality that the Method had given contemporary drama. At the same time he felt an almost messianic commitment to making Shakespeare freely available to what he called "a great dispossessed audience — both the ordinary theatregoers who have been priced out of the theatre, and those who have never seen a live professional production" [Papp 11]. He founded his Shakespeare Workshop in a Lower East Side church in 1954, and in the summer of 1956 gave his first season of free Shakespeare in the band shell of a nearby park, on a trailer truck that traveled throughout the city, and finally in Central Park.

Typical of Papp's skill and commitment as champion of his theatre was a skirmish with the city's Parks Commission in 1959. At its core it was a simple financial dispute — the city wanted Papp to pay some of the costs of his Central Park season, and to charge admission to raise the money — and most of Papp's dealings were with minor bureaucrats. But Papp effectively cast himself as the populist hero and Robert Moses, the Commissioner, as a snobbish patrician offended by the prospect of the wrong kind of people in his park, and marshalled public support that forced the city to retreat. Two years later Papp convinced the city and philanthropist George Delacorte to build him a permanent outdoor Central Park theatre, where the New York Shakespeare Festival has provided free summer seasons ever since.

Photo: The New York Shakespeare Festival

Joseph Papp

In the years that followed, Papp's limitless energy and vision would lead the New York Shakespeare Festival to a permanent year-round home, seasons of award-winning new plays and classics, traveling theatre-in-the-streets companies, television productions, and artistic and commercial successes on, Off- and Off Off-Broadway. In the 1950s his contribution was in creating another noncommercial alternative to Broadway and in providing a place for the Off-Broadway generation of actors and directors to find their way into Shakespeare; among his early actors were Roscoe Lee Browne, Colleen Dewhurst, James Earl Jones, and George C. Scott. And as that list suggests, Papp also pioneered a colorblind philosophy of casting that expanded the range of roles available to black, Hispanic, and Asian actors while also liberating the imaginations of audiences, who quickly adjusted to the sight of a black King Lear with white daughters or a mixed-race Roman senate.

There were other notable Off-Broadway companies during this first decade, many of which had commercial and artistic successes that helped increase public awareness of the alternative theatre. The Shakespearewrights, founded and supported by Shakespeare-lover Donald Goldman in 1953, anticipated and paralleled Joseph Papp's work with productions designed to be clean, clear, and entertaining, frequently performed for high school and college audiences. David Ross led the 4th Street Theatre through a successful cycle of Chekhov plays, while the Irish Players explored that national dramatic heritage.

There were individual hits as well. The biggest, and up to that time the longest-running musical in New York theatre history was Marc Blitzstein's adaptation of Kurt Weill and Bertolt Brecht's *The Threepenny Opera*. The satiric musical opened for a brief run in March 1954 as part of a repertory season at the Theatre de Lys, and then reopened in September 1955 and ran for over six years. Blitzstein's version softened some of the anger in Brecht's depiction of criminal society as a logical extension of the capitalist system, which may have helped make the play acceptable to American audiences. Weill's alternately brassy and haunting music, the intimacy of the tiny theatre, and a strong cast led by Weill's widow Lotte Lenya in the role she had created in 1928 also contributed to making this still the most successful American production of any of Brecht's plays. The original cast album sold hundreds of thousands of copies, and "The Ballad of Mack the Knife" was a popular hit for almost every singer who recorded it.

The Threepenny Opera was also an early hint of the direction toward which Off-Broadway would evolve. Although its small theatre and modest production were keys to a success it probably would not have had on Broadway, it was not inherently different from the Broadway product but rather a variant of it. While it was still running, critic Robert Brustein complained in a different context that "Off Broadway was originally established as an alternative theatre for serious works of art... The accumulation of musicals in the minority theatre is a depressing sign of commercial accommodation" [*Seasons* 43]. Increasingly in the following years Off-Broadway would take a shape that was not so much an alternative to Broadway as an alternative version of it.

In addition to the actors and actresses already mentioned, the generation that got its start or early experience Off-Broadway during this period included Beatrice Arthur, Ben Gazzara, Joel Grey, Tammy Grimes, Hal Holbrook, Jack Palance, and Kim Stanley. (Off-Broadway continued to be a breeding ground of future stars: the 1960s produced, among others, Faye Dunaway, Dustin Hoffman, Stacy Keach, Frank Langella, and Al Pacino; the 1970s Judd Hirsch, William Hurt, Michael Moriarty, Christopher Reeve, Meryl Streep, and Sigourney Weaver; and so on.)

Other than Jose Quintero, the most successful Off-Broadway director of the 1950s was Stuart Vaughan, who began with the New York Shakespeare Festival and directed the Phoenix Theatre during its two-year experiment as a repertory company. The cornerstone of Joseph Papp's attempt to create an American style of producing Shakespeare, Vaughan filled the plays with movement and inventive business, although he was only intermittently successful in helping untrained actors handle the verse. His most successful work at the Phoenix was also in Shakespeare, and his experience in organizing and operating one of the first large-scale repertory companies in contemporary America led to a career in the regional theatre movement.

☆

The London production of John Osborne's *Look Back in Anger* in 1956 introduced a revolutionary new voice into the staid and conventional British theatre, and the next few years showed that there was a whole generation of young British dramatists with new things to say and new dramatic vocabularies to express them in. There was no equivalently shocking moment in the American theatre, but a comparable group of new young American dramatists did appear in the early 1960s, their plays giving shape to the second period in Off-Broadway's development.

The generating factor in America may have been the discovery of the important new European playwrights, itself one of Off-Broadway's significant contributions. Samuel Beckett's *Waiting for Godot* was produced on Broadway in 1956, but his other plays received their first American productions Off-Broadway, starting with *Endgame* in 1959, *Krapp's Last Tape* in 1960, and *Happy Days* in 1961. Eugene Ionesco's *The Lesson* and *The Chairs* were produced by the Phoenix Theatre in 1958, and *The Bald Soprano* appeared Off-Broadway in the same year. In addition to *The Threepenny Opera*, Brecht was represented by the Phoenix's *Good Woman of Setzuan* in 1956 and the Living Theatre's *In the Jungle of Cities* in 1961; and Jean Genet's *The Balcony* was a big success for the Circle in the Square in 1960.

The first indication that a new generation of American writers was going to challenge the conventions of Broadway drama came in 1959, when the Living Theatre produced Jack Gelber's *The Connection*. Gelber showed a group of heroin addicts waiting for their dealer to arrive, in what was not only a shocking piece of social realism but also a series of challenges to middle-class complacency. Although his junkies were presented as burned out and unsalvageable, they could be eloquent and even persuasive in their praise of the fix and in their argument that heroin addiction was just a variant on more accepted compulsions toward sex, money, or power. The form of the play also threatened comfortable preconceptions: Gelber's premise was that a playwright had cast real junkies in his play about junkies, and their refusal to follow the script attacked the audience's expectation of the sort of safe, controlled, comfortable theatrical experience that conventional theatres offered.

The Connection was an important turning point for the Living Theatre. By accident more than design their 1959 season was made up of three plays set in the theatre: Pirandello's *Tonight We Improvise*, William Carlos Williams's *Many Loves*, and *The Connection*. This coincidence helped Beck and Malina find the "extension of the boundaries of theatrical expression" that they had declared as a goal and had been feeling their way toward for a decade. From this point on the Living Theatre would be committed to breaking down the comfortable distance between audience and play, and would directly influence the styles of companies and directors throughout the world.

The staging of *The Connection* was designed to reinforce the script's threats to complacency. The audience entering the theatre found the performers already there, involved in improvised actions and conversations that imperceptibly moved into the start of the play. Musicians in the group broke into improvised jazz pieces at seemingly random moments. During intermission the actors stayed in character and mingled with the audience, engaging in conversations, starting arguments, and demanding handouts. The interruptions of the "playwright" when the junkies refused to follow his script seemed unrehearsed, while the onstage depictions of the mechanics of shooting up and the results of an overdose were frighteningly real. Even the most sophisticated theatregoers had to leave the play uncertain whether those actually were real addicts — according to one source [Tytell 157], some of them were — and whether everything that happened had been part of the script.

The Connection was panned by the newspaper reviewers and was kept alive in the repertoire by the more popular *Many Loves* for the first few weeks of its run. But as more supportive reviews appeared in weekly and monthly magazines, and as word of this new play and this challenging theatrical experience spread, everyone who was interested in theatre wanted to see it. *The Connection* became the mainstay of the Living Theatre's next few seasons and of its European tours in 1961 and 1962. More than that, it signaled a new identity for Off-Broadway as a home for the avant-garde in plays and productions, and its style and staging devices were widely imitated.

But the Living Theatre itself could not enjoy this success for long. The artistic nonconformity of Beck and Malina had evolved into a political commitment that extended beyond play choice or acting styles. "Julian Beck was a revolutionary leader," at least in his own eyes, according to Gelber. "The theatre was Julian's principal but by no means only vehicle to achieve his anarchist-pacifist goals" [6-7]. Despite the importance of *The Connection* to the Living Theatre's financial health, the Becks refused the opportunity of a Broadway run as a matter of principle.

For the rest of its existence the directors of the Living Theatre would think of it as a political force first, and an artistic enterprise only second. No longer just an alternative to the mainstream culture, they were aggressively antagonistic toward it, and assumed it felt the same way toward them. In fact, for the most part it hardly noticed them; as an essentially sympathetic historian acknowledged, "by choosing anarchism, Beck and Malina made themselves marginal in America" [Tytell 56].

A little less sympathetically, Gelber suggests that politics directly interfered with the Living Theatre's artistic growth:

> The kind of actor the Living Theatre sought was necessarily inexperienced. Political leaning, sexual inclination, and willingness to follow Judith's direction . . . were more important. . . . Each prospective actor was scrutinized as to his or her values and whether or not they measured up politically. [8, 15–16]

Indeed, as late as 1996 Judith Malina was far more interested in discussing the Living Theatre's role as a political agent than its theatrical history [Interview].

In 1963 the company staged Kenneth Brown's *The Brig*, a critical picture of life in a Marine stockade, in a brutal and unrelenting production designed to exhaust and frighten the audience rather than entertain them. When the Internal Revenue Service seized their theatre in October 1963 for failure to pay back taxes, the Becks cried censorship. "Most of the company believed that the IRS seizure had just been a pretext and that actually The Living Theatre was being harassed for daring to perform a play offensive to the Marine Corps," writes Tytell [189], although Gelber believes that the real problem was that they hadn't paid their rent and that Beck himself engineered the IRS raid in order to create a scandal that would inspire support and donations [18-19].

While vocal support did come from the artistic community, funding didn't, and their arrest and trial only reinforced Beck and Malina's belief that the government was repressing their art for political reasons. After their conviction and brief imprisonment — actually, the sympathetic judge allowed them to play a London engagement (where they picketed their own theatre in a dispute with the landlord) before returning to serve their terms — the Becks exiled themselves and their company to Europe, where the Living Theatre evolved again into a new form that would once more shake theatrical preconceptions when it returned to America in 1968.

Meanwhile, other new voices were being heard. Edward Albee's *The Zoo Story*, first produced in Berlin in 1959, had its American premiere Off-Broadway in January 1960. *The Sandbox* opened in May, *The American Dream* the following January, and *The Death of Bessie Smith* in March 1961. Albee's Off-Broadway plays were clearly the work of a beginning writer, but one whose talent and distinctive voice overcame his technical limitations. He owed obvious debts to older writers, most notably to Ionesco in *The American Dream* and to Tennessee Williams in both his

Margo Skinner and Richard Kneeland in
Who's Afraid of Virginia Woolf?

sympathy for social outcasts and his poetic and musical use of dialogue, and he repeatedly fell into the trap of long, essentially nondramatic monologues. But the plays also showed a striking control of language and a startling new view of contemporary America as a threatening and spirit-destroying place.

The Zoo Story and *The American Dream* are the strongest of the four. In the first a complacent middle-class New Yorker sitting on a park bench is accosted by a troubled young man who launches into an extended monologue describing his rootless, haunted life and his desperate need to make contact with someone or something that will convince him of his own reality. He finds that comfort only in death when his story destroys his listener's own sense of security and reality, and leads to a mortal battle over possession of the bench.

In *The American Dream*, the conversation of an archetypal American family—Mommy, Daddy, Grandma, and a Young Man—echoes the banalities and absurdities of Ionesco's *Bald Soprano*, particularly in the comically literal use of metaphors and cliches. But Albee presents this linguistic abuse as a symptom of their misuse of each other: both language and social norms are consciously used to deny the value of the individual, and the American Dream is of sterile and lifeless beauty.

Albee's first full-length play was produced on Broadway in 1962, quickly establishing him as the most important American dramatist since Miller and Williams. *Who's Afraid of Virginia Woolf?* is one of the very best plays in the American canon, and the first to fit the new Off-Broadway sensibility into the conventions of mainstream Broadway drama. A realistic domestic melodrama with four characters, a single living room set, and a fictional time identical to its playing time, it is both frightening and inspirational in its depiction of contemporary America.

Albee's protagonists George and Martha are a middle-aged couple seemingly trapped in a Strindbergian marriage built on lies, fantasies, infidelities, and alcohol. They spend much of the play attacking each other with brilliantly caustic wit, and horrify the younger couple who are their guests for a night of abusive and damaging psychological games. But through all the horrors Albee forces us to see that this marriage *works*—that it supports, reinforces, and protects, giving George and Martha the energy and the tools for facing the same painful and uncertain experience of life that destroyed the young man in *The Zoo Story*. Meanwhile the supposedly healthier marriage of their guests is exposed as false and cowardly, devoted to escape from the challenges of reality rather than commitment to dealing with them. The vision of ordinary daily existence as demanding all the mental and emotional resources one can muster came in part from Tennessee Williams, but the eloquence and raw energy of Albee's presentation was original, announcing the arrival of a new generation of dramatists.

Albee's subsequent plays continued to challenge Broadway audiences with the Off-Broadway sensibility. *Tiny Alice* (1964) was an intriguing if somewhat obscure examination of the demands of religious faith, while *A Delicate Balance* (1966) restated his conviction that security and politeness are a very thin veneer over the frightening emptiness of life. As Stuart W. Little notes,

> Edward Albee more than anyone else opened up off-Broadway to new writers. It was partly his visible success that gave encouragement to new writers.... It was also the quality and the character of his writing that alerted the theater and excited and challenged his contemporaries. For he had opened a new vein of dramatic writing. [*Off* 216]

In fact, Albee's success had an even more direct benefit for Off-Broadway writers. His producers, Richard Barr and Clinton Wilder, were committed to the presentation of new plays, and Albee joined with them in devoting some of *Virginia Woolf*'s profits to the establishment of a Playwrights Unit, a workshop for young dramatists where their scripts-in-progress could be read, analyzed, and given modest stagings. Practically every notable young American dramatist of the 1960s passed through the Playwrights Unit, and eighty-five of their plays were commercially produced by its sponsors between 1963 and 1969.

Two star graduates were LeRoi Jones and Mart Crowley. In Jones' best play, *Dutchman* (1964), a white seductress and a middle-class black man meet on a New York subway and act out a violent paradigm of the growing racial tensions in American society. Crowley introduced audiences to the perspective and experience of another minority in *The Boys in the Band* (1968), presenting a group of homosexual men adjusting with varying degrees of success to guilt, loneliness, and social opprobrium. Both of these plays, along with most of Albee's, have become staples of the American theatrical repertoire, with successful revivals attesting to their continuing power.

Meanwhile, the Phoenix Theatre's biggest commercial success came shortly after its move to a smaller theatre in 1961, with Arthur Kopit's *Oh Dad Poor Dad Mama's Hung You in the Closet and I'm Feeling So Sad*, a surrealistic farce about an overpowering mother and her thoroughly cowed son; audiences' enjoyment of Kopit's parody of the conventions and attitudes of Off-Broadway drama was evidence of how quickly the new styles had taken hold. Jack Richardson's *The Prodigal* (1960) and *Gallows Humor* (1961), and Murray Schisgal's short comedies *The Typists* and *The Tiger* (1962) were also impressive. New playwrights of another sort were the specialty of the American Place Theatre, a company dedicated to allowing established authors from other fields to experiment with dramatic writing. Its first success was with poet Robert Lowell's double bill *The Old Glory* (1964), dramatizations of stories by Melville and Hawthorne. Two scholar-poets followed: Ronald Ribman with *Harry, Noon and Night* (1965) and *The Journey of the Fifth Horse* (1966), and William Alfred with *Hogan's Goat* (1965).

It was during this same period that Off-Broadway also developed a distinctive variant on that Broadway staple, the musical comedy. The success of *The Threepenny Opera* showed that audiences would accept a musical without Broadway's large casts, elaborate production values, and full orchestras. But the modest production style had to be an integral part of the show, not a limitation placed on it; the Phoenix Theatre's *The Golden Apple* (1954) and *Once Upon a Mattress* (1959) were really displaced Broadway shows (*Mattress* quickly transferred to Broadway for a successful run).

Closer to the mark was the 1959 Off-Broadway revival of Jerome Kern's 1917 musical *Leave It to Jane;* the production's affectionate and slightly patronizing tone toward its simple story and innocent world underscored a delicateness that would have been buried in a more elaborate staging. In the even more overtly satiric *Little Mary Sunshine* (1959), Rick Besoyan's parody of Nelson Eddy-Jeanette MacDonald operettas drew much of its humor from the disparity between its grand passions and the small stage on which they were played. And it would be hard to imagine a more fragile musical than Tom Jones and Harvey Schmidt's *The Fantasticks* (1960), a dreamlike story of lovers overcoming obstacles that were really placed in their way just to encourage their love; yet with its appropriately modest production and its appropriately tiny theatre it settled in for the longest continuous run in American theatre history. Later Off-Broadway musical successes generally had the same unassuming quality: for example *You're a Good Man, Charlie Brown* (1967), songs and sketches based on the "Peanuts" cartoons; *Godspell* (1970), a festive retelling of the Gospel story; and *Nunsense* (1985), a mock-amateur show. Off-Broadway theatre owner Eric Krebs comments about the last,

Nunsense played in my Douglas Fairbanks Theatre for nine years.

Nunsense never belonged on Broadway, and had it moved there it would have closed in fifteen minutes. Yet Off-Broadway in a 199 seat theatre it was able financially to play week to week at the beginning on a very low amount of money until it could build a word-of-mouth and a following. [Interview]

☆

Between 1950 and 1962 Off-Broadway theatres presented close to one thousand productions, of which a third were new American plays. Starting in 1957 there were more theatres in operation and more productions each season Off-Broadway than on. But as the 1960s progressed, Off-Broadway's vitality and creative energy seemed to wane. The dramatic renaissance that the Albee generation had seemed to promise failed to materialize, at least Off-Broadway. Many of the new playwrights proved unable to follow up on their first successes, while others sought their fortunes elsewhere. Albee, Murray Schisgal, Tom Jones, and Harvey Schmidt went to Broadway with varying degrees of success; Jack Gelber turned to directing; LeRoi Jones left the theatre (and changed his name to Amiri Baraka) to devote himself to political and social action in the African-American community; and some playwrights, evidently less revolutionary than they seemed, were soon happily working in film or television.

Other artists also found themselves moving on. Jose Quintero continued through the 1950s to have success as a director at the Circle in the Square, which had moved from its original home to another Greenwich Village theatre but retained its trademark arena stage. In 1961 artistic and personal differences with Theodore Mann led Quintero to leave the company, with Mann taking over both artistic and business management; Quintero's final Circle production was the very successful staging of Genet's *The Balcony*. The leading new director of the period was Alan Schneider, who had previously staged some light comedies and melodramas on Broadway and who directed the American premiere of *Waiting for Godot* in 1956. That led to the Off-Broadway production of Beckett's *Endgame* (1958), to the American premieres of each of Beckett's other plays, and to most of Albee's Off-Broadway and Broadway plays. Schneider's special strength lay in giving these new and potentially bewildering works a solid reality of setting and characterization, so that audiences could make the connection between the world of the plays and their own experience of life.

Gene Frankel was a skilled director and teacher with a particular affinity for plays of political and social comment. As director of Genet's *The Blacks* (1961), he experimented with a rehearsal technique that would become very popular later in the decade, leading his actors through discussions, encounter sessions, and improvisations in which they discovered and harnessed their own passions and convictions about the play's racial themes. (This production of *The Blacks* is important for another reason: during its one thousand-performance run it employed hundreds of African-American actors, giving experience and exposure that boosted many careers.) After Stuart Vaughan left the New York Shakespeare Festival, Gerald Freedman and Joseph Papp himself continued the work of making Shakespeare come alive for contemporary audiences.

Meanwhile inflation and rising audience expectations made the shoestring operations of Off-Broadway's early years no longer viable; in the mid-1960s a production could cost over $25,000 to mount, and Off-Broadway began to feel the hit-or-flop pressures of Broadway as producers became more cautious and more concerned with attracting audiences. Edward Albee spoke for those who wanted to believe things hadn't changed when he said in 1964,

> Off-Broadway is a losing economic proposition. The actors are not in it for money. The producers are not in it for money. The playwright is not in it for money. The off-Broadway theater simply has to be subsidized by the actors, the producers, the playwrights, the directors. [qtd in Little, *Off* 229]

But a year later his own producers, Barr and Wilder, were forced to admit they could find no new plays they could risk staging, and marked time with a season of revivals of their previous successes.

Two of the four leading companies from Off-Broadway's first period were in apparent decline. The Living Theatre spent the mid-1960s in Europe; although they were developing a new style and repertoire there, it would not be until their return to America in 1968 that its power would be recognized. The Phoenix Theatre, constantly beset by financial problems and unable to support itself even in its new small theatre, withdrew from Off-Broadway production and served as host-producer for the APA. The Circle in the Square was perhaps the least affected; having established a place and an audience for itself as the home of sensitively staged revivals and classics, it had successful runs with such plays as Webster's *The White Devil* (1965) and O'Neill's *A Moon for the Misbegotten* (1968).

A 1969 Circle in the Square production drew attention to a new relationship between Broadway and Off-Broadway: Jules Feiffer's *Little Murders*, which had failed on Broadway only a year earlier, was successfully reconceived and redirected for the smaller Circle theatre. As the earlier revivals of Williams and O'Neill had suggested, Off-Broadway's intimacy, sensitivity, and more sophisticated audience could provide a congenial home for plays originally intended for Broadway.

Alone among the older companies, the New York Shakespeare Festival actually grew and flourished through the decade and beyond. Joseph Papp, using all his skills as salesman, politician, and arm-twister, successfully cajoled money and support from the city, the foundations, and a loyal group of private donors. In 1962 the Delacorte Theater in Central Park opened; in 1964 a bus-and-truck company began to tour New York's other parks and neighborhoods; and in 1966 Papp realized his dream of a permanent year-round theatre. Private donations enabled the Festival to buy the landmark Astor Library building in downtown Manhattan and convert it into the Public Theater, with three playing spaces and a film theatre. In 1971 Papp would pull off an even greater coup by convincing the city to buy the building from him and lease it back for a dollar a year, thus replenishing the Festival's coffers and freeing it from the enormous mortgage expenses.

Meanwhile, the Festival's summer Shakespeare seasons maintained a remarkably high quality, with such successes as *The Merchant of Venice* with George C. Scott as Shylock in 1963 and *Othello* with James Earl Jones in 1964. The first production at the Public Theater was a new rock musical called *Hair* which, in a revised version, would become the first of many Festival shows to move to Broadway and national success. The highlight of the Public's second season was Charles Gordone's *No Place To Be Somebody*, the first Off-Broadway play and the first by a black writer to win the Pulitzer Prize.

Papp would continue to be the entrepreneur, guiding spirit, artistic leader, and virtually the personification of the New York Shakespeare Festival until his death in 1991. Inevitably, not all was perfect about his tenure. The benign despotism of his reign meant that the Festival's offerings were to an enormous degree a reflection of his own tastes and enthusiasms, and both were frequently open to question: his taste was too esoteric for some — Bernard Gersten: "Joe wanted to persuade people who did not want to go to the theater to see plays he felt they should see" [qtd in Epstein 179] — and too conventional for others — John Simon: "vulgar, nouveau riche, insecure notions of what culture is" [Epstein 6].

The Public Theater

Papp occasionally championed writers, theatre companies, or plays that turned out not to merit his commitment of Festival resources to them. He tended to adopt and absorb young writers (e.g., David Rabe) until his protégés, for all their gratitude, were obliged to break with him to keep their sense of independence. He never did succeed in creating or inspiring the new American style of playing Shakespeare that had been one of his earliest goals. Like any enthusiast, he could occasionally be as abrasive as he was often charming, and he was not immune to the seductions of egotism (Broadway transfers of Festival shows were as likely to be advertised as "Joseph Papp presents..." as "The New York Shakespeare Festival presents...").

One of his greatest accomplishments, as explained in later chapters, was finding ways to exploit the commercial theatre to support his not-for-profit organization; the transfer of *A Chorus Line* to Broadway and international productions led to profits of close to forty million dollars for the Festival. But it may also have permitted a kind of fiscal complacency that left the Festival underprepared for the day the money ran out.

Still, there can be no question about Papp's importance. He produced more than seven hundred plays; provided New Yorkers with free Shakespeare in the park for four decades; played a part in the creation of *Hair, A Chorus Line*, and the plays of David Rabe.

> Hundreds of writers, actors, directors, composers, designers, producers, arts administrators, stage managers, journalists and critics traced the beginnings of their careers to the Festival. Thousands more dated their first exposure to Shakespeare to a production in Central Park. Millions of others had seen his productions on television and on Broadway. [Epstein 11]

As innovator, as missionary, as support to some artists and model to others, as tireless defender of his theatre and the arts in general against philistines and politicians (often, in his mind, the same), as boundlessly enthusiastic lover of theatre in every form, and as a colorful figure in his own right, he contributed far more than the Shakespeare Festival and its productions to the American theatre. One critic's comment on Papp's 1974 season could easily serve as his epitaph: "No one who likes theater could fail to applaud Papp's energetic determination to lift the American theater out of its doldrums into the heavens, single-handed if necessary" [Guernsey 272].

Charles Gordone's *No Place To Be Somebody*, a loosely structured picture of growing frustration and anger among the patrons of a Harlem bar, was part of one of Off-Broadway's important accomplishments in the 1960s and 1970s, contributing to the appearance and growth of a new black American theatre and drama. The civil rights and black power movements and the example of LeRoi Jones led a number of African-American writers and performers to turn to the theatre as a platform for self-expression. And although Off-Broadway's audience remained predominantly white, it was liberal and sympathetic, and hungry for new plays. The work of the black dramatists ranged from simple agitprop pieces to poetic reveries, spiritual-based musicals to absurdist farces. Few of the writers had mastered all the technical requirements of structure and characterization, but the best were able to overcome their awkwardness through the power of their moral commitment or the freshness of their vision. Among the successes were *Ceremonies in Dark Old Men* (1969), Lonnie Elder's quietly tragic study of the generation of urban blacks who were too old and tired to dream of revolution, and Douglas Turner Ward's *Day of Absence* (1966), in which black actors in whiteface parodied the reactions of a southern town on the day all the blacks disappeared. In 1968 Ward and actor Robert Hooks founded the Negro Ensemble Company, which was soon followed by the Black Theater Workshop and the New Lafayette Theater. All maintained high standards of play selection and production, encouraging a slowly growing black audience while helping black writers communicate with concerned whites.

Other social forces of the late 1960s were also reflected Off-Broadway, which was often quicker to respond than more commercial art forms. The antiwar movement found voice in several plays, among them Megan Terry's *Viet Rock* (1966) and Barbara Garson's *MacBird!* (1967), which presented President Lyndon Johnson as Shakespeare's murderous Macbeth. Broader criticism of American society was expressed in Jean-Claude van Itallie's *America Hurrah* (1966) and in the group creations with which the Living Theatre toured the country in 1968 and 1969, openly calling for social and political revolution. There was a lighter side as well: 1968 became the year of the nudes and the dirty words as Off-Broadway playwrights and directors topped each other in breaking the taboos of censorship and taste.

☆

The outlines of the entire American theatre were changing during this period, inspired and instigated to a great extent by Off-Broadway's successful challenge to the Broadway monopoly in the 1950s. As the next chapter will show, repertory companies and resident theatres were being established all over the country, and some of them quickly generated satellite "Off-Broadways" of their own. Even in New York City, something calling itself Off Off-Broadway had appeared in the early 1960s, and this second generation of shoestring theatres housed in cabarets, coffeehouses, and churches was taking over Off-Broadway's former role as the home of the avant-garde.

Meanwhile, the economic pressures that led Off-Broadway producers to caution and greater commercial considerations in the 1960s only grew worse in the 1970s, when the costs of producing a play or musical Off-Broadway reached the levels of Broadway production twenty years earlier. Critic Robert Brustein had been somewhat premature in 1961 when he complained that

> Accompanying [Off-Broadway's] heightened prestige . . . has come a growing reluctance to take chances. . . . The rise in ticket prices and production costs, the employment of high salaried actors from the commercial stage, the burgeoning of new high-rent theaters, the marked increase in press-agentry and advertising — all these tokens, along with a general decline in the quality of off-Broadway fare, suggest that powerful economic pressures are putting the squeeze on off-Broadway's aesthetic freedom. [*Seasons* 42–43]

But there is no doubt that the more conservative Otis L. Guernsey, Jr. was a bit overdue in coming to the same conclusion twelve years later:

> Shrinking straight-play and expanding musical volume; reluctance to experiment, with a consequently lower level of invention; rising production costs and substantial ticket prices.... Off Broadway appears to be changing from a free-swinging adventure into some sort of mini-commercial theater, inheriting all the problems which have for so long burdened Broadway. [257]

If Off-Broadway came to resemble Broadway more and more, as Guernsey suggested, much of that resemblance was caused by the fact that Broadway had become more like it. By 1970 Albee, Kopit, and Schisgal had become Broadway writers, as had Pinter, Brecht, and Ionesco. Jose Quintero and Alan Schneider were Broadway directors, and *Hair* and three seasons of the APA-Phoenix had played uptown. Beginning in the 1970s, transfers from Off-Broadway to Broadway became even more frequent, with the New York Shakespeare Festival in particular becoming the source of some of Broadway's biggest commercial and critical successes.

Meanwhile, as Chapter Five will explain, economic forces were reducing Broadway's vitality, and plays that in another period would have been Broadway fare were increasingly being staged Off-Broadway because it was cheaper. As Broadway and Off-Broadway producer David Richenthal explained, "Your capital costs are much less than on Broadway, and if you've produced correctly and your weekly operating budgets are reasonable, you can recoup your investment in a few months" rather than the years it could take on Broadway [Interview]. It was not so much that Off-Broadway, having had its experimental fling, had retreated back into the theatrical mainstream. Rather, the mainstream had been altered and expanded so that artists and sensibilities that had once been peripheral now made up a significant part of the center.

From the audience's perspective, the distinction between Broadway and the more commercial wing of Off-Broadway eventually became completely blurred. Geography played a part in this mingling of images, as more and more Off-Broadway theatres opened in the Broadway district. When the American Place Theatre was founded in a church a block from Broadway, and the Circle in the Square moved uptown to a building shared with a new Broadway theatre, and a number of companies converted a rundown section of Forty-second Street into "Theatre

Row," going to the Off-Broadway theatre could mean getting off the subway at the same stop as Broadway.

When important playwrights (Tennessee Williams, Edward Albee, Lanford Wilson, David Mamet, even Neil Simon) were produced Off-Broadway as well as on, and when movie and TV stars (Anthony Hopkins, Judd Hirsch, Jessica Tandy, Richard Thomas, Al Pacino) were as likely to be seen Off-Broadway as on, the only difference a theatre-goer was likely to notice was the cost of the ticket (as a general rule, about half the Broadway price) and the size of the house. (Actually, the only real difference was a legal one, as Actors Equity and the theatrical craft unions developed different contracts and pay scales based on little more than the number of seats in the auditorium.)

Meanwhile, the more radical and experimental energies in New York City theatre moved in the opposite direction, even further away from the commercial mainstream, as the self-consciously ironic label Off Off-Broadway suggests; that movement will be discussed in Chapter Four. What, then, of the essentially non-experimental but still artistically ambitious young playwrights, actors, and directors, the artistic heirs of the first Off-Broadway generation? This splintering of Off-Broadway, one part moving closer to Broadway and one further from it, would have left a vacuum in the center were it not for the appearance of a third force in the American theatre scene.

As Chapter Three will demonstrate, during the same years covered in this chapter a theatrical revolution of another sort, and ultimately far more significant, was taking place across America: the appearance and very rapid spread of a noncommercial, subsidized resident theatre movement. Established, continuing companies, legally defined as not-for-profit corporations and thus eligible for support from charitable foundations as well as individual, corporate, and government donors, represented the new face of the American theatre. A branch of this movement, adapted to the special circumstances of New York City, picked up the flag of classics, revivals, and new American plays, and became an important part of Off-Broadway in the 1970s and 1980s. As Marshall W. Mason, then Artistic Director of the Circle Repertory Company, said in 1975, "We're a regional theatre whose region is New York" [Interview 108].

It is becoming apparent that the story of Off-Broadway in the last quarter of the century is so bound up with other segments of the theatre that it would be repetitive at best (and false at worst) to insist on speaking of it separately; and various aspects of the history begun in this chapter will be picked up in later chapters. For now, let this be said. The first significant contribution of Off-Broadway to the history of the American theatre was the very fact of its existence. By breaking the Broadway monopoly and demonstrating that theatre could happen in physical spaces and economic structures other than those that ruled Times Square, Off-Broadway began the revolutions described in this book. The second essential contribution is the ongoing body of work, by actors, directors, designers and playwrights, that has found a congenial home in this alternative arena.

And, when Broadway's creative energies flagged, it was Off-Broadway — particularly the not-for-profit institutional theatre companies — that took up the challenge and responsibility of presenting new plays and playwrights to the New York audience. As the importance of Broadway — and indeed of New York — waned, Off-Broadway would become, in the last years of the century, the theatrical center of what could be seen as just one theatre city among many.

Frank Langella, Roscoe Lee Browne in *The Old Glory*

3

REGIONAL THEATRE

The Civic Light Opera Companies of Los Angeles and San Francisco were formed to produce annual seasons of Viennese operetta. But around 1950 they found themselves in a new role as co-producers and, in essence, underwriters of the national companies of such Broadway musicals as *Where's Charley?* and *Guys and Dolls.* Most Broadway successes had one or more touring companies during or after their New York run, but it was generally agreed that there were few profitable cities west of Chicago, and producers of elaborate and expensive shows were reluctant to make a long western trip just to play two stops in California. So the California organizations had to guarantee the New York producers' profits and occasionally make up their losses to be included in the national tours. For much the same reason many touring dramas and comedies never reached the West Coast either, as the original producers found it safer to license local restagings. Thus, for example, while some cities elsewhere in the country were visited by the New York-based touring company of *The Cocktail Party* in 1951, Californians saw a production that originated at the La Jolla Playhouse.

About the same time the phenomenon of summer stock was booming. Summer theatres, amateur and professional, had existed since the Elitch Gardens in Denver started offering plays in 1890. The traditionally slow season in New York led actors and producers to follow vacationing audiences to their rural retreats and resort towns, and by the summer of 1949 there were at least 125 professional repertory companies and about the same number of amateur groups performing in barns, tents, resort hotels, and theatres. The professional companies alone presented more than 450 plays, usually for one- or two-week runs, and frequently with established Broadway and Hollywood stars in the leading roles. Writing in 1978, summer stock veteran Harold J. Kennedy remembered this as a golden age:

> Summer stock thirty years ago was an experimental experience. Actors did it for almost no money and they did it usually for the opportunity to play some glorious part, which they were usually wrong

for, in some artsy-craftsy play that no sensible commercial manager would ever allow them to do .... It was much more adventurous and in many ways better for the theater. [195]

But the record doesn't really support Kennedy's memory. Except for a couple of Shakespeare festivals and an occasional stab at Chekhov or Restoration comedy, the summer stock seasons were made up almost entirely of recent Broadway hits: in 1949 twenty-six professional theatres offered *The Heiress,* twenty-one did *John Loves Mary,* and so on. And Theodore Mann remembers how the Circle in the Square attempted to do summer stock in 1951:

> That summer we toured in the Catskills wherever we could get a booking. I remember once going to this famous cultural hotel in New Hampshire [with] Christopher Fry's *A Phoenix Too Frequent....* The first line begins "Oh, Zeus," and at that point they started to get up and leave. At the end of the play there were four people left in the house; they were the kitchen crew and they loved it. [Interview]

Mann and his cast had to stage a sit-in at the manager's office to be paid their $125 for the performance.

There were some new plays offered in summer stock. In 1949 about a hundred new scripts were performed, but all were pre-Broadway try-outs looking for producers or underwritten by Broadway producers; the Theatre Guild, for example, frequently used the Country Playhouse in Westport, Connecticut, to test new scripts before investing in full productions. (Only four of the one hundred new plays in 1949 actually got to Broadway, and only one—William Inge's *Come Back, Little Sheba*—succeeded, a typical ratio for the period.)

And summer stock was really a rather local phenomenon. A fifth of the 250 professional and amateur theatres operating at the end of the 1940s were in New York State, and almost all the rest were in New Jersey, Pennsylvania, and the New England states—i.e., where the Broadway audience went for the summer. Most of the stock companies were formed in New York with New York actors, and many were managed from there. And most of the big stars, like their counterparts a century earlier, appeared in only one play all summer, arriving at a theatre in time for a quick run-through with a local cast that had rehearsed without them, playing a week, and then moving on to another theatre offering the same play. Kennedy recalls being in one local company when the visiting male star suddenly began playing a love scene to him, because he was sitting where the heroine had sat at the last theatre [65–6].

A few years later, in a further repetition of the nineteenth-century pattern, this system was replaced by complete touring casts, almost exclusively in crowd-pleasing light comedies and Broadway hits, eliminating the need for many local companies and turning local producers into little more than landlords.

These two examples — the California productions and the summer stock companies — demonstrate Broadway's total domination of the professional American theatre at mid-century. There was theatre outside Manhattan, but it was either Broadway-based, Broadway-bound, or a Broadway surrogate. There were hundreds of theatres and, at peak season, thousands of actors at work in America. But there was no real American theatre independent of New York. When a national theatre appeared — or, rather, when a number of companies began to establish independent identities around the country — the roots were not in Broadway or its professional outposts, but in the amateur community theatre movement.

☆

Margo Jones was a talented and dedicated director who had worked with the Pasadena Playhouse and the Ojai, California, Community Players before founding the Houston Community Players in 1936. After several years in Houston, she concluded that really high quality productions required the rehearsal and preparation time that only a professional company could afford, and chose Dallas as a city likely to support such a company. She spent most of the 1940s organizing what was to become Theatre '47 (later Theatre '48, and so on), the first not-for-profit professional resident repertory theatre in America.

The significance of Theatre '47 does not merely lie in the fact that it was first; Jones's accomplishments and her messianic zeal directly influenced many of the theatres that followed. Although she herself thought that her advocacy of theatre-in-the-round staging was her biggest contribution, it was really her vision and her call to action, as expressed in her book *Theatre-in-the-Round*:

> The dream of all serious theatre people in the United States in the middle of our twentieth century is the establishment of a national theatre.... What our country needs today, theatrically speaking, is a resident professional theatre in every city with a population of over one hundred thousand.... Every town in America wants theatre! It is the duty and business of a capable theatre person to go into the communities of this country and create fine theatres. [3–5]

Photo: Lucas Pritchard; Billy Rose Theatre Collection, New York Public Library at Lincoln Center

Margo Jones

Theatre-in-the-Round became, in Joseph Wesley Zeigler's words, "the nearest thing to a bible in the regional theatre world" [*Regional* 17]; and Jones's accomplishments, public statements, and willingness to counsel and encourage others made Theatre '47 a model for other companies in its organization and operation.

In purely practical terms, it is likely that Margo Jones's decision to incorporate her theatre as a not-for-profit organization had the most far-reaching effects. She recognized that a resident repertory company was too expensive an operation to support itself entirely through the box office; a not-for-profit corporation, with a board of directors made up of civic and social leaders, not only encouraged donations but also involved the community in the theatre's future. Virtually every subsequent regional theatre has chosen not-for-profit status; and the influx of private, foundation, and government donations has changed the entire financial set-up of the American theatre.

Other pattern-setting elements were the adoption of a found space for the actual playhouse, in this case a building on the State Fairgrounds that was vacant most of the year, and the establishment of a permanent organization with a professional staff and resident professional company. For her repertoire Jones deliberately turned her back on the light Broadway hand-me-downs that were the staples of amateur companies, and committed herself to classics (Ibsen, Chekhov, Shakespeare) and new plays (the premieres of Tennessee Williams's *Summer and Smoke* and an early version of William Inge's *Dark at the Top of the Stairs* in the first season). Audiences were encouraged to subscribe for an entire season, as much to cement their commitment to the theatre as to provide working capital.

Although each season included at least one week of rotating repertory, the bulk of the schedule was made up of two- or three-week runs of each play in turn. (Actual rotating repertory — that is, a different play each night — is expensive and very rare in American resident theatre, and even those companies with "Repertory" in their titles generally schedule a sequence of continuing runs.) Finally, although Jones acknowledged that the jobs of managing director and artistic director were ideally separate, she filled both roles in her theatre. This proved unfortunate for the Dallas company, which disbanded soon after her untimely death in 1955, but as Stephen Langley acknowledged in a guidebook on production, "It is important to note that every significant resident theatre was founded and operated by a single if not singular personality who could easily qualify as 'dynamic'" [*Theatre Management* 118–19].

Two such figures appeared on the scene almost immediately. In 1947 Nina Vance formed an amateur company in Houston, where Jones's Community Players had become inactive. Two years later she moved from her rented dance studio to a converted factory reached through a back alley, where the Alley Theatre's seasons of Williams, Miller, O'Neill, and light comedies inspired enthusiastic community support. This, along with the urging of Margo Jones, encouraged Vance to hire occasional professional guest actors and then, in 1954, to convert the Alley to a fully professional company.

(The operative date for such changes generally when a company "goes Equity" — that is, when its actors sign contracts approved by Actors' Equity, the performers' union. There are some non-Equity professional theatres; and many amateur companies that eventually go Equity pass through a preliminary stage in which amateurs work alongside professionals or actors are paid less than the union minimum.)

Meanwhile, in 1950 Zelda Fichandler formed the amateur Arena Stage in a converted movie house in Washington, D.C., and after one seventeen-play season also made the leap to professional status. When its original structure as a commercial for-profit operation could not be sustained, the Arena was reorganized as a not-for-profit corporation; and both the Washington and Houston companies flourished in the

Photo: Alley Theatre Collection

Nina Vance

Photo: Tess Steinkolk

Zelda Fichandler

years that followed, moving to larger homes, doubling and redoubling their subscription bases and, in the 1960s, building multimillion-dollar theatres to house their expanded activities.

What might be called the Alley-Arena model — the formation under the direction of a charismatic leader of an amateur company that graduates to professional status — was repeated in several other cities. Mack Scism founded the amateur Mummers Theatre in Oklahoma City in 1949 and led it as it grew from a summer tent company producing comic nineteenth-century melodramas to a year-round community theatre in the 1950s and to a professional repertory company in the 1960s. Herbert Blau and Jules Irving began their Actor's Workshop in a San Francisco loft in 1952 and went Equity in 1955; they quickly gained a national reputation for innovative productions and an adventurous repertoire built around such authors as Brecht, Beckett, and Pinter. George Touliatos began the amateur Front Street Theatre in a Memphis hotel ballroom in 1957 and progressed to professional status in 1959.

The example of such ventures inspired some already-functioning amateur companies to transform themselves into professional theatres, in what might be called the Cleveland Play House model. The Play House, one of the oldest community theatres in America, had had a professional executive director and business staff since the 1920s but had retained its amateur status even as its activities expanded to include an annual summer Shakespeare festival; it finally made the change in 1958. Similarly, the Studio Arena Theatre in Buffalo, New York, begun as an acting school and amateur company in 1927, went Equity in 1965. The Dallas Theater Center evolved out of the amateur Dallas Little Theatre in 1954, under the direction of Paul Baker; long a student/professional mix, it achieved full professional status in 1981. Theatre Atlanta was formed in 1957 through the merger of several older amateur groups, hired a professional managing director in 1965, and became a professional company in 1966.

The Goodman Theatre, an acting school and community theatre associated with Chicago's Art Institute since 1925, formed a professional repertory company in 1969; the company stayed on even after the acting school split away to join a local university. Two theatres that began as professional stock companies (i.e., by booking individually cast productions, frequently with guest stars) in the 1950s reorganized themselves as not-for-profit repertory theatres in the 1960s: the Fred Miller Theatre, later the Milwaukee Rep; and the Charles Playhouse in Boston.

The Alley Theatre

Arena Stage

A third group of regional theatres was born full-grown in a pattern most glamorously exemplified by the Tyrone Guthrie Theater in Minneapolis. In 1959 three theatre professionals — world-famous director Guthrie, Broadway producer Oliver Rea, and stage manager Peter Zeisler — decided that the next career challenge they wanted to face was the creation of a professional repertory company. As associates of theirs later admitted, "In the beginning, at least, theirs was not an attempt to build a theatre to fit and serve a particular community, but to find a community that would fit and serve a particular theatre — Guthrie's theatre" [Morison 5].

They considered several cities and chose Minneapolis as much because it was the farthest removed from other theatre centers as for any other reason, and so impressed civic and community leaders with their plans that the 2.25 million-dollar Tyrone Guthrie Theater was built for them. In 1963 a star-filled company directed by Guthrie began its first season and almost overnight gave the entire regional theatre movement what Zeigler called "enhanced legitimacy and new attention":

> The emergence of The Guthrie Theater was [a] major turning point of the regional theatre revolution because it further legitimized the movement and gave it national weight. It gave hope to all regional theatres that they too could become known on a national level, that the *Times* might soon cover their opening nights, and that actors like Hume Cronyn and Jessica Tandy might soon set aside a season for them. [*Regional* 75]

The Guthrie was not immune to the financial and audience-building problems that beset less famous companies, but it remained one of the strongest and most prestigious in the country. On a somewhat more modest scale, several other energetic individuals created full-grown theatres in the 1960s: actor-director Ellis Rabb formed the touring Association of Performing Artists in 1960; Smith College professor Jacques Cartier founded the professional Hartford Stage Company in 1964; and Yale Drama School students Harlan Kleiman and Jon Jory opened New Haven's Long Wharf Theatre in 1965.

A variant on this pattern came with the spread of university-based professional theatres. Colleges and universities had long served as cultural centers in many parts of the country, but their theatre programs were as often as not merely extracurricular clubs, and their theatre departments strictly academic in their focus. In a speech to the Association

Photo: Tyrone Guthrie Theater Collection

Tyrone Guthrie

of Graduate Schools in 1961, W. McNeil Lowry of the Ford Foundation warned that

> The university has largely taken over the functions of professional training in the arts but in the main has sacrificed professional standards.... The future of professional training in the arts depends, first, upon a radical shift in the university atmosphere surrounding students considered potential artists, and, second, upon the provision of postgraduate opportunities for professional apprenticeship. [106]

To Howard Stein, later Professor of Theatre at Yale and Columbia, the message was clear: "'I will not give you any money because you teach people to teach people, and we want to support artists and the training of artists.' It changed the training of theatre people in this country" [Interview].

Of course some university theatre programs already had a pre-professional focus, but during the 1960s many others changed their structure to involve working theatre artists and professional training. And for many universities this meant either developing a close relationship with a professional theatre company or creating one of their own. The Dallas Theater Center was associated with Baylor College and later with Trinity University; the Syracuse Repertory Theatre, begun as a Syracuse University student program in 1961, evolved into a professional company in 1966; and the Yale Repertory Theatre (Yale, 1966), Loretto-Hilton Center (Webster College, St. Louis, 1966), McCarter Theatre

(Princeton, 1972), and American Repertory Theatre (Harvard, 1979) are among others in this category.

In 1969 the University/Resident Theatre Association was founded to encourage the development of university-based professional theatres or ties between universities and existing professional companies. Executive Director Scott L. Steele explains,

> They went about this by establishing criteria that members had to follow: using more professional guest artists, having faculty members who were also practicing professionals, and, most importantly, creating associations with professional theatres for internships, etc. [Interview]

In addition to those schools already named, the University of Connecticut developed a relationship with the Connecticut Repertory Theatre, Florida State with the Asolo Theatre Company, the University of Minnesota with the Guthrie, and so on. As Steele points out, such connections have significant benefits for the theatres as well, aside from providing them with interns and potential company members. "The Alabama Shakespeare Festival associated itself with the University of Alabama, and I think it had a major impact on that theatre company eventually becoming a line item on the state budget" [Interview].

Finally, a number of resident theatres were born by outside fiat, as civic groups or government agencies decided that a particular city needed a repertory company and ordered its creation. Although this group included some of the resident theatre's biggest success stories, companies in this category—which might be called the Lincoln Center model in honor of its most spectacular failure—generally suffered the greatest birth and growing pains, in part from the absence of the highly motivated leaders typical of other theatres and in part from the proprietary instincts of the founding bodies. As John Glore pointed out about the Seattle Repertory Theatre,

> It is significant that the theater was first conceived by the citizenry; and their committee carried the embryonic idea through to its realization. From the beginning then, the citizens rightly held the belief that SRT was their child and must answer to them.... This, in part, accounts for SRT's somewhat erratic history. [64]

The Seattle Rep was brought into being by a local committee in 1963, to make use of a theatre building left over from the Seattle World's Fair. Stuart Vaughan, who had led New York's Phoenix Theatre during its repertory company period, was hired as artistic director but was fired after two seasons as a result of artistic differences with the board of directors. A similar fate befell Andre Gregory, hired to direct the new Theatre of the Living Arts in Philadelphia in 1965. As he explained later, "The Board and I were both working to create a theatre in Philadelphia. The difficulty was that we were trying to create two different kinds of theatre" [20]. Gregory's theatre featured imaginative productions of Beckett, Anouilh, and Rochelle Owens; the Board and the Philadelphia audiences evidently wanted *Room Service* and *The Time of Your Life* (which Gregory also staged) Gregory was fired and the theatre put in the hands of a more conservative director.

Also in 1965, William Ball was hired by the board of the Pittsburgh Playhouse when that veteran amateur theatre chose to start afresh as a professional company rather than follow the Cleveland model. Ball had long dreamed of a combination theatre and conservatory in which professional actors could continue to study their craft while performing, and the company he created for Pittsburgh was the American Conservatory Theatre. His first season of Albee, Pirandello, Shakespeare, Molière, and the like was evidently too much of a contrast to the Playhouse's past menu of Broadway comedies, and Ball was dismissed within a year. And while the Seattle Repertory Theatre survived its growing pains, the Pittsburgh Playhouse and the Theatre of the Living Arts did not; one lapsed back into amateur status and Broadway hand-me-downs, and the other went bankrupt.

Meanwhile, in one of the success stories of this category, William Ball's American Conservatory Theatre spent 1966 in a critically triumphant tour of the country that resulted in invitations to settle in Chicago and San Francisco. For a while ACT considered spending half the year in each city, but fundraising was more successful in San Francisco, and the company opened there in 1967. A couple of overly ambitious seasons threatened to sink the new theatre, but some belt-tightening got it through the shaky period and it went on to become one of the most active and prosperous resident repertory companies in the country.

The Repertory Theatre New Orleans and the Inner City Repertory Company in Los Angeles were created in 1966 by the federal Office of Education and the National Endowment for the Arts to perform classic plays for students bussed in from area high schools and, incidentally, for paying adult audiences. Both companies had to deal with interference and censorship by local school boards as well as the inherent difficulty of satisfying the disparate tastes and needs of their student and adult au-

William Ball

diences. Without a local base of support, the New Orleans theatre died with the end of its federal funding; and the Inner City Rep survived only in a reduced form on the government and foundation grants for its associated community cultural center. (A third theatre in this federal project, Trinity Square Repertory Company in Providence, Rhode Island, was already functioning as a community theatre and was helped in its advancement to professional status by the government grant; it survived and flourished afterward.)

☆

Curiously, one of the biggest successes in the resident theatre movement and its greatest disaster have similar backgrounds: both were created externally to fill massive multimillion-dollar arts centers. But the Center Theatre Group flourished in Los Angeles's Music Center, while the Repertory Theater of Lincoln Center in New York City collapsed under its own weight four separate times. This makes them worthy of special analysis.

The Los Angeles Music Center is one of the many downtown arts centers built in the culture revival and urban renewal fervor of the 1960s. It consists of three theatres: the 3250-seat Dorothy Chandler Pavilion, home of the Los Angeles Philharmonic and the Light Opera Company; and the 2100-seat Ahmanson Theatre and 742-seat arena-stage Mark Taper Forum, both built to be operated by a resident play-

The Music Center of the County of Los Angeles
From top: Ahmanson Theatre, Mark
Taper Forum, Dorothy Chandler Pavilion

producing organization. One key to the Center's success, undoubtedly, is that it did not attempt to create a new theatre company, but rather adopted and expanded one that had already developed an identity and an audience.

The Theatre Group, as it was then called, was formed in 1959 in a loose alliance with the University of California in Los Angeles. Led first by John Houseman and then by Gordon Davidson, it did not employ a permanent company, but drew on the pool of Hollywood-based actors eager to do stage work. Despite its challenging repertoire of classic and contemporary plays and its relative poverty and inaccessibility — the Group received no subsidy from UCLA but was merely allowed to borrow whatever campus theatre, lecture hall, or classroom was not being used by university groups on a given date — the Theatre Group built up a loyal following. When Davidson was invited to move his operation downtown in 1967 he brought along a subscription base of eleven thousand and a reputation that attracted twenty thousand more.

The Center Theatre Group's activities were divided between its two theatres. At the Mark Taper Forum Davidson continued to do uncompromisingly challenging and provocative plays, with a special emphasis on American premieres such as John Whiting's *The Devils* (1967) and Heiner Kipphardt's *In the Matter of J. Robert Oppenheimer* (1968), and world premieres such as Conor Cruise O'Brien's *Murderous Angels* (1970). An integral part of the Taper program was New Theatre for Now (later, Taper Too), workshop productions of new American plays, some of which graduated into the regular season. New Theatre for Now's early alumni list challenges that of the Barr-Wilder-Albee Playwrights Unit in New York: John Guare, Oliver Hailey, Israel Horovitz, Adrienne Kennedy, Terrence McNally, Leonard Melfi, Robert Patrick, Lanford Wilson.

The larger Ahmanson Theatre hosted visiting productions and staged more conventional works, many of them essentially Broadway tryouts. In a variant on the old use of summer stock to test plays, Ahmanson productions would be offered to New York producers or co-produced with them. The New York producer got the opportunity to test the project with the Center Theatre Group bearing or sharing the initial expense, while the Group was able to mount productions and attract stars it might otherwise not have been able to afford, and to participate in the profits, if any, from the New York run. The Center Theatre Group's first Ahmanson production in 1967 was the American premiere of Eugene O'Neill's posthumous *More Stately Mansions*, directed by Jose Quintero and starring Ingrid Bergman and Colleen Dewhurst. In the years that followed it would also send such plays as

Photo: Mark Taper Forum Collection

The Mark Taper Forum

Photo: Mark Taper Forum Collection

Gordon Davidson

Alan Ayckbourn's *The Norman Conquests* (1975) and several of Neil Simon's successful comedies on to New York.

The first of the great urban renewal arts centers of the 1960s was Lincoln Center for the Performing Arts, about a mile north of the Broadway theatre district in New York. With homes for the Metropolitan Opera, the New York Philharmonic, the New York City Opera and Ballet companies, the Juilliard School, and the New York Public Library's performing arts collection, all it needed was a resident theatre company. The Lincoln Center Board of Directors hired experienced Broadway producer Robert Whitehead and director Elia Kazan to form and direct such a company; and they in turn recruited director-critic Harold Clurman, playwright Arthur Miller, and an acting company led by Hal Holbrook, Ralph Meeker, David Wayne, and Jason Robards.

Since the 1100-seat Vivian Beaumont Theater (with a smaller studio theatre in its basement) that was to be its home was not completed, the Repertory Theater of Lincoln Center played its first two seasons (1964–1965) in a temporary theatre especially built for it in Greenwich Village. The opening production was Miller's new *After the Fall*, directed by Kazan. It was followed by Eugene O'Neill's *Marco Millions*, directed by Jose Quintero; S. N. Behrman's new comedy *But For Whom Charlie*, directed by Kazan; Middleton's *The Changeling*, also directed by Kazan; *Incident at Vichy*, another new Miller play, directed by Clurman; and William Ball's production of Molière's *Tartuffe*.

Clearly, this was a high-powered operation, involving artists of established reputation and talent. It was also a disaster, with only *After the Fall* achieving any critical and popular success. In December 1964 the Board fired Whitehead, leading Kazan, Miller, and Clurman to resign in protest. Zeigler reconstructs the next step in the thinking of the Lincoln Center Board of Directors:

> The Repertory Theatre of Lincoln Center in this first phase had been an attempt to form a National Theatre out of the best of Broadway, and it failed. If talents like Kazan's and Whitehead's could not create a National Theatre, none from Broadway could — and therefore the talent for the job would have to come from beyond. [*Regional* 145]

Herbert Blau and Jules Irving of the Actor's Workshop in San Francisco were hired to create a new company and start all over for the Beaumont's opening in 1965. Their first New York season was a challenging and adventurous one: *Danton's Death, The Country Wife, The Condemned of Altona,* and *The Caucasian Chalk Circle*. It was also a critical and box office flop.

After an equally unsuccessful second season Blau resigned in despair, leaving Irving to struggle on for five more years, during which the repertory company was disbanded and individually cast productions, generally of such safe classics as Shaw's *St. Joan*, were offered to shrinking audiences and growing deficits. By the end of the decade the Beaumont was losing $800,000 a year, and in 1971 the Lincoln Center Board seriously considered a proposal to turn the building into a complex of movie theatres. In 1972 Irving finally gave up. (The curse that haunted the Beaumont had meanwhile cast its spell across the country: without Blau and Irving the Actor's Workshop disbanded in 1966.)

Lincoln Center for the Performing Arts
**From lower left: New York State Theater, Guggenheim Bandshell
in Damrosch Park, the Metropolitan Opera House, the New York
Public Library at Lincoln Center: Library & Museum of the
Performing Arts, Vivian Beaumont Theater and Mitzi Newhouse
Theater, Juilliard School and Alice Tully Hall, Avery Fisher Hall**

In 1973 the Board of Directors called in the one man in the country
who seemed likely to be able to defy the curse, and the Beaumont Theater became part of Joseph Papp's New York Shakespeare Festival em-
pire. Papp announced a policy of producing new plays in the main
theatre and a year-round Shakespeare festival in the smaller house, but
after two money-losing years he dropped the Shakespeare, moved the
new plays downstairs and offered a series of safe revivals and classics in
the main theatre. After two more years he too quit, complaining that the
Beaumont's losses were draining the New York Shakespeare Festival's
resources and threatening its other operations.

The Beaumont Theater remained dark until the end of the decade,
when the parent Lincoln Center Board decided to run it directly, creating the Lincoln Center Theater Company, to be directed by Richmond
Crinkley. Devoting most of his energy to raising money and looking for
solutions to real or perceived problems with the building itself, Crinkley
managed only three badly-received productions before the Board pulled
the plug; and the house remained empty, except for a couple of outside

Photo: David Hirsch/Lincoln Center for the Performing Arts, Inc.

Vivian Beaumont Theater

Photo: Brigitte Lacombe

Bernard Gersten, Greg Mosher

bookings, for another four years while the Lincoln Center Board considered converting it into a skating rink.

The curse was only lifted with the fifth attempt. In 1985 Gregory Mosher of Chicago's Goodman Theatre was hired as artistic director and Bernard Gersten, formerly of the New York Shakespeare Festival, as executive producer of the Lincoln Center Theater. Giving up any pretense to establishing a resident repertory company like Whitehead's, or to offering a significant artistic alternative like Papp's, Mosher and Gersten wisely offered New York what it wanted: another Broadway producer in the mold of the no-longer-active Theatre Guild. The Lincoln Center Theater became, in effect, a subsidized venue for productions on the more artistically ambitious end of the Broadway spectrum: revivals (*House of Blue Leaves*, 1986), imports (*Sarafina*, 1987), safe classics (*Our Town*, 1988), and the occasional new play by established writers (David Mamet's *Speed-the-Plow*, 1988).

Some of these ran only as part of the Lincoln Center season, some transferred to Broadway, and some opened directly on Broadway. By the mid-1980s Broadway had given up producing this sort of work, and there still remained an audience for whom Off-Broadway (which *was* doing similar productions) was intimidating, unwelcoming, or, because of its lower budgets, unsatisfying; and so the Lincoln Center Theater found a niche. When Andre Bishop, previously of Off-Broadway's Playwrights Horizons, succeeded Mosher as Artistic Director in 1992, he continued essentially the same (finally) winning formula.

There is no single reason why the theatre in Los Angeles succeeded immediately and the one in New York failed again and again, but the contributing factors illuminate the problems and triumphs of other resident theatres. The fact that Lincoln Center began by trying to create a mature repertory company out of thin air while Los Angeles allowed a going concern to flourish under its sponsorship is certainly an important difference. As Andre Bishop notes, "Unlike most theatres that started with a man or a woman and an artistic impulse to fill a need, this place started with a building that filled no need, and then they hired people to run the building" [Interview]. Bernard Gersten says much the same thing:

> This building was not built for an existing theatre company; that was one of its disadvantages. The Met Opera was built for a known artistic entity, and so was Avery Fisher Hall, and so was the State Theatre; and Juilliard School certainly knew what it was. But the theatre was just an abstraction: there "should be" a theatre here. [Interview]

The Center Theatre Group started with at least some of its growing pains behind it; it had established a reputation and a following at UCLA, and working with a low budget and borrowed spaces helped Gordon Davidson learn how to use a bare stage. Lincoln Center's first directors had to learn how to operate a repertory theatre as they went along, and Bishop feels that this was the largest factor in their failure:

> When the Beaumont was built they decided to build this art theatre based on a European model, based on a thrust stage, based on a repertory company doing the classics—everything New York had never seen. And so Kazan and Whitehead simply were trying to do something they did not have any feeling for. [Interview]

Elia Kazan himself later wrote,

> I've often wondered why I accepted an executive post, responsible not only for the creation of a company of actors but also for administering a kind of theatre that was new to me and to us all in New York. [586]

Part of their difficulty in the first two seasons arose from the very basic error of choosing an acting company primarily to meet the needs of one play, *After the Fall,* and then having to squeeze the actors into the other plays. Another part came from having Broadway's most talented director of contemporary American dramas discover his (and his actors') limitations with Jacobean tragedy and even boulevard comedy in full view of the whole world:

> Sam Behrman's *But For Whom Charlie* not only could have been done on Broadway but should have been done there. It desperately needed the services of stars.... Our company had been populated with actors who'd served Art's play and who were to my own taste of realistic psychological drama. To put them in Sam's play was unfair to him—and to them. [Kazan 689]

The Center Theatre Group also had an artistic identity and a core audience from the start, and its three-tier structure (conventional plays in the Ahmanson, more adventurous productions in the Taper, and new plays in the Monday night workshops) allowed audiences with different tastes to come with some idea of the sort of theatrical experience they were going to have. Despite occasional adverse reactions to Taper plays—Gordon Davidson recalls then–Governor Ronald Reagan walking out in the middle of the opening performance of *The Devils*—"for every person [we] lost because of what we were doing, there were others we could bring in for the first time." The Lincoln Center operation changed leadership, styles, and repertoires every few years in its desperate attempt to find something that worked, and never gave a loyal audience time to find it.

Identity problems of this sort threatened the Tyrone Guthrie Theater as well; when the novelty of the new building wore off and the star-studded first company left, subscriptions fell alarmingly and the management had to work hard to build an audience that would come to a resident company for its own sake. Similarly, when Gregory Boyd became Artistic Director of the Alley Theatre in 1989 he expanded the repertoire from its safe conservative pattern and found that such tinkering had repercussions on the subscription base: "When I first got here in '89 we did some fairly radical productions and we lost a lot of our traditional Alley audience. Since then we've replaced it and more, with a lot younger audience" [Interview]

More basically, the Center Theatre Group met an authentic need that the Lincoln Center theatre did not. By 1967 Los Angeles was theatre-hungry and the Center Theatre Group was to a great extent the only game in town. Audiences, financial supporters, and even critics were primed to like it and to want it to succeed. In a very real sense the Repertory Theater of Lincoln Center had no reason for existing; while it would have been nice, in theory, for New York City to have a world-class repertory company, it filled no real audience hunger. The first version was essentially a Broadway operation, and New York already had a Broadway. *After the Fall* certainly would have found a Broadway producer, and *But For Whom Charlie* was in fact scheduled for Broadway production by Whitehead, with Kazan directing, and was slotted into the Lincoln Center schedule instead.

The Blau-Irving and Papp versions were essentially Off-Broadway, and New York already had an Off-Broadway. Many of Blau and Irving's plays would eventually have been done Off-Broadway, and Papp's Beaumont seasons were simply extensions of the work he was already doing elsewhere in the city. Audiences came to the Metropolitan Opera in Lincoln Center because the old Opera House had been torn down, but there was no built-in reason to come to the Beaumont. The successful resident theatres across America were those that satisfied an audience hunger for good theatre; where that hunger didn't exist (in Pittsburgh and New Orleans, for example), simply creating a theatre didn't create an audience. On the other hand, the fact that William Ball's ACT arrived in San Francisco the year after the Actor's Workshop died undoubtedly contributed to its enthusiastic welcome.

Another inescapable cause of Lincoln Center's repeated failures was the public perception of the theatre and its offerings. While the second and third versions may have had more in common with such Off-Broadway operations as the Circle in the Square, the public and the critics always saw and judged them in Broadway terms. Certainly the backgrounds and offerings of the first directors did little to discourage this identification, and the impressive new Beaumont Theater with its classy neighbors did not inspire the kind of lowered expectations and willingness to experiment that New Yorkers had learned to bring to Off-Broadway. One curse that haunted the Vivian Beaumont Theater was the smash-hit-or-flop syndrome of the commercial Broadway theatre, where anything less than overwhelming success was total failure.

The experience of the Papp years illustrates the power of the Beaumont's false image most clearly. The Shakespeare Festival's productions at Lincoln Center were no different in range and style from those at the Public Theater downtown, and any single Beaumont season had about the same proportion of strong and weak plays as a typical Public season. But audiences came to the Public and came back again even if what they had seen the previous time wasn't any good, because of their faith in and affection for the Festival as a continuing operation. Going to a Festival production at the Beaumont just wasn't the same thing; it was like going to Broadway — or, even worse, like going to the opera — and audiences demanded perfection every time out. As Joe Papp complained,

> Putting on a new play at Lincoln Center is extraordinarily more important and more significant than putting on that same play either off-Broadway, off off-Broadway, on Broadway or in a regional theater . . . . Because Lincoln Center represents a certain idea of official culture. [Qtd in Epstein 305]

No repertory theatre can produce equally high quality work in every production every season, and this is something that Public Theater audiences and audiences in other cities either sensed from the start or came to understand. Audiences who understand this are committed to theatre as an ongoing part of their lives rather than as isolated distractions; and that understanding and commitment, never achieved at Lincoln Center, gave the resident theatre movement its vitality and significance.

And then, inevitably, there were questions of societal expectations and personality conflict. Like some of the other theatres across the country that had boards first and artists later, there was always a question of what group and what sensibility was to dominate. Kazan recalled with some bitterness that "To start with, we were naive. We never faced the fact that we were not partners, but employees" [687] and blamed much of the opening years' troubles on "real estate operators and bankers who demand, not effort in a new direction, but reliable returns on an investment" [613].

In contrast, Davidson had the support of leaders of all of Los Angeles' power and money factions. Founder and guiding force behind the Music Center was Dorothy Chandler, wife of the publisher of the *Los Angeles Times*, while Lew Wasserman, one of the most powerful men in Hollywood, was president of the Center Theare Group's board, and Franklin Murphy, Chancellor of UCLA, chaired Los Angeles County's oversight committee. Davidson credits all of them for supporting his work and respecting his independence:

> I felt I had allies rather than adversaries.... I think they felt the Taper was doing something worthwhile and that I was doing what I beleived in.... Another thing I came to appreciate was the fact that they never pulled rank on me.

Scott Steele, who was Richmond Crinkley's Deputy Director, says that every Artistic Director was subject to excessive and inappropriate demands, not only from the board, but from the critics, the audiences, and the general *zeitgeist*. Crinkley, for example, wanted to start small, with modest productions in the studio theatre. But the expansive 1980s had begun, and New York — and thus the board — demanded "opening large, opening big, going for the glitz as opposed to nurturing, developing and growing" [Interview]. So Crinkley mounted a Broadway-sized season of plays including a large-scale *Macbeth* and a Woody Allen comedy, and predictably failed.

As late as 1996 even the successful fifth version of the theatre was being second-guessed, as *The New York Times* ran an article under the headline "It's a Success, but Is That Enough?" that acknowledged that Lincoln Center was "the pre-eminent institutional theater in the country, a theater with a slew of critical hits to its credit," but still criticized it for being too commercial and not "a repertory company or a purveyor of the classics in the mode of a traditional national theater" [Marks, "Success"].

And why did the fifth version of the Lincoln Center Theater finally succeed? Bernard Gersten credits "a stronger and more able Board" (and, Scott Steele adds, a less interfering one), along with a greater success in managing the administration and finances and an eclectic repertoire [Interview]. Andre Bishop believes it is partly an accident of architecture and history:

> It was a configuration of stage — thrust — that simply had never

been seen in New York....I think now, for one thing, time has caught up. There are theatres shaped like the Beaumont all over the country, which there were not in 1965. There are also several generations of directors now who know how to direct in these sorts of theatres, which there were not in 1965. [Interview]

And Gregory Mosher agrees that the very large Beaumont stage had virtually guaranteed that any production trying to fill it would seem inadequate. His solution, inspired by a Peter Brook-directed *Carmen* that had been booked into the house during one of its dark periods, was to mask off most of the stage and play on the apron; and he claims he can show a direct correlation between the failure of any Beaumont production and how far upstage it was played [Interview].

But surely the most significant factor is that the Mosher-Bishop-Gersten version was finally filling a need, doing Broadway when there was no longer a Broadway. As Chapter Five will show, by the mid-1980s economic and artistic forces had led the commercial New York theatre to withdraw almost entirely from producing anything but the safest of musicals and star vehicles. Off-Broadway theatres filled the gap by doing new plays, classics, and revivals, but inescapably on a small scale. For the first time in its history there was an audience hunger that the Lincoln Center Theater could properly satisfy, for larger-scale, fully professional productions of a sort unavailable elsewhere in the city.

> I think we are known for the variety of work we do, for the excellence of our productions and the scale of them. The policy is simply the best of world plays and musicals, and clearly that is not what most other theatres in New York can do. [Bishop interview]

☆

The importance of timing, of meeting audience hungers, of being in tune with the *zeitgeist*, and of plain luck cannot be underestimated, as Los Angeles discovered when it attempted to repeat the Center Theatre Group achievement two decades later. To help revitalize a decaying downtown area in 1985, the city converted vacant buildings into the four-house Los Angeles Theatre Center; the hope was that the theatre would attract people, people would attract restaurants and other service businesses, and they in turn would attract residents to the newly "gentrified" neighborhood.

Meanwhile, the Los Angeles Actors Theatre, a socially-conscious company that had been founded by Ralph Waite in 1975 and was subsequently directed by Bill Bushnell, was looking for an inner-city base from which it could serve nontraditional audiences. The company was invited into the new theatre, just as Gordon Davidson's Theatre Group had been offered the Taper. But, despite an ambitious and frequently praised program, particularly strong in serving minority artists and audiences, the LATC was defeated by a mix of factors, some of which recalled the Lincoln Center experience.

Members of the theatre's board had different visions of the theatre's role and mission, and its proper financial operation, from those of its director. One of the theatre's strongest supporters in the city's funding agency left his position, and "his successor had no vested interest in us, and his successor's successor had no vested interest in us." A downturn in the economy kept the expected gentrification from ever happening; and there was a change in the social atmosphere. Bushnell believes that a spirit of harmony and optimism in Los Angeles, the kind of unspoken commitment to multicultural unity that supported his work, reached a peak just at the time the LATC was founded.

> I think the illusion was that everything was still in ascension and going up, when in actual fact we may already have crested the hill. But the descent was real fast so that by 1991 we were into the beginning of what is now obvious in the state of California, incredible [racial and cultural] polarization. [Interview]

"Multiculturalists like myself are held in high disrepute in today's world," concludes Bushnell, and the values, the goals and the actual work produced by the LATC were simply out of step with the times.

And then there was the fact that the LATC wasn't the only game in town; by 1991 there were close to five hundred theatres and theatre companies in the Los Angeles area competing for audiences and funding. For these, and probably several other reasons, after six money-losing years the city could no longer afford the experiment, or no longer wanted to, and the LATC closed in 1991. Similar fates befell some other attempts to create resident companies to fill existing theatres; for example, at the Brooklyn Academy of Music in 1979 and Washington's Kennedy Center in 1984. For similarly complex reasons, the Brooklyn company folded in two years, the Washington in three.

☆

Not all of the regional theatres born in the 1950s and 1960s survived. The Theatre of the Living Arts, the Pittsburgh Playhouse, the Charles Playhouse, the Front Street Theatre, the Repertory Theatre New Orleans, and some others fell victim to financial pressures, personality clashes, or the simple fact that their cities were just not ready to support a resident theatre. Others had artistically and even financially successful runs of a decade or more before being forced to disband, usually by accumulated and insurmountable deficits. Still others, born in the political and social ferment of the 1960s, lived out what proved to be their natural life spans and died when their era was done: the Free Southern Theatre, for example, formed in 1963 to tour the rural South creating plays about the lives of audiences who had perhaps never seen a play, ceased operating in 1980 and formally disbanded in 1986.

Still, the blossoming of professional regional theatre activity in the three decades following Margo Jones's planting of the seed in Dallas came very close to fulfilling her dream of a national theatre. In 1950 there was Theatre '50. In 1960 there were a dozen professional resident theatres spread across the country. By 1966 there were thirty, and Actors' Equity reported that more actors were employed in resident theatres than in all the Broadway and road companies combined. At the close of the 1970s the League of Resident Theatres had more than sixty members, and the National Endowment for the Arts estimated that there were ten times as many smaller "alternative" theatres around the country. For the first time in the twentieth century the term "American theatre" was not synonymous with "New York City theatre."

☆

Although every resident theatre had unique features resulting from its origins or location, a number of common patterns, many traceable back to Margo Jones and Theatre '47, were evident. The most significant, aside from the geographical spread, was the fact that each theatre was meant to be a permanent institution and not the *ad hoc* producing operation typical of Broadway. This meant continuity and a very different relationship to the audience. The goal of every resident theatre was to become a cultural fact of life in its community — not a special event like the once-a-year appearance of the circus, but a continuing resource to be visited as casually and frequently as the local movie house.

> People who sign up for the year...know damn well that they're going to get some plays they're going to like and some they're not....It no longer involves hits or misses, but it's simply an institution they wish to support because it's part of their lives. We never had that in America — America's always been hits or misses — until the 1960s when the resident theatres came. [Stein interview]

To the extent that individual companies have succeeded in achieving this goal they have not only made professional theatre available where it had not been before, but have given it a role in American life that it had not had for a hundred years.

The majority of companies offered their plays in seasons of sequential two- to six-week runs, and some were able to sell 80 or 90 percent of their tickets through season subscriptions. This was at first simply a fiscal necessity, enabling theatres to raise much of a season's budget in advance. But it also had significant artistic implications, partly freeing artistic directors from the need to choose plays based on their ticket-selling potential; as Robert Falls of Chicago's Goodman Theatre explains,

> Knowing that you're going to have bodies in your seats throughout the course of a year gives you tremendous freedom, much more than if you were producing commercially, to produce a body of work that has true artistic purpose. One can make daring choices and go out on the limb far more than in the marketplace. [Interview]

The greatest significance of the subscription system, however, was the revolutionary change in audience psychology it generated: in every city thousands of people bought tickets months in advance to plays that did not come bearing the glory of Broadway success or rave reviews — plays, indeed, that the ticket buyers may not even have heard of before. New York and road company audiences went to see particular plays and stars; resident theatre audiences went to the theatre.

The repertoire of a particular resident company reflected the tastes of its artistic director (and, occasionally, of its governing board), the strengths and limits of its actors and physical resources, and the level of sophistication and adventurousness of its audience. The Mark Taper Forum could offer a much less orthodox selection than, say, the Indiana Repertory Theatre; and Edward Albee might be as radical as one company wanted to get, while another considered him as traditional as Arthur Miller. In most cases the theatre felt an obligation to fill in the gaps in its audience's experience of the classics while also introducing it to new works, and the practicalities of attracting and holding ticket buyers required the inclusion of some light and familiar plays in all but the most adventurous repertoires.

Generally a season struck a predictable balance between the familiar and the challenging. A typical five- or six-play package was likely to include one Shakespeare play (or, in a more ambitious company, Jonson, Marlowe, Congreve, or even a Greek tragedy); one modern European classic (probably Shaw or Chekhov, possibly Ibsen, Gogol, or even

Pirandello); one major American writer (Williams, Miller, O'Neill, Wilder); one safe crowd-pleaser to reassure those who might be frightened by the prospect of so much culture (a Neil Simon comedy, *Charley's Aunt*, a musical); possibly one contemporary and vaguely avant-garde play (Brecht, Beckett, Pinter, Albee — usually something validated by a recent New York run); and, increasingly from the 1970s on, a new American play, possibly one developed through the theatre's own playwriting workshop.

Finding the proper balance for the local audience was one of an artistic director's greatest challenges. Serious misjudgments in either direction could alienate subscribers and endanger a theatre's survival: the Pittsburgh and Philadelphia theatres died because their repertoires were too adventurous for their audiences, while the Inner City Repertory Company lost many Los Angeles subscribers by capitulating to Board of Education censorship in its first season. In contrast, whatever their original ambitions, both the Seattle Rep and the Studio Arena in Buffalo achieved community acceptance only by acknowledging the limits of their audiences' adventurousness and retreating to conservative repertoires.

Even the experienced Zelda Fichandler could guess wrong. After fourteen years of relatively orthodox classics at the Arena Stage, she decided in 1965 that her audience was ready for less familiar Pinter, Brecht, Anouilh, and the like. In two seasons the Arena lost half of its sixteen thousand subscribers, and quickly returned to a menu of *Macbeth* and *The Inspector General*. (To be fair to the Washington audience, within the next few years it was ready to support such challenges as Arthur Kopit's *Indians*.)

In addition to the regular season, most theatres offered such special projects as holiday shows, children's theatre, touring productions, student performances, and apprentice or training programs (the Guthrie sponsored a Boy Scout troop) — operations that not only attracted new audiences and brought in additional funds but also inspired civic pride, increasing the community's emotional commitment to the theatre. "When we tour nationally," explains Gregory Boyd of the Alley Theatre,

> the reviews from New Haven and Chicago and San Diego are all printed in the local papers. When we play England or Italy or Russia or Japan it tells the local people that this is an organization that is known in all parts of the world. It creates a sense of the Alley being a place to be. [Interview]

New play workshops and staged readings became very popular in the 1970s as financial support for such projects appeared, and as directors and audiences were drawn to the idea of the resident theatre as source of original plays as well as caretaker of the classics. As companies expanded their activities many opened second and even third playhouses, generally smaller studio theatres for their children's shows or experimental productions.

With occasional exceptions such as the Mark Taper Forum, almost all regional theatres began with a commitment to employing resident acting companies, usually for one- or two-year contracts, though in some cases actors might stay with a company for more than a decade. A regional theatre contract offered actors a continuity of employment and an opportunity for growth hitherto virtually unattainable in the American theatre; and while one early fear was that actors could not be lured away from New York and Hollywood, a remarkable number chose to build their careers moving from company to company and developing their skills in a larger variety of roles than they would ever have had occasion to play otherwise. Jane Alexander, Rene Auberjonois, Robert Foxworth, George Grizzard, Stephen Joyce, Stacy Keach, Frank Langella, and Anthony Zerbe are among many whose regional theatre experience helped shape their talents and reputations.

One early sign of the regional theatre movement's strength and significance was the number of New York-based artists who became involved in it. Hume Cronyn and Jessica Tandy joined the Guthrie Theater company for its first seasons, and other established Broadway actors soon began to play in regional theatres with increasing frequency. Directors Stuart Vaughan and William Ball left promising New York careers to commit themselves to regional companies, while others such as Alan Schneider moved freely between New York and regional assignments; in 1959 Schneider used a Ford Foundation grant to subsidize a year spent directing plays at several regional theatres that could not have afforded his services otherwise.

Authors who could easily have found Broadway producers began to give their plays to resident companies instead, in many cases because of the authors' dissatisfaction with the commercial theatre. Paddy Chayefsky's *The Latent Heterosexual* had its first production at the Dallas Theater Center in 1968; Edward Albee gave his *Box-Mao-Box* to the Studio Arena Theatre in the same year; Robert Anderson's *Solitaire/ Double Solitaire* began at the Long Wharf in 1971; and Jerome Lawrence

Photo: Fletcher Drake/Arena Stage Collection

James Earl Jones and Jane Alexander in *The Great White Hope*

and Robert E. Lee premiered several plays at regional theatres. In 1970, through a program called American Playwrights Theater, Lawrence and Lee's *The Night Thoreau Spent in Jail* was produced concurrently by more than one hundred professional and university theatres; the authors happily noted that more people saw that play in one season than had seen their biggest Broadway hits, *Inherit the Wind* and *Mame*, in their total combined runs.

Further evidence of regional theatre's vitality and fertility lay in its original contributions to the American dramatic repertoire. Two generations of young American dramatists — Oliver Hailey, Terrence McNally, David Mamet, Sam Shepard, Marcia Norman, Beth Henley, August Wilson, and others — were discovered or nurtured by regional companies. Such plays as Arthur Kopit's *Indians*, first done at the Arena in 1969; Michael Cristofer's *The Shadow Box* (Mark Taper Forum, 1975); David Mamet's *A Life in the Theatre* (Goodman Theatre, 1976), Beth Henley's *Crimes of the Heart* (Actors Theatre of Louisville, 1979) Sam Shepard's *True West* (Magic Theatre, 1980), and August Wilson's *Fences* (Yale Rep, 1985) have been staged around the country as frequently as *Hamlet* or *St. Joan*.

To the list could be added Paul Zindel's *The Effect of Gamma Rays on Man-in-the-Moon Marigolds* (Alley Theatre, 1965), Howard Sackler's *The Great White Hope* (Arena, 1967), the musical *Raisin* (Arena, 1973), David

Rabe's *Streamers* (Long Wharf, 1976), Arthur Kopit's *Wings* (Yale, 1979), and virtually all the plays of Mamet, Shepard, Norman, Henley, and Wilson. (Because they moved so freely between large and small regional theatres, between other cities and New York, and among New York's several theatrical worlds, these and other playwrights will be discussed more fully in later chapters.) Regional theatres also introduced Americans to European plays too challenging or risky for commercial producers: the first professional production of Brecht's *Caucasian Chalk Circle* (Arena Stage, 1961), Edward Bond's *Bingo* (Cleveland Play House, 1965), David Storey's *The Changing Room* (Long Wharf, 1972), Joshua Sobol's *Ghetto* (Mark Taper Forum, 1986), and dozens of others.

A final proof that the vital roots of the American theatre were now elsewhere than that square mile of Manhattan was a striking change in the role of Broadway. Instead of being the source of all new plays and productions, New York became more and more a showcase for work originated someplace else. Most of the plays already mentioned were picked up by New York producers after their regional premieres (as opposed to being conceived of from the start as Broadway tryouts) and given Broadway or Off-Broadway runs.

☆

Although many companies were born without theatre buildings and had to follow the lead of the Arena and Alley, playing in converted warehouses and other found spaces, the rapid expansion of the resident theatre movement in the mid-1960s coincided with a period of national economic strength and the era of urban renewal. For a while it seemed as if every city in America was attempting to revitalize its downtown with an arts center of some sort. Lincoln Center in New York, the Los Angeles Music Center, and the Kennedy Center in Washington are the best-known products of this flurry of building.

Private, government, and foundation money also created multi-million-dollar homes for the Alley Theatre, the Arena Stage, the Mummers Theatre, and the Milwaukee Rep; indeed, more than 170 theatres and arts centers were built between 1962 and 1969, with more than 60 percent of all private, government, and foundation support for the performing arts devoted to construction. Building continued even after the urban renewal fervor subsided; between 1980 and 1984 new theatres were built in Indianapolis, Syracuse, Seattle, San Diego, and Cleveland. Those cities that didn't construct new homes for their resident companies at least converted and refurbished older theatres or grand old movie palaces, so the majority of resident companies born during this period soon found themselves in relatively luxurious playing spaces.

The importance of this extensive theatre-building can't be underestimated. A new theatre was a tangible sign of local commitment, an indication that the resident company was seen as a permanent part of the community. It also had direct artistic and economic effects; as a Twentieth Century Fund task force concluded in 1970, "The largest single controllable factor in the health of the performing arts is the attractiveness, technical adequacy, and financial efficiency of their housing" [2]. Aside from the artistic freedom and opportunities a fully equipped theatre provided for an acting company, it had a measurable psychological effect on an audience: civic pride, a sense of occasion, and simple physical comfort could significantly increase the attractiveness of theatregoing and the pleasure of the experience.

While there were certainly other factors involved, it is notable that the Center Theatre Group's subscription base in its first year at the Music Center was almost three times what it had been at UCLA. The Arena Stage was ten years old, with a strong identity and loyal following, when it moved to its new theatre, yet subscriptions jumped 45 percent in the first season there. The Milwaukee Repertory Theatre more than doubled its subscriptions with the move to the Performing Arts Center, and the Tyrone Guthrie Theater — the building itself — was a big drawing card in that company's first season. In contrast, of course, is the Lincoln Center debacle, though it should be noted that the Center's other components — the opera, ballet, etc. — flourished in the new complex, and by 1996 Andre Bishop could report that his members "would rather come here than to the West Forties. The parking is better, the location seems more attractive, it seems less dangerous, the restaurants are more gracious" [Interview].

On the other hand, analysts for the Twentieth Century Fund, considering the urban renewal and arts center bandwagon in general, concluded that

> Perhaps the most important question to be raised about cultural centers is whether as much thought has been given to the nature of their presentations as to the design of the buildings. One suspects that the planners of some of the centers have not really considered in any detail what should be done with the buildings once they were completed, but have proceeded on the assumption that quality of performance would somehow take care of itself. [Baumol 41]

While the Lincoln Center Repertory Theater was the grandest and most expensive example of this sort of shortsightedness, the case of the Oklahoma City Mummers was perhaps the saddest. An amateur company founded in 1949, the Mummers became a pet project of the Ford Foundation, which gave the company almost two million dollars between 1959 and 1970 to help it make the leap to professional status. But most of that money, along with an almost equal amount from other sources, went to the building of a massive (and excellent) new theatre; when it opened in 1970 Ford and the Mummers were startled to discover that Oklahoma City, which had supported its modest little local amateur troupe, didn't really want a company of professional actors in a big new building. The professional version of the Mummers folded in a year, leaving the expensive new theatre vacant.

A variant of this error was the experience of Atlanta, Savannah, Indianapolis, St. Paul, and several other cities that chose to build a single large auditorium to house symphonies, rock concerts, and touring shows as well as plays, and generally found that compromise designing made it equally not-quite-adequate for all its planned uses. (In another sort of misplanning, the Beaumont Theater in Lincoln Center, designed for a classical repertoire and a resident company that never developed, was left with a stage too large for most productions and with extensive and useless backstage space other companies could envy.)

The building boom of the 1960s had another effect on the American theatre, whose significance took a while to be fully felt. There are fads in theatre design as in other things, and a rebellion against the proscenium arch made the three-sided thrust stage very fashionable at the time that all these buildings were being designed and constructed. As a result some of the most important theatre buildings in America — the Tyrone Guthrie, the Mark Taper Forum, the Vivian Beaumont, and the homes of the Alley Theatre, the Dallas Theater Center, the Long Wharf Theatre, the Loretto-Hilton Repertory Company, the Studio Arena Theatre, and the Yale Rep, among others — have permanent full or modified thrust stages, with audiences sitting on three sides of an open playing area.

This is a very flexible arrangement, but one that poses some problems. As Andre Bishop pointed out, most American directors had no experience with this sort of stage in the 1960s, and had to learn by trial and error as they went along. Shakespeare is much easier to do on an open stage, once you get the hang of it, but plays written for proscenium the-

Photo: Ezra Stoller ® ESTO

Vivian Beaumont Theater (interior)

atres are not; it is difficult, for example, to achieve the full effect of a powerful curtain line when there is no curtain.

By the mid-1980s a new generation of artistic directors, tired of coping with these problems; a new generation of stage designers, frustrated by the limited set-design opportunities of the open stage; and a new generation of audiences, their appetite for spectacle whetted by the elaborate musicals of the period, gave the first signs of rebellion against the thrust stage. During the late 1980s and early 1990s the Tyrone Guthrie Theater went through several redesigns, bringing the audience-stage relationship closer to the head-on configuration of the proscenium. At Lincoln Center, Gregory Mosher repeatedly closed off most of the stage, creating a smaller, more intimate playing area at the front. Some newer theatres, in America and Europe, have been designed in more traditional shapes.

Meanwhile, though, at least two generations of dramatists raised on non-proscenium theatre have unquestionably been affected by this setting in the construction of their plays. Two structural elements that have become commonplace in even the most realistic plays of the last quarter of the century can be traced partly to the influence of arena staging: the replacement of extended action by a more cinematic flow of brief scenes (made possible by the more impressionistic set and lighting design of an open stage) and the use of narration and direct audience address (less of a break with the illusion than in a "fourth wall" proscenium setting). It is possible that the next wave of theatre design, whatever it may be, will find these plays as awkward to stage as proscenium plays are on a thrust stage.

☆

The growth of the resident theatre movement and the spread of vital and fertile theatrical activity independent of New York is clearly the most significant development in the American theatre since 1950. But it was accompanied — and, in fact, made possible — by a second innovation whose importance may eventually be even greater: the partial liberation of the American theatre from the marketplace.

The fact is that every regional resident theatre company loses money, and loses big. According to annual surveys by the Theatre Communications Group, total earned income (primarily from ticket sales, but also including royalties, theatre rentals, merchandising, etc.) averages between 50 and 65 percent of expenses, with some theatres making as little as one-third of their expenses at the box office. When that happens on Broadway a show closes and its backers lose their money, just as if they had invested in a company that went bankrupt. In the resident theatres for the most part, the company happily continues operation, with the missing 35 or 66 percent being made up by sources who believe that the arts aren't *supposed* to be profitable and who don't expect to be repaid. These modern Medicis count among their number some millionaires, such as the benefactors for whom the Ahmanson, Taper, Beaumont, and Delacorte buildings were named, and many more individuals willing to pay a hundred dollars above their subscription to be "Friends" of their favorite theatre. But they were led by the nation's venerable philanthropic foundations and, in a revolutionary development, by the federal, state, and local governments.

Charitable foundations in America were, to a great extent, the byproduct of the federal income and inheritance taxes, leading one analyst to comment, "The American counterpart to European government subsidy of the arts is not, as many think, the National Endowment for the Arts plus a collective body of state and local arts councils. It is the tax law" [Jeffri 3]. Early in the twentieth century the very richest individuals and families discovered that they could keep more of their millions by giving some of them away, thereby qualifying for deductions that put them in a lower tax bracket.

Thus were born the Ford Foundation, the Rockefeller Foundation, and others, devoted to supporting educational and social causes, scientific research, and the like. While some of these, notably the Rockefeller Foundation, also supported the arts indirectly through their educational grants, the real beginnings of subsidized theatre in America came in 1957, when the Ford Foundation tentatively inaugurated its program in the arts.

Under the direction of W. McNeil Lowry, a former teacher and journalist who joined Ford's education-funding program in 1953 and became head of its arts and humanities program in 1957 (he became Vice President of the Foundation in 1964, and retired in 1974), the Foundation studied the experience and work of such companies as the Alley, the Arena, and the Mummers (all three of which would later become leading beneficiaries of the Foundation). It then decided that increasing the availability of the arts to the American population was a legitimate extension of its social mandate, and that the resident theatre movement was the great hope of the American theatre.

Ford's arts program began relatively modestly with travel grants allowing the directors of fledgling companies to visit other theatres to observe their operations, and with student internships in theatre management. To test whether ambitious young actors would be willing to commit themselves to repertory companies, the Foundation underwrote the payrolls of four theatres — the Arena, Alley, Actor's Workshop, and Phoenix — for three seasons beginning in 1959.

Evidently satisfied with the experiment, Ford upped the ante radically in 1962 with a total of $6.1 million in grants to nine theatres: the Actor's Studio in New York, the Actor's Workshop, the Alley, the American Shakespeare Festival, the Arena, the Fred Miller Theatre in Milwaukee, the Mummers, the UCLA Theatre Group, and the Guthrie Theater. The Alley alone received $2.1 million, half of which was designated for the construction of its new theatre; Ford later gave another $1.4 million to that project. The Mummers, still an amateur company barely out of its summer tent state, got $1.25 million, part of a series of grants that pushed it toward full professional status.

In the decade that followed, six-figure grants from the Ford Foundation became almost commonplace as the foundation's total arts giving averaged $9.5 million a year. In 1971, for example, Ford gave $365,000

W. MacNeil Lowry

to the American Place Theatre in New York; $320,000 to Baltimore's Center Stage; $240,000 to the Hartford Stage Company; $305,000 to the Seattle Rep; $150,000 to Stage/West in West Springfield, Massachusetts; and $357,000 to the Trinity Square Rep. The APA-Phoenix partnership got $900,000 in 1967; the Arena Stage got $600,000 in 1970; the Guthrie received $619,000 in 1972; the New York Shakespeare Festival got $1.5 million in 1973; and San Francisco's ACT got a total of more than four million dollars in various grants. (To put these figures in some perspective, remember that by the mid-1970s a single Broadway musical cost more than a million dollars to produce. At the same time the Arena, on an annual budget of about $2.5 million, produced as many as nine plays in addition to workshops, readings and touring productions.)

Many of these grants were unrestricted gifts to be used by the theatres to make up their deficits and keep themselves in operation. Some went to support specific programs, such as new play workshops, or special projects, such as the construction or renovation of a theatre building; Ford built new theatres for the Alley and the Mummers, and bought and renovated theatres for ACT and the Actors Theatre of Louisville. In the mid-1960s the Foundation helped create several ethnic and minority-oriented theatres, including New York's Negro Ensemble Company, the Free Southern Theater, and the Inner City Repertory Company. Another grant program focused on more experimental companies such as Off Off-Broadway's Cafe La Mama.

Not content to stay in his office reading grant applications, Lowry toured the country, exhorting changes in theatre training, encouraging new companies, and studying what worked in one place and might be of use elsewhere. At Chicago's opera company, for example, ticket-sales expert Danny Newman had developed a seemingly foolproof method for selling subscriptions. Arguing that the potential subscriber base for any arts institution was a tiny and demographically definable segment of the population, Newman counselled targeting all marketing at that segment, foregoing general advertising in favor of repeated mailings to carefully-chosen mailing lists. Soon Newman, too, was touring the country, preaching his gospel to new and established resident theatres who found that it virtually always worked.

Other advisors and managers were also turned into trouble-shooters; Bill Bushnell, who worked at the Cleveland Play House, Center Stage, and the ACT early in his career, jokingly referred to himself as "one of Mac Lowry's hired guns":

> I could go into any theatre in America and give you theatre in ten minutes because I knew exactly how to do it. I'd studied with Danny Newman. I had been a manager. I bailed out [several theatres] that were going to close. [Interview]

In 1961 Ford established the Theatre Communications Group, a national service organization for not-for-profit theatres large and small. TCG operates a central casting and personnel service; provides expert assistance in management, fundraising, and subscription sales; publishes *American Theatre* magazine; and organizes conferences and workshops for its member companies.

The Ford Foundation's original plan was to stimulate regional theatres to self-sufficiency through seed money, but it soon discovered that this was an unreasonable hope. A study commissioned by the Twentieth Century Fund in 1966 reached the conclusion that "performing organizations typically operate under constant financial strain — that their costs almost always exceed their earned income;" and, even more significantly, "Because of the economic structure of the performing arts, these financial pressures are here to stay, and there are fundamental reasons for expecting the income gap to widen steadily with the passage of time" [Baumol 161]. Later studies by Ford and by the Rockefeller Brothers Fund reached the same conclusion: a resident theatre company, like a symphony orchestra or a museum, is by its very nature a money-losing operation.

As a result, the pattern and purpose of foundation giving began to change in the 1970s. As a Ford Foundation working paper explained a decade later,

> Institutional operating grants diminished and funds were concentrated on the ... "stabilization strategy," ... [which] attempted to arrest the pattern of crisis management of arts organizations .... Over the course of a decade the stabilization program significantly improved the financial condition of arts organizations by emphasizing incentives and rewards for sound management practices [Mayleas 16]

The hope was that theatres and other arts organizations, if never able to support themselves, would develop solid infrastructures that enabled them to function on the money available from other sources. As the author of the working paper later explained, "Ford believed it was now the responsibility of local communities, in conjunction with the newly established National Endowment for the Arts, to take the premier responsibility for their own institutions" [Interview].

By 1977 the Ford Foundation had given away more than $35 million to theatre companies throughout the country, and in the process had stimulated further millions in contributions from other sources, since many of its grants required the recipients to raise matching funds elsewhere. In addition Ford spent about $11 million on ancillary grants: underwriting of new play production, support of theatre education, individual travel and study fellowships. Stephen Langley could later write, with some justification, that neither Margo Jones nor Joseph Papp but "W. McNeil Lowry conceivably influenced twentieth century theatre in this country more than any other individual" [*Theatre Management and Production* 171].

The Ford Foundation was the original and for a long time the largest patron of the noncommercial theatre, but not the only one. The Rockefeller Foundation, whose traditions lay in sponsoring individual researchers in the sciences and social sciences, translated that pattern into its arts giving: "the Rockefeller Foundation really committed itself to supporting the creative individual, within the context of a producing organization" [Sato interview].

Rockefeller grants went to individual playwrights and to many companies dedicated to the production of new American plays or the exploration of unconventional production methods; the Foundation funded the Center Theatre Group's New Theatre for Now, the Milwaukee Rep's Theatre for Tomorrow, and ACT's Plays in Progress programs, among others. The Andrew W. Mellon Foundation, the Rockefeller Brothers Fund, the Twentieth Century Fund, the Wallace Funds (several funds associated with *The Reader's Digest*), and the Shubert Foundation have also been active contributors, as have hundreds of smaller foundations.

More significantly, public money was made available to the theatre. Until the 1960s the United States was almost alone in the developed world in having no history of direct government support of the arts. (Depression-era exceptions like the Federal Theatre were primarily employment programs, and had little lasting artistic effect.) In 1966 Congress created the National Endowment for the Arts with an annual grant budget of $2.5 million; by 1978 that had risen to over $100 million, and by 1994 to $170 million.

The NEA funds music, dance, art, and broadcasting projects as well as theatre, but it has still been able to support hundreds of companies and individuals. Some established regional theatres have received sizeable grants ($125,000 to the New York Shakespeare Festival; $117,500 to the Arena; $95,000 to ACT, for example, all in 1971), but the National Endowment's mandate has generally been in favor of individual artists, smaller companies, and theatres and writers doing new work. The bulk of its giving has been in the $5000 to $25,000 range, allowing a greater breadth and diversity of support than is typical of the private foundations; by 1980 the NEA had disbursed almost a billion dollars through 40,000 grants.

In addition, following the lead of New York State, which began offering grants to its artists and art institutions in 1960, every state in the union has a Council on the Arts which disburses taxpayers' money, often to organizations too small or local to attract the attention of national funding sources. Some resident theatres also receive support from state and local boards of education, community development agencies, parks departments, and even zoning commissions.

Foundation and government subsidy has even found its way into the Broadway theatre. The Theatre Development Fund was established in 1967 by the Twentieth Century Fund, the Rockefeller Brothers Fund, and the NEA to explore the possibilities of injecting subsidy money into the commercial theatre. It began by buying up blocks of tickets to forthcoming plays of artistic merit but uncertain commercial strength and reselling them at a discount to students and similar groups, thereby encouraging new audiences while giving the productions a financial buffer. TDF takes credit for helping such plays as *The Great White Hope*, *The Changing Room*, *The Hot l Baltimore*, *That Championship Season*, *The Shadow Box*, *Sweeney Todd*, *Wings*, and *The Elephant Man* weather their first weeks until they caught on with the general public.

In 1973 TDF, in partnership with the League of New York Theatres, opened a discount ticket booth in Times Square, where Broadway and Off-Broadway shows that were not sold out offered tickets on the day of performance for half price. Soon the discount booth was selling more than a million tickets a year and helping Broadway hold on to the segment of its audience that rising ticket prices were driving away; TDF estimated that up to three-quarters of its customers would not have bought full-price tickets. TDF also instituted a discount voucher system for Off Off-Broadway theatres, supplying the difference between the voucher price and the full ticket price; a costume rental service for not-for-profit theatres; and aid to other cities, notably Boston, Chicago, and Minneapolis, in developing their own voucher systems.

The Shubert Organization, owner of Broadway theatres and producer of shows, is actually owned (through a uniquely complex legal structure) by the not-for-profit Shubert Foundation; while the not-for-profit Lincoln Center Theater and Manhattan Theatre Club (among others) frequently produce plays on Broadway alongside commercial producers. In the 1990s, the Cameron Mackintosh Foundation, established by the very successful British producer of musicals, combined with the New York Times Foundation to fund the Alliance for New American Musicals, funding the development of what might turn out to be future Broadway hits.

Without question the establishment of resident theatres all across America and the broad cultural acceptance of theatre as a not-for-profit activity deserving of subsidy were the most positive things to happen to the American theatre in the twentieth century, and without question the theatrical situation in the last quarter of the century was healthier and more exciting than it had been in a hundred years. But of course it was not perfect; and as the euphoria of the first decades of explosive growth waned, some ongoing problems became apparent.

The first to become clear was the discovery that subsidy was not a universal panacea. As the experience of the Mummers and the Repertory Theatre New Orleans showed, money unwisely spent could be even more harmful than lack of funds. Looking back with some pride on its involvement in the performing arts since 1957, the Ford Foundation was forced to admit that it might have done some companies a greater service (and saved itself some money) by guiding them toward greater stability and community acceptance before overwhelming them with massive grants [Magat 128].

More insidious was the danger that financial support implied some artistic control. Cases of direct artistic interference or censorship by funding agencies have fortunately been rare, although some school boards, for example, have demanded a say in the choice of plays their students would see, and the NEA was subject at almost predictable intervals to threats of abolition by politicians claiming to be offended by art they called obscene or un-american or just weird.

But self-censorship was always a possibility, as Martin Gottfried warned in 1967: "There can be no greater loss to the artist than that of self-reliance. Once he becomes dependent upon outsiders, he can no longer be free.... There is a pressure to be inoffensive, an inclination to be sleek, proper and bland" [*Theater* 93]. Gottfried suspected that the charitable foundations consciously planned to influence the theatres they funded, but Joseph Wesley Zeigler, who served as executive director of Ford's Theatre Communications Group, saw a different danger:

> The pervasive power of Ford support tended to homogenize and codify theatres, although the villain in this was not really or directly Ford but rather those theatres which homogenized themselves in hopes of thereby gaining Ford support. [*Regional* 184]

A resident theatre's artistic director might not even realize that he or she was choosing a repertoire or production style with an eye toward catering to the tastes or prejudices of a potentially friendly foundation. In 1985 Peter Zeisler saw clear evidence of this in the subtle evolution of the typical resident theatre repertoire over a thirty-year period. Certainly one of the important services of the regional theatre was the development of new scripts and new writers, but was that cause or effect, and what were its repercussions? "As nonprofit theatres increasingly started working with original scripts...many funding sources restricted their grants to 'premiere' productions. As a result,...the classical repertoire has languished" [3].

Zeigler admitted that even the innocent programs of the Theatre Communications Group had artistic implications:

> TCG homogenized theatres through its casting service, which prompted the appearance of the same actors in various theatres over the years; through its visitation program, which encouraged artists and managers to think and act alike; and through Danny Newman's peregrinations, which provided promotional tools that looked and worked alike. We helped theatres to become more stable but at a high cost to them — a threatened loss of individuality. [*Regional* 185]

While some of the "homogenized" structures would eventually be questioned, as companies sought individual ways of responding to local conditions, Zeigler's criticism of TCG is far too harsh. The pool of floating actors, to the extent that there was one, meant a steady supply of experienced and growing performers for each company; and the similarities in bookkeeping and advertising were the results of sharing ideas that worked rather than letting each theatre stumble through its own trial-and-error process.

But Zeigler's underlying fear that financial support inevitably had some artistic effects was valid. Broadway folklore is filled with tales of producers forced to hire the untalented sweethearts or nephews of their financial backers. Nothing as grotesque happens in the subsidized theatre, but an accumulation of small artistic compromises and adjustments could be as stultifying.

This became particularly apparent in the 1980s when some of the most relied-upon funding sources began to change the philosophy of their giving. As Robert Brustein points out, the original purpose of the National Endowment for the Arts was very high-minded:

> It was never the intention of the Endowment to subsidize popular taste, because the cultural appetites of the demographic majority were thought to be adequately represented by the market — by Broadway shows, bestselling books, [etc.] . . . . No, the National Endowment was designed as a counter-market strategy, in the hope that by subsidizing cultural offerings at affordable prices the works of serious art could become available to all. ["Arts Wars" 111]

But the NEA was subject from the beginning to internal debate and external criticism on the issue of elite vs. popular — that is, should taxpayers' money go to individuals and institutions producing the highest quality work, even if they served only very small audiences, or should it support art that spoke to a larger number of those who were paying for it, even if the quality and importance of the work were questionable? Virtually all resident theatre companies saw themselves as being in the first camp, striving to do excellent work even if it appealed only to an elite audience, and as long as the elitist/excellence philosophy dominated NEA giving, all was well. Beginning in the 1980s, however, the NEA committed itself more and more to the populist position, directing funds away from its traditional recipients and toward local folk festivals and the like. (The impetus for this shift came from both the political left, in the name of populism and cultural diversity, and the right, out of suspicion of obscure, presumably radical artists.)

To complicate matters, while NEA and other federal grants were traditionally small and rarely made up more than 5 percent of any company's budget, theatres discovered that the loss of even a small NEA grant had rippling repercussions. Other funding sources, particularly those (like corporations) sometimes lacking the resources to make informed artistic judgments, tended to look to more expert givers for guidance, and NEA funding was used by many as an imprimatur that gave them the confidence to donate to a particular theatre. "You don't get much from the National Endowment," explains Theodore Mann, a founder of Circle in the Square. "And if the National Endowment isn't giving you much, then corporations and foundations feel that's an indication that maybe you're not worth it" [Interview]. It was little comfort to a theatre to be assured that an NEA grant had been denied only for policy reasons, when that change in policy took with it the chance to get two or three times as much from other sources.

About the same time, another significant shift was visible in the pattern of both government and foundation funding, following a general cultural awareness that the Eurocentric tradition of much of American art was becoming less reflective of the realities of American society. "Multiculturalism" became the buzzword of the era, the idea that art, and theatre in particular, should better reflect the experience of the non-white, non-Anglo portions of the population. Both the Ford and Rockefeller Foundations, traditionally the leaders in artistic support, specifically redirected their giving to companies that could demonstrate cross-cultural projects.

Meanwhile, the 1980s brought other social awakenings as well, with a growing sense that theatre had an obligation to reflect the experience of women, homosexuals, Vietnam veterans, the homeless, the disabled. The NEA and the arts-funding agencies of several states wrote multicultural requirements into their criteria for awarding grants: for example, "outreach to new and underserved audiences" (Vermont), "degree to which the project would involve/benefit minorities" (Alabama), "evidence that the project/program/organization is serving the needs of traditionally underserved populations" (Kansas), and "include representation of [the] diverse cultural, ethnic and artistic plurality of its community in the planning, execution and evaluation of its programs" (Oklahoma) [Qtd in Pankratz 78–79].

No one could possibly criticize those impulses — and in fact funding sources acknowledged that many theatres had actually preceded them in the awareness of these artistic imperatives. But, as Stephen Langley warned, "When the NEA or any other major funder announces that it will award grants for certain types of programs, there will always be a number of applicants who will invent projects just to fit those program guidelines" [*Theatre Management and Production* 558].

Any funds earmarked for a special purpose, whether they were board of education subsidies for student performances or foundation grants to support minority arts, ran the risk of diverting a company from its central purposes or tempting it to overextend itself. So, as funds for general operations began to give way to grants earmarked for work that met specific social agendas, it was the rare theatre company that was not faced with an artistic dilemma. Warren Kliewer encapsulated the problem in this hypothetical challenge:

> You are the artistic director. For next season's new play slot, you've narrowed the choices down to two scripts. One is dramaturgically inept, but it deals with a social problem much discussed in the news media — let's say, homelessness. The other play is witty, skillful, finished, even thoughtful, but has nothing to say on any topic that will ever become trendy.... A major foundation... has just announced a huge new initiative to address the problem of homelessness. Which play do you choose? [66]

The deck needn't be that badly stacked to pose artistic problems. Suppose the choice were between equally interesting plays on Anglo and Hispanic topics. Was an all-white theatre company, trained only in traditional dramatic forms, actually serving the desired social agenda by doing an inadequate job on a play about characters it didn't understand in a theatrical mode with which it had no experience? Did a theatre become multicultural simply by hiring some minority actors or recruiting minority millionaires or civic leaders for its board? Indeed, did a theatre have the right to make a claim on the time and resources of minority artists, millionaires, or civic leaders just to improve the theatre's funding chances? Should a theatre qualify for an NEA grant by doing a local folk play instead of Shakespeare, when the audience was going to be the same old subscription list anyway?

These questions were not unanswerable, and some artistic directors, such as Lloyd Richards of the Yale Rep, found artistically and culturally satisfying ways of meeting these new challenges:

> Our student body was integrated, our casts were integrated, and people became aware that certain playwrights were part of the family of the theatre. Our company of playwrights included not only Shakespeare, Shaw, Sheridan and Chekhov; it included Wole Soyinka, Derek Walcott, August Wilson, Athol Fugard. [Interview]

But they *were* challenges, and, as Langley warned, less sensitive and less clearly motivated directors than Richards ran the risk of stumbling: "art that follows the funding has usually lost both integrity and purpose" [*Theatre Management and Production* 400].

Such questions were compounded by an increasingly frantic scramble for resources as not only the types of funding but the actual dollar amounts changed. The very success of the regional theatre movement had led inevitably to greater expenses, as shoestring companies grew into institutions with multimillion dollar annual budgets; and the inescapability of inflation meant that there was always need for more money.

Meanwhile, some of the most relied-upon funding sources became less certain. Changing conditions and social agendas at the Ford, Rockefeller, and other foundations meant that the almost annual six- and seven-figure general purpose grants that some companies had come to rely on were a thing of the past. Most of the richest foundations were not established primarily to fund arts institutions, after all, and the 1980s brought social problems (homelessness, educational reform, AIDS) that had as least as legitimate a claim to foundation attention as the theatre.

And most foundations got their funds from stock investments, and the 1970s and 1980s saw several waves of recession and corporate downsizing that reduced profits and dividends; the Ford Foundation's total budget for giving, to all causes, dropped by over 50 percent from 1974 to 1979. Coincidentally, changes in the tax laws in the 1980s took away some of the incentive for both foundation and private contributions. So, after two decades of extraordinarily generous support for the not-for-profit theatre, some of the largest donors pulled back significantly. In 1981 Ford reduced its total arts funding to about three million dollars a year; in 1989 its theatre program gave out a total of $1.5 million, less than it had given to a single theatre in earlier years.

Foundation support did not disappear overnight, of course—although for a theatre that suddenly lost an essential grant it might just as well have. In fact, according to annual TCG surveys, foundation giving was the one funding source that grew at annual double-digit rates through the 1980s. But the nature of the funding changed, with less encouragement to growth and support for general operating funds, and more and more earmarked for specific productions or not-purely-artistic social services. And the sources also changed, with the traditional leaders—Ford, Rockefeller, Mellon, Twentieth Century—disappearing from the top ten lists, supplanted by smaller, frequently local foundations generally making smaller, project-focused grants and forcing theatres to begin anew the slow process of proving their worth and developing relationships.

Replacing Ford and the others as leading donors to not-for-profit theatres were the several arts funds associated with the founders of *The Reader's Digest*, generally grouped under the name of the Wallace Funds, and the Broadway-based Shubert Foundation. (As mentioned earlier, the for-profit Shubert Organization is wholly owned by the nonprofit Shubert Foundation, heir to the original Shubert brothers. The Foundation, which began as a general-purpose charity funding hospitals, universities, and the like, redefined itself in 1975 to support theatre and other performing arts.)

Meanwhile, public funding also came under siege. Ronald Reagan became President in 1981 after running on a platform of reducing government spending, and one of his first proposals was a 50 percent cut in the NEA. While that was defeated, the exponential growth in NEA allocations that had marked the previous decade was brought to a stop, and its effective grant budget remained flat (i.e., shrank, taking inflation into account) for the next decade and beyond. In the early 1990s the Endowment barely survived another censorship-based political attack, but only in a severely crippled form; from 1994 to 1995 its budget was cut almost 40 percent.

As a result the NEA had to change its philosophy of giving, devoting much of its energies and allocations not to direct grants, but to finding ways to help the arts community adjust to the fact that the NEA wasn't giving as many grants:

> We're now trying to find ways to encourage organizations to adapt flexibly to a changing environment. We're hoping to find ways to place arts organizations more solidly within the context of the community. We're hoping to mobilize government, private and business interests so that not only will there be more dollar support but also a better sense of connection. [Bolt interview]

Budgetary and political forces kept the NEA under pressure, and indeed under threat of extinction, for the remainder of the century, and its supporters could only measure success in terms of limiting the severity of cuts in funding.

☆

So one of the fantasies of the not-for-profit theatre, that the artists would be wholly liberated from the marketplace and free to concentrate on their art, proved elusive. The hunt for money would always be a part of the job, and adjusting to that discovery proved traumatic for some. By the 1980s there was a generation of theatre artists and administrators who had grown up knowing nothing but subsidized theatre, and some of them fell into the psychological trap of considering subsidy their due. This "entitlement" mentality led too many companies to the casual assumption that the money would always be there, so that the case for support need not be presented more than perfunctorily. In a few cases it led to an unattractive truculence, as companies that didn't get a hoped-for grant complained as if the funding source owed them the free cash; there is, for example, more than the hint of a whine in this 1990 protest by Ellen Stewart of Off Off-Broadway's LaMama Theatre:

> We have never, ever received money, or artistic consideration or monies, like the Public Theater or BAM [the Brooklyn Academy of Music].... The Public Theater pays a dollar a year for all of its real estates. LaMama has to pay rent. The utilities, the repairs, everything that BAM needs the city pays for.... They don't give us a dime for those things, and they never have. [Qtd in Horn 35]

Ironically, one of the people Stewart envied, Joe Papp of the Public Theater, was just as susceptible to the same trap of assuming support as a right. When a severe fiscal crisis in the late 1970s led the city of New York, rather than abandoning free Shakespeare in Central Park, to seek out private sponsors to replace its grants, Papp refused the alternative money: "If I took that money I would be letting the city off the hook and I have no intention of doing so" [Qtd in Epstein].

"By the end of the 1980s, many in the arts community—especially individual artists—had come to believe that they were entitled to federal funding.... In a world ruled by entitlement, the denial of a grant is going to be seen by the rejected grantee as censorship" [Zeigler, *Arts* 153–55]. This was particularly apparent whenever some politician threatened the NEA and the not-for-profit artistic community in general reacted with self-righteous outrage instead of presenting its positive case to Congress and the public. When the NEA briefly imposed an anti-obscenity provision on grantees in 1990, Joe Papp and some others publicly refused grants they had already been awarded, but with a truculence that won them few friends in or out of the arts community; poorer artists saw that the New York Shakespeare Festival could afford to reject a relatively small grant that would have been life-or-death to them, while outsiders saw the protesters seeming to defend obscenity.

"We had to learn to reframe the argument," notes Gigi Bolt, Director of Theatre and Musical Theatre at the NEA. "Not only speaking in terms of our own values, but recognizing that there were genuine concerns on the part of the critics and the community at large." To be fair, some of this criticism is the product of hindsight, as Bolt points out:

> I don't think the special confluence of social, political and economic forces that came together to create this situation could have been foreseen. The 1980s seemed to offer the opportunity of continued growth, and I don't think many people in the arts community had a sense of what would transpire. It's taken some years to be able to understand the forces that have been in play, and therefore how to respond to them. [Interview]

One more product of this passive "entitlement" fallacy was a pattern in the not-for-profit theatre of unwise or just neglectful financial planning, and a slowness in developing new sources of funding; it was late in the 1980s, for example, before more than a handful of theatres began to establish endowment funds to provide some continuity of income. As TCG surveys showed, the single largest group of donors through the 1980s was individuals, but these were almost entirely "Friend" or "Patron" subscribers who gave $100 or so over their annual subscriptions in return for their name in the program and an invitation to a cocktail party. With a few exceptions (e.g., Joe Papp) not-for-profit theatres failed to cultivate the individual millionaires who were the prime benefactors of museums, opera companies, and universities. (To be fair, recruiting millionaires was difficult; the Ford Foundation noted that "individual patronage . . . is directed, by and large, to established arts organizations, most notably art museums and symphony orchestras . . . . It is, as a rule, less supportive of smaller or alternative institutions or innovative programs [Mayleas 7].)

A fourth area of funding, corporate donations, was aggressively cultivated in the 1970s and 1980s, though with limited results. Actually, many American corporations do have a long history of philanthropy; the Dayton Hudson Company, owner of several retail chains, has given 5 percent of pre-tax profits to charity for fifty years, and AT&T's support of the arts goes back to the Bell Telephone Hour on radio. Ben Cameron, Senior Program Officer of the Dayton Hudson Foundation, calls it "enlightened self-interest:"

> We do recognize that the arts are integral to creating better living places and marketplaces. There is a recognition that they build more livable communities, and that in itself will attract a better quality of worker in our stores and a more satisfied customer to shop there. [Interview]

But, while some corporate support for the arts came from a company's philanthropic budget—for example, a series of grants by Exxon to such theatres as the Taper, Guthrie, Long Wharf, and Alley—much new corporate money in the 1980s came, directly or indirectly, from the marketing or public relations departments. This meant, in Langley's words, that "Corporate sponsorship . . . is money given with the expectation of getting something in return" [*Theatre Management and Production* 559]. Corporations are not primarily in the charity business, and to support a not-for-profit theatre the relevant executive had to be convinced that a grant was a good investment for the company; in 1989, for example, AT&T gave forty-three theatres grants averaging about $17,000 each to sponsor individual productions, hoping that prominent mention of the gift in programs and press releases would "establish the company's presence in key markets [with the] target audience—upscale decision-makers" [Shewey 32].

Such corporate sponsorship frequently comes with very attractive fringe benefits, such as the use of the company's expert marketing and public relations resources. As Suzanne Sato, Vice President, Arts and Culture, of the AT&T Foundation, explains,

> To be very clear, the ads we're buying are AT&T ads, that trumpet our involvement in the production, but for most theatres it's more ad impressions than they are able to manage out of their own budget. And also our ad agency designs an image. We don't require theatres to use our image, but for a lot of them that's another expense they don't have to incur. [Interview]

And the selfish benefits for the corporations can be so indirect as to be almost free of the taint of crass commercialism; as Sato points out, if the primary objective was return on investment, "Naming a sports arena is going to give you a lot more public impressions."

> We have thematic guidelines [for our giving] that aim to make these points, not just about our philanthropy but, by extension, about the company, that we're an innovative and creative company, that we are committed to the diversity of our employee base and the diversity of the community. We want to associate ourselves with excellence. [Interview]

Still, the self-serving agendas of corporate sponsors, however muted, meant a new minefield for theatres to walk through in their search for funding. Virtually all corporate giving, predicated as it was on visibility for the donor, was for specific projects and productions rather

than the less exploitable ongoing institutional support the big foundations had earlier supplied. (Some of Dayton Hudson's funding was an
exception to this rule, though most of its general operating support
grants were focussed in its Minneapolis base, making the Guthrie Theater a prime beneficiary.) Most corporations, like AT&T, had a specific
image they wanted to project and associate themselves with, which
meant that corporate grants were likely to have pre-set parameters.
Dayton Hudson's Target branch, for example, promotes a family image.

> So we tell potential applicants, if the perception is that a family can't
> afford to go because of cost, the chances of support [from Target]
> are nominal to nonexistent, whereas if you're doing something like
> family free days your chances are going to be more persuasive.
> [Cameron interview]

By all accounts the Tyrone Guthrie Theater's annual Target-
sponsored Open House, with tours of the building and family fun with
costumes and makeup, is a great success; the thousands of people who
come into the theatre for the first time include some who will return as
ticket-buyers. But if a foundation grant earmarked for a special purpose
might tempt a theatre to create a project to fit it, or if local government
money might have explicit or implicit censorship attached, the same
dangers lay in corporate dollars.

Meanwhile, not-for-profit theatres, accustomed to dealing with
funding sources that shared their values, have had to learn to speak the
corporate language and package their needs in terms corporations would
respond to. Betty Blondeau Russell, Director of Development for the
Alliance Theatre in Atlanta, turned philanthropy into a product by offering local companies a tickets-and-party package for $7500: "We felt
that corporations were still going to have to be doing some marketing
and entertaining, and our corporate package offers entertainment opportunities" [qtd in "Advance or Retreat" 44]. Similarly, San Diego's Gaslamp
Quarter Theatre got a grant from a nearby condominium developer by
convincing him that the theatre was a neighborhood amenity he could
use as a selling point [Reiss *Applaud* 115].

☆

All these financial pressures led, inevitably, to belt-tightening at all
but the most fortunate theatres. One of the first casualties was the full-
time resident acting company, as theatre after theatre reduced the size of
its core company or eliminated it altogether, casting each play separately
as the commercial theatre did. Gregory Boyd of the Alley, one of the few

theatres able to retain an ongoing company, sees the elimination of resident companies as both an artistic and a financial error:

> When the League of Resident Theatres was founded, the key word was "resident," which meant that they were companies of artists. Very few companies exist in America right now. Buildings exist, that put out six or seven or ten projects a year, but companies — that is, where you can have a season-long or ten-season-long dialogue with an audience — that is rarer.... The audience has a proprietary interest in the theatre because of the team, the same company of actors every season. [Interview]

Ancillary activities — tours, education programs, children's theatres, and the like — began to fall by the wayside; and in many cases the number of plays in a season or the length of each run was reduced. There were several experiments in co-production, with two or more companies sharing the cost of a play and running it in each of their theatres. As later chapters will show, the commercial theatre was turning more and more to the noncommercial sector for its new plays; and the temptation to select the repertoire with an eye toward profitable commercial transfers was one that some artistic directors could not afford to resist. In 1984 the NEA bemoaned what it called an "artistic deficit," which Robert Brustein later identified explicitly as "a hesitancy to produce projects considered too controversial to move to New York" ["Arts Wars" 20].

The not-for-profit theatre in America was not destroyed by these financial pressures. Some theatres, generally the oldest and largest, either continued to grow or at least held their own, while most others were able to adjust successfully to the changing economic realities. Still, individual companies were wounded and some — the BAM Theatre Company (closed 1981), Phoenix Theatre (1982), California Repertory Theatre (1985), Hartman Theatre (1987), Alaska Repertory Theatre (1988), Philadelphia Theatre Company (1989), Actors Theatre of St. Paul (1990), Chelsea Stage (1990), and Los Angeles Theater Center (1991), among others — were forced to cease operations. A total of twenty-three companies closed down between 1987 and 1992, according to the Theatre Communication Group, and half those remaining faced mounting deficits [Janowitz "92"].

Adjustments of another sort, resulting more from success than from the danger of failure, put other unexpected pressures on the regional theatre after the first euphoric decades. Companies that had begun with the enthusiasm of youthful amateurs found themselves established institutions with multimillion dollar budgets. Benjamin Mordecai, then

Managing Director of the Yale Repertory Theatre, complained in 1984 that "Maintaining 'product' in a multi-million dollar facility places a weight of responsibility around the neck of artistic ambition" [28]. Six years later Zelda Fichandler explained, "It's very expensive to do all that Arena does.... A little over half of its money goes directly to the art, to what you see on the stage. The rest goes to maintaining the surround — the institution" [8].

Artistic directors who just wanted to make theatre evolved into executives of what were, in effect, medium-sized corporations. "When I walked into the [Actors Theatre of Louisville] twenty-seven years ago I think there were about six of us on the staff," muses Producing Director Jon Jory. "Now we have a staff that, depending on the time of year, including actors, might run anywhere from eighty to one hundred fifty.... You sometimes spend more time meeting than anything else" [Interview]. Joe Dowling, Artistic Director of the Guthrie, adds, "These days, we have to be administrators and evangelists.... Forty percent of my time is spent talking to community groups" [qtd. in Weber "Birth"].

Theatres that were the product of one forceful individual's driving energy faced identity crises as well as leadership vacuums when that individual left or died. Boards of directors, who in many cases had been recruited by a theatre's charismatic founder and were happy to stay out of artistic issues, were faced with hiring the founder's successors and otherwise involving themselves in the theatre's operation; "the old days of 'join the board and we won't ask you to do anything' [were] all but gone" [Reiss "Arts" 30]. Zelda Fichandler's successor at the Arena Stage, Douglas C. Wager, was chosen in-house, but when he announced his departure in 1997, "he left its board of trustees on unfamiliar ground.... The board hadn't a clue where to look" [Weber "Birth"].

Margo Jones set the pattern for the success of the resident theatre movement, so it is sadly ironic that her theatre set the pattern for one kind of failure. An artistic institution so closely associated with its founder and so much a reflection of her artistic vision could not survive her. After her death in 1955, the board of directors that she had selected to support her found itself making artistic choices for which it was unprepared. The theatre went through several "managing directors," none with real artistic vision or power, before dying in 1959.

As noted earlier, San Francisco's Actor's Workshop was unable to outlive the departure of its founders, Herbert Blau and Jules Irving, and closed in 1966. The Tyrone Guthrie Theater continued to function after the departure of its charismatic founder and star-filled first company, but experienced several uneven patches in the decades that followed, as subsequent artistic directors discovered how very fragile the theatre's hold on its audience was and how easy it was for even the most successful institution to have money-losing years. The Alley Theatre survived Nina Vance's death in 1980, but weathered an artistically unfocused and deficit-creating decade until a strong artistic director, Gregory Boyd, redefined the repertoire and rebuilt the audience.

After being turned down by Meryl Streep, Jerry Zaks, Mike Nichols, and James Lapine (all of whom saw that their talents did not extend to the executive), Joe Papp hand-picked JoAnne Akalaitis to be his successor as artistic director of the New York Shakespeare Festival, presumably with full knowledge of her strengths and weaknesses. But the Festival board was less open and patient; citing a too-challenging repertoire and a failure to attract funding, they fired her after eighteen months. (Her replacement, George C. Wolfe, was a writer-director with experience in both the commercial and not-for-profit theatre; he continued Papp's tradition of mixing new works and classics, and of using Broadway to the Festival's benefit, while gradually putting his own stamp on the theatre.)

Companies whose founders stayed were not immune to growing pains. It should be no criticism to say that some of the most admired artistic directors in the American theatre were less talented as administrators, except that in some cases that limitation threatened the lives of their theatres. William Ball of the American Conservatory Theatre and Adrian Hall of Trinity Square and the Dallas Theater Center both created exciting theatre while accumulating deficits, losing subscribers, and alienating their boards of directors.

Ball founded the ACT and ran it for twenty years until waning artistic powers, falling subscriptions, and estranged financial supporters led to his departure in 1986. Hall actually defeated a board attempt to fire him from Trinity Square in 1975, but subsequently went through thirteen business managers in fifteen years of mounting deficits before leaving in 1989 to concentrate on Dallas (where he had been serving simultaneously as artistic director); he was fired by the Dallas board within a year. (Meanwhile, Hall's successor at Trinity Square was Anne Bogart, a talented director of experimental theatre with little experience in the conventional repertoire or in administration; she resigned after a year's conflict with the board.)

In this light, it is worth noting that the most successful artistic directors around the country are quick to share credit with strong co-administrators—

Any artistic director needs a partner — a managing director, executive director, whatever. It is not a one-person job. The reason my career has turned out OK so far is that I was blessed with working with two brilliant partners [at Playwrights Horizons and Lincoln Center] whose contributions to those theatres and my own growth are beyond my describing. [Bishop interview; similar comments from Arvin Brown, Gregory Mosher, Theodore Mann, and Tim Sanford]

— or to recognize that their own jobs include administrative and institutional obligations —

For the pleasure of being able to spend time in a rehearsal room with a playwright and actors, there is the responsibility to communicate to a board of directors, and therefore to the community, the necessity of my particular vision and why it needs to be supported. It's really part of the job description to communicate, to advocate, to raise money, or at least to bring people around you who have those particular skills and to encourage them to do it. [Falls interview; similar comment from Jon Jory]

By the 1980s most theatres in America were into their second or third generation of leadership: to take years almost at random, in 1980 new artistic directors were named at the Guthrie, Studio Arena, Hartford Stage, Philadelphia Drama Guild, Loretto-Hilton, Yale, and North Light Rep; 1989 saw new people heading the Dallas Theater Center, East West Players, Trinity Rep, Williamstown Theatre Festival, Alabama Shakespeare Festival, Alley Theatre, and StageWest; 1991 had changeovers at the Arena, Actors' Company, Yale, Center Stage, New York Shakespeare Festival, Oregon Shakespeare Festival, Lincoln Center, and Playwrights Horizons; 1992 added ACT, Classic Stage Company, Indiana Rep, Group Theatre of Seattle, Syracuse Stage, Dallas, and Portland Stage; 1996 witnessed changes at Long Wharf, Seattle Rep, Guthrie, and Circle in the Square.

Not all of these represent failures, of course; some were the results of deaths or retirements, others of a chain reaction, as an artistic director leaving one theatre to take a position elsewhere left a vacancy behind. Still, almost every change in leadership signalled identity problems for a theatre, as artistic directors attempted to put their mark on the repertoire, audiences waited warily to see how much would change, and boards of directors became more closely involved in artistic and administrative matters. As in some of the examples mentioned earlier, second artistic directors often proved to have much shorter tenure than their predecessors, as boards belatedly became aware of their power and their responsibility to what were now sizeable institutions; and some observers saw a pattern of declining energy and artistic vision. "When you have something to conserve, you become conservative," warns Gregory Mosher [Interview]; and Todd London complained:

> The impetus to break away, found and pioneer has been replaced by the need to maintain, hold on, secure. The language of the visionary has been watered down into the corporate jargon of the successor, one, two, three, four generations young. [22]

If we measure by the productive life of Broadway as the dominant force in American theatre — about a half-century — then the not-for-profit regional theatre was facing middle age.

As suggested earlier, the regional theatre's maturity brought another set of financial and artistic dilemmas arising out of its shifting and always uncomfortable relationship to the commercial theatre, but that subject can best be discussed later, in Chapters Five and Six. The point being made here — that the euphoria of the resident theatre movement's early decades was tempered somewhat by the discovery that maturity involved ongoing struggles both financial and artistic — should not blind us to the extraordinary change in the scope and structure of the American theatre.

For the first time in a century, virtually every American lives within driving distance of a professional theatre offering high-quality productions. For the first time in a century, audiences outside New York City are more likely to see both classics and world premieres than those in New York. For the first time in a century, theatres have established a place in their communities as permanent cultural resources to be sustained and supported. And for the first time in its history, the dominant segment of the American theatre is at least partly liberated from the marketplace, able to make artistic choices that are not entirely determined by commercial considerations. The resident theatre has produced artistically vital theatrical activity throughout America; and the general cultural acceptance of its need for — and perhaps even its right to — subsidy is evidence of a national commitment to the theatre as a link with the past and an explorer of the future, and not merely as a source of idle entertainment.

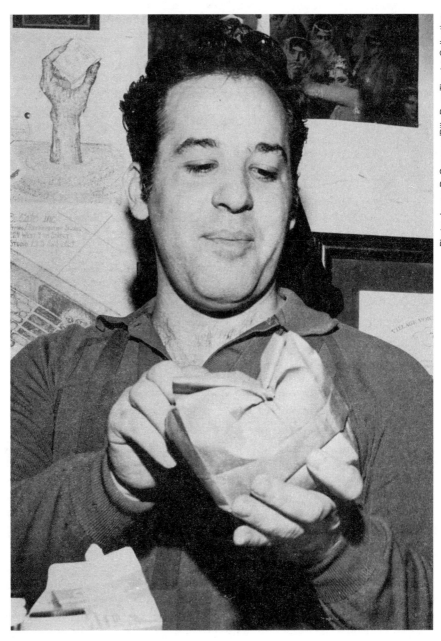

Joe Cino

4

OFF OFF AND OTHER ALTERNATIVES

Joseph Cino was an overweight ex-dancer, a homosexual, an alcoholic, a drug-taker, and a flamboyant Greenwich Village "character." Having given up his stage ambitions by 1958, he opened the Caffe Cino, one of many coffeehouses that sprang up in the Village in the late 1950s. The Caffe Cino quickly became a haven for other outcasts, misfits, and failed or would-be performers; the long, narrow storefront cafe had a tiny stage in the middle, where the loving host let his guests live out their fantasies by performing for each other and for any unsuspecting tourists who wandered in. Eventually some of the Cino regulars put on a play, and Off Off-Broadway was born.

That at least is the myth, and as myths go it's a pretty good one, with a happy blend of truth and almost-truth. The truth lies in the basic facts — there was a Joe Cino, and he did give his stage to anyone who wanted to use it, with a determined disregard for questions of talent or commercial appeal. Plays were produced at the Cino for almost ten years and there were even a couple of financial successes, most notably the parody musical *Dames at Sea* (1966).

The mythic elements include the larger-than-life Cino himself and the collection of fellow misfits who formed around him, particularly as filtered through memory in the years since Joe Cino's suicide in 1967. (A fictionalized but highly evocative picture of the Caffe Cino's rise and fall appears in the play *Kennedy's Children* by Cino alumnus Robert Patrick.) The myth also comes in trying to pinpoint the birth of Off Off-Broadway.

The first use of that term is generally attributed to *Village Voice* critic Jerry Tallmer, who was trying to call attention to a wide range of theatrical activity in New York City in 1960, theatres and productions with little in common beyond obscurity, poverty, and inexperience. Actually, the roots of Off Off-Broadway are indistinguishable from the roots of Off-Broadway; for every Circle in the Square that rose from nowhere to fame and something approaching institutional status in the 1950s, hun-

**Leonard Melfi, Paul Foster, Ellen Stewart,
Tom O'Horgan and Kevin O'Connor (l to r)**

dreds of other companies died at birth or struggled on unnoticed by most of the world — the Living Theatre, for example, was quintessential Off Off-Broadway for its first ten years.

But it wasn't until the early 1960s, when Off-Broadway as a theatrical environment had achieved some stability, and its budgets, production values, and commercial ambitions had risen significantly above the shoestring level, that some new label became necessary to point out that theatre of a different sort was still going on in lofts, coffeehouses, and vacant stores all around Manhattan.

Even the staunchest defenders of early Off Off-Broadway — for example, Michael Smith, editor of several collections of its plays — admit that "much of the new work was tentative, lacking in craft, technically crude" [12]. Inexperience and shoestring budgets do not magically guarantee great theatre; and actors, directors, and authors willing to work for free are sometimes actors, directors, and authors that no one will pay.

From the beginning a large number of Off Off-Broadway productions were conceived of as showcases (a term that later came to have specific legal and contractual meanings), essentially self-subsidized auditions to which agents and producers were invited in the hope that they might remember and someday hire the participants. The distinction between showcases and vanity productions was not always clear, and even those performers and writers who did have legitimate aspirations and some talent were almost always lacking in experience and thus in control over their craft.

But it was this very freedom from minimum standards and commercial pressures that allowed the alternative-to-the-alternative theatre to grow and, at least briefly, to become a fertile ground for theatrical experiment. Except perhaps for the determined showcasers, the only motivation for Off Off-Broadway artists was the desire to work; in Michael Smith's words, "satisfaction in the doing was the only satisfaction to be had . . . . With neither money nor careers at stake, caution is unnecessary, you can do anything" [16]. The assumption of commercial failure was virtually built into the system, and the opportunity to fail and fail again without shame meant, at least for some, the opportunity to learn their craft and develop their powers.

Pulitzer Prize-winning dramatists Lanford Wilson and Sam Shepard were both in the large group of writers who had their first plays produced Off Off-Broadway, Wilson's *So Long at the Fair* at the Caffe Cino in 1963 and Shepard's *Cowboys* at Theatre Genesis in 1964. Tom O'Horgan, one of the most colorful and influential Broadway and Off-Broadway directors of the late 1960s, began at LaMama; Robert DeNiro, Judd Hirsch, Nick Nolte, Al Pacino, and Bernadette Peters acted Off Off-Broadway at the beginning of their careers; and through the decades after 1960 scores of plays first seen Off Off-Broadway went on to commercial productions Off- or on Broadway and to become staples of the regional theatre repertoire.

Despite its enormous output (a new play every week or two for almost ten years), the Caffe Cino did not produce many plays or artists of particular merit. Lanford Wilson's *The Madness of Lady Bright* (1964) and Sam Shepard's *Icarus's Mother* (1965) stand out, along with *Dames at Sea*; and director Marshall W. Mason, O'Neill Center founder George White, and Off-Broadway producer Eric Krebs served part of their apprenticeships at the Cino. Generally, though, Joe Cino's determined rejection of objective standards — he put on what he liked or what his friends wanted to do, and his tastes and his associates ran to the outlandish and extravagant — made the Caffe Cino one of the more self-indulgently amateurish of Off Off-Broadway venues.

Its importance, even at the time, was largely symbolic: it was *there*, and its continued operation in spite of zoning laws, financial pressures, and creative failures seemed to demonstrate that some unquenchable artistic force was present and had chosen Off Off-Broadway as its home. The Cino proved that a theatre of experiment, of violated rules, and of personal vision could still exist after Off-Broadway had become commercialized; and even its coterie quality allowed for positive interpretation, suggesting that drama and theatre could be a vehicle for communal unity and expression.

The connection between alternative theatre and the counterculture movements of the 1960s is a complicated one. Certainly, not all of the shoestring theatre groups in New York and around the country were politically radical or even politically aware. Still, the alternative theatre was for the most part a young theatre and inevitably reflected to some degree the concerns and awareness of a younger generation of artists and audiences. Whether this manifested itself in antiwar plays, communally organized companies, attempts to reach new audiences, or coterie productions that rejected new audiences, there was an extra-artistic quality to the movement, an overt or implicit belief that theatre could play a social role.

In this light it is not surprising that several early Off Off-Broadway theatres were established by churches as a service to their congregations and communities. Ralph Cook, director of St. Mark's Theatre Genesis, spoke of

> a truly indigenous theatre [in which] the actors, directors, and writers are members of a geographical community and are presenting plays . . . as an integral everyday part of the life of the community . . . and the artist is assuming his original role of tribal actor and artificer. [94]

St. Mark's-in-the-Bouwerie served the neighborhood formerly known as the Lower East Side but beginning to be labeled the East Village as it became the center of New York's hippie community in the mid-1960s. Theatre Genesis was established in 1964 with a mission as much social as artistic; later in the decade it received some of its funding from the federal Office of Juvenile Delinquency for involving neighborhood kids in its activities. Still, Cook ran it as a playwrights' workshop, utilizing private and public readings, improvisations, and full productions to guide playwrights "who are at that point where they need a continuing relationship with a stage and actors in order to evolve" [93]. Theatre Genesis gave Sam Shepard his first productions, and also staged plays by Tom Sankey, Murray Mednick, and Leonard Melfi.

The Judson Memorial Church in Greenwich Village began its involvement with theatre even earlier by offering a room to a member of the congregation who wanted to give a poetry reading. The church formed the Judson Poets' Theatre in 1961 to serve both the community and itself; the Reverend Al Carmines, assistant minister and head of the church's arts program, explained,

> One need in our community was a space where new playwrights could be produced....Another concern was [that] the church... might be exposed to the work of these playwrights and thus hear the secular prophets in our city. [123]

Although Judson introduced a number of artists, its biggest discovery turned out to be Carmines himself, a talented composer and lyricist who virtually created a genre of Off Off-Broadway chamber musicals, ranging from Christmas cantatas to literary adaptations. Other churches in New York, from Riverside Church on the edge of Harlem to St. Clements on the edge of the Broadway theatre district, also saw Off Off-Broadway theatre as a way of serving their communities.

Of course, not all Off Off-Broadway entrepreneurs were social workers. The most artistically significant and successful Off Off-Broadway venue of the 1960s came into being and survived because its founder worshiped playwrights, loved live performance, and found her life's work in bringing the two together. If Joseph Papp of the New York Shakespeare Festival was the modern American theatre's most extraordinary producer-director-fundraiser-talentspotter-hustler-workaholic, then Ellen Stewart of LaMama must run a very close second.

A fashion designer by profession, Stewart became an Off Off-Broadway producer in 1961 because she knew someone who had written a play he couldn't get staged. She founded the Cafe LaMama in frank imitation of the Cino — as she later explained, young playwrights sought her out "because they didn't feel experienced enough to go to Caffe Cino" [Horn 15] — and operated it in a variety of locations and manifestations. When city officials closed down the cafe for one violation or another it moved and then moved again and then became a private club (the LaMama Experimental Theatre Club, open only to members; its fliers and advertisements did not give its address, since those who could get in already knew where it was), and finally a theatre.

Totally committed to her playwrights, Stewart subsidized LaMama with her fashion earnings until the foundation and government grants began to come in in the late 1960s. She fought or found her way around any obstacles — commercial producers when they mistreated her alumni, the actors' union when it tried to keep its members from working for her without pay, even the Immigration Service when it caused trouble for foreign companies she invited to play at LaMama.

When publishers rejected LaMama plays in the early 1960s because the authors were unknown and newspaper critics refused to come to the cafe and write the reviews that would make the authors known, Stewart accepted invitations from drama festivals in France and Denmark and sent a company to Europe in 1965 at her own expense. She got her reviews there, which led to her being taken more seriously at home; and also impressed the foreign alternative theatre community so much that there were soon satellite LaMama companies in Paris, Munich, Tel Aviv, Melbourne, Manila, Buenos Aires, and Tokyo. "By 1967, a distinctive group of young experimental playwrights had emerged, as had the distinctive acting style under the tutelage of [Tom] O'Horgan, and this was the artistic imprint that LaMama was leaving on the major theatrical capitals of the world" [Horn 25].

Stewart also lent her stage and prestige to other companies, notably the Open Theatre, that needed playing space, and had an important role in introducing Americans to the European avant-garde. LaMama co-sponsored the first American visits of Jerzy Grotowski (1969) and Andrei Serban (1970); and in 1971 Stewart founded the Third World Institute of Theatre Arts Studies as a vehicle for sponsoring productions by theatre companies from Africa and Asia.

LaMama playwrights of the 1960s included Tom Eyen, Israel Horovitz, Leonard Melfi, Megan Terry, and the ubiquitous Sam Shepard. Lanford Wilson's *Balm in Gilead*, generally recognized as Off Off-Broadway's first original full-length play — the combination of beginning writers and low budgets usually produced one-act plays — was directed at LaMama in 1965 by Marshall W. Mason, with whom Wilson would later work so successfully in the Circle Repertory Company. LaMama's most impressive and notorious director was Tom O'Horgan, whose explorations of ritual, mime, choric speaking, and, when his graduation to Off-Broadway and Broadway brought him larger budgets, elaborate staging effects had wide influence in the late 1960s. Ellen Stewart and LaMama continued through the following decades to be the New York City theatre's most receptive and nourishing haven for beginning artists, experimenters, and foreign companies.

A list of early Off Off-Broadway companies could take up an entire volume, but a sampling of the longer-lasting groups will give some sense of the variety available to New York City theatregoers in the 1960s. Joseph Chaikin, a former member of the Living Theatre, formed the

Open Theatre in 1964 to explore the possibilities of collaborative creation and the evocation of dream and myth in performance. Similar experimentation was done by the Performance Group, led by Richard Schechner, also editor of *The Drama Review*, which functioned for a while as a kind of house organ of the experimental theatre movement, and by Andre Gregory's Manhattan Project. The Bread and Puppet Theatre used masks and larger-than-lifesize heads and bodies of the sort sometimes seen in parades in their plays of political and social criticism, often performed in the streets.

The Circle Stage Company (later renamed the CSC Repertory Company and then the Classic Stage Company, with changing repertoires) experimented with new stagings of classical dramas, sometimes with more ambition than success. The Barr-Wilder-Albee Playwrights Unit was essentially an Off Off-Broadway operation. The American Theatre for Poets did poetic drama; the Joseph Jefferson Theatre Company revived American classics; the Octagon Theatre produced musicals; the AMAS Repertory Theatre did new black plays; INTAR's repertoire mixed new Hispanic-American plays and Spanish classics; the Ridiculous Theatrical Company offered wildly campy comic extravaganzas; and dozens of less specialized theatres provided a constant flow of new plays.

☆

Off Off-Broadway was a New York City phenomenon, the product of a concentration of unemployed actors and a theatrically sophisticated and adventurous audience. But theatrical sophistication was coming to other parts of the country in the 1960s, and a by-product of the growth of regional theatre was a satellite system of smaller, sometimes just barely professional companies. In a sense, a measure of a regional theatre's success was the speed with which it became the establishment and inspired the appearance of self-styled alternatives: before the end of the decade Washington, Los Angeles, San Francisco, Minneapolis, and other resident theatre centers had small Off- and Off Off-Broadways of their own; and Boston, Denver, and other cities developed alternative theatres even in the absence of a resident establishment.

As in New York, some of these groups had extra-theatrical agendas. The political and social ferment of the 1960s produced a lot of new, alternative companies who were exploring the use of theatre as a tool for social education and persuasion. The Free Southern Theater, an integrated — later, all-black — company founded in 1964, toured small

Southern towns bringing such plays as *In White America* and *Waiting for Godot* to rural black audiences, in the faith that they would understand them in spite of their cultural deprivations, and be inspired by the opportunity to share their responses with the black performers. El Teatro Campesino grew out of the Mexican-American farm workers' strikes of the mid-1960s as a traveling improvisational company devoted to boosting the strikers' morale, and later expanded its mission to include dramatizing the Chicano experience for Anglo audiences.

In similar ways the Florida Studio Theatre, based in Sarasota, and The Playgroup Inc. of Knoxville, Tennessee, produced company-created works drawn from the experiences and history of their rural audiences. The San Francisco Mime Troupe and the Bread and Puppet Theatre in New York took to the streets with plays of political satire and criticism. There were as many as one hundred feminist theatre companies around the country by the late 1970s, and theatres expressing the positions or dramatizing the experiences of Marxists, pacifists, prisoners, homosexuals, and the physically handicapped.

These politically-inspired companies aside, "alternative" did not always mean "antagonistic" around the country, as it generally did in New York, where the Off Off-Broadway community prided itself, with perhaps a hint of sour grapes, on the distance between it and the commercial theatre. Many smaller regional theatres were born as friendly supplements to the local mainstream. The Washington Theater Club, for example, grew from an amateur community theatre to a professional company in the early 1960s, and credited the larger Arena Stage for much of its success; as Artistic Director Davey Marlin-Jones explained in 1970, "Arena Stage . . . created an appetite for the theatre [but] there are things they can do better than anybody and things that are prohibitive because of their size. That automatically opened opportunities for us" [290].

The opening was for new plays, European plays, and what Marlin-Jones called "theatre of the second chance," plays that had failed in New York but could be rediscovered in modest but imaginative productions. In short, the Washington Theater Club filled exactly the same role that the Circle in the Square and other companies had filled in New York; it even advertised for a time as "Washington's professional Off-Broadway theater." It was joined in the 1970s by the Folger Theatre, a sort of mini-Royal Shakespeare Company formed by the Folger Shakespeare Library to alternate Shakespeare with new plays; the New Playwrights' Theatre of Washington; and DC Black Repertory Theater.

In Boston the Charles Playhouse opened in 1957 and slowly built to modest success as a conservative resident company; and the Theater Company of Boston followed as an Off-Broadway-type alternative, offering the first American productions of such plays as Ann Jellicoe's *The Knack* and John Arden's *Live Like Pigs* along with new American plays, with casts that included at various times Stockard Channing, Blythe Danner, Robert Duvall, Dustin Hoffman, Al Pacino, and Jon Voigt. Through the 1960s Boston also saw the People's Theatre, the Caravan Theatre, the Hub Theatre Centre, the Players Theatre of Boston, and a half-dozen others; and as some of these died off in the 1970s they were replaced by Theatre Workshop Boston, the Reality Theatre, Boston Arts Group, Cambridge Ensemble, Boston Shakespeare Company, and others, providing a fairly consistent mix of conventional and experimental theatre.

In Minneapolis the Firehouse Theater was formed in 1963, the same year the Guthrie Theater opened, as an Off-Broadway alternative, but soon found this role inadequate. As director Marlow Hotchkiss recalled,

> Our goal ... was hardly more specific than a desire to be relevant, ... which practically meant that we staged last year's better Off-Broadway offerings.... But to try to do the Off-Broadway thing with unskilled actors was simply to wed the worst of both worlds. In two years the Firehouse Theater moved from a vague promise of relevance to spiritual bankruptcy. Ironically, the solution to this problem was found in yet another New York model, Off Off-Broadway. [qtd in Sainer 30]

The Firehouse experimented with a variety of avant-garde styles and techniques and gradually developed its own focus: scripted and group-created works that purposely incorporated elements of chance and audience involvement to make the actual moment on stage part of the fictional story.

The Firehouse Theatre moved to San Francisco in 1969 and found not only the resident American Conservatory Theatre but also such alternative companies as the San Francisco Mime Troupe, a political street theatre that used spoken plays as well as mimes; the Julian Theatre, which began as a classical repertory company but gradually changed its focus to new plays by West Coast writers; and the Magic Theatre, also devoted to new plays (Sam Shepard's Pulitzer Prize play *Buried Child* was developed with the Magic Theatre while he was a writer in residence there, and premiered in 1978).

Chicago was a little later in developing an alternative movement, in part because it was a leading "road" city, with several touring ex-Broadway shows each season to satisfy audiences; and in part because its young theatre artists were drawn to a different arena. In the early 1950s the generation that might have formed Chicago's Off-Broadway, many of them alumni of the University of Chicago's student theatre, were doing the same mix of classics and modern European plays as their New York counterparts. A core group formed the Compass Players, where they were strongly influenced by legendary improvisation teacher Viola Spolin, whose exercises in freeing the imagination would later help shape the styles of companies such as the San Francisco Mime Troupe and the Open Theatre. Under the direction of Spolin's son Paul Sills, the Compass repertoire gradually shifted from scripted texts to group-created plays, to shorter improvised-on-the-spot sketches.

Sills' artistic impulse—as Compass producer David Shepherd recalled, "Paul was more interested in what he called 'little entertainments' that mixed together songs, blackouts, and psychological pieces. In other words, revues." [qtd in Coleman 83]—along with the special talents of such performers as Mike Nichols, Elaine May, Severn Darden, and Shelley Berman, helped create a whole new type of entertainment that

Photo: Ron Blanchette

The San Francisco Mime Troupe in *False Promises*

blended improvisation, stand-up comedy, revue, and traditional theatre. In 1959 the Compass Players evolved into the Second City, and Chicago-style improvisational comedy not only inspired similar groups in other cities but continued to flourish in Chicago through several decades and generations of talented young performers.

Chicago had to wait another decade until the establishment of the Goodman Theatre's professional company in 1969 helped reawaken audience and performer interest in traditional theatre, but within a few years the Goodman was supplemented by a sizeable "Off-Loop" theatrical community. Noting that many of these new companies were founded by recent college graduates, Scott Steele of the University/Resident Theatre Association sees them as a direct product of the shift toward professionalism that took place in university theatre training in the 1960s; "It took a number of years of developing the right attitude about theatre in campus before folks like that rolled out and said, 'Hell, let's start something'" [Interview].

The Organic Theatre Company developed out of a student group in 1969 and earned a reputation for inventiveness and professionalism with such productions as *Warp*, a three-part Flash Gordon-style science fiction epic, and the premiere of David Mamet's *Sexual Perversity in Chicago* (1974). Mamet himself was co-founder of the Evanston Theatre Company, later the North Light Repertory Company, and subsequently contributed to the St. Nicholas Theatre Company. Another group of students came together as the Steppenwolf Theatre in 1976, and rapidly attracted attention and praise for their intensely realistic acting and production style.

The Body Politic, Performance Community, Victory Gardens, Wisdom Bridge — by 1978 there were fifty theatre companies in the Chicago Alliance for the Performing Arts, ranging from such well-established (though always financially fragile) groups as those just named, all committed to new and experimental works, to more marginal and barely professional companies offering a typical community theatre fare. (The Alliance, a mutual support organization, disbanded in 1980, partially as a result of the size and disparate goals of its membership.)

The list is potentially endless. By the late 1970s Los Angeles had about one hundred Off Off-Broadway-type theatres, many of them primarily showcases for unemployed actors, but including the experimental Odyssey Theatre Ensemble and LaMama Hollywood, the multilingual Los Angeles Actors' Theatre, the oriental-American East-West Players, and others from Actors Alley through Words and Music;

two decades later there were more than five hundred theatre companies in southern California. The Association of Philadelphia Theatres had eleven members by 1975; at various times there were new-play-producing theatres in Buffalo (American Contemporary Theatre), Omaha (Omaha Magic Theatre), Milwaukee (Theatre X), Iowa City (Iowa Theatre Lab), Seattle (Empty Space Theatre), Denver (Changing Scene), and dozens of other cities.

In the early 1960s the Waterford, Connecticut, site of Eugene O'Neill's boyhood home was offered to the theatre community as the Eugene O'Neill Theater Center. Founder George White explains that its important contributions to the American theatre were not all planned: "It started as a way to save a bunch of old buildings from being torn down; it was a place looking for a project. I think a lot of people had in their minds a summer stock theatre." White convened the grandly-titled National Playwrights Conference in 1965.

> I hocked a life insurance policy and we got people in the community to provide bed-and-breakfast, and we invited twenty playwrights out of Caffe Cino, Cafe LaMama [and other Off Off-Broadway theatres], people like San Shepard, John Guare, Lanford Wilson. They were so angry at the world, and frustrated by not being able to be heard. [Interview]

White concluded that the best service the O'Neill Center could provide was a far-off-Broadway site where playwrights could try out new plays, "a place where they could try, where they could fail, where they could test things outside the glare of the hit-or-flop syndrome of New York" [Interview]. After a false start of attempting full-scale productions, he and Artistic Director Lloyd Richards organized staged readings of as many as seventeen works-in-progress each summer. On a relatively bare stage, with professional actors led by professional directors but still using their scripts, a playwright's early draft could display its strengths and weaknesses and guide the writer toward revision.

New York began to take notice when the works in progress turned out to be such plays as John Guare's *House of Blue Leaves* (1966), Israel Horovitz's *The Indian Wants the Bronx* (1966), and Lanford Wilson's *Lemon Sky* (1968), and ground rules (no published reviews, no contract-signing on the spot) had to be established to preserve the Center's value to developing artists. These young playwrights, and subsequently scores of others, learned from their O'Neill stagings, reworked their plays, and saw them go on to New York and regional theatre runs. The O'Neill Center continued to serve as a nursery for writing talent while expanding its operations to include complementary workshops for young directors, choreographers, and critics, and also serving as the home base of the National Theatre of the Deaf, a professional touring company offering spoken and signed productions of classics and new plays.

☆

In September 1968 the Living Theatre returned to America after a four-year self-imposed exile in Europe, where Julian Beck, Judith Malina, and their company had developed a wholly new style of creation and performance. In a six-month tour that began at Yale University and stopped at colleges and alternative theatres across the country, the Living Theatre offered a four-play repertoire that shocked purists and puritans, excited audiences, and disturbed critics everywhere.

The most conventional play they performed was a new adaptation of *Antigone* by Judith Malina that stripped away the poetry and philosophy to leave an open confrontation between a repressive state and an idealistic youth in the context of an immoral war, with obviously intentional parallels to contemporary America. The nearest to a critical success among the four was a staging of *Frankenstein* as an allegory of uncensored primal forces accidentally turned loose by a repressive society and hunted down, only to turn and destroy some of the hunters while liberating the others in a climactic orgy of love and unification. Again the topical application to the era of Woodstock, student riots, and the generation gap was undisguised, although the real inventiveness of *Frankenstein* lay in the production, which featured a multi-level gridwork on which the actors stood or hung at the end of Act I to form with their bodies the outline of the giant Creature, and which was then divided into compartments representing aspects of the Creature's psyche, whose functions were dramatized in turn as the Creature came to life and self-awareness.

The third Living Theatre program, *Mysteries and Other Pieces*, was actually a collection of rehearsal exercises: an actor stood absolutely still for six minutes; a group went through a Yoga breathing exercise; another group "passed" improvised movements and sounds back and forth among themselves; members of the company scattered around the theatre died horrible deaths and were carried to a growing pile of bodies on the stage until there were none alive.

The fourth piece, *Paradise Now*, was, in John Tytell's words, "the defining experience of The Living Theatre" [198]. It combined elements of the other three works but went beyond them in stretching traditional definitions of a theatrical event. In a frequently obscure sequence of group-created "rites" (The Rite of Study, The Rite of Universal Intercourse, etc.) the company simultaneously dramatized a catalogue of contemporary social evils (e.g., "Bolivia: A Group of Revolutionaries Plot their Strategy"), a call for social action ("Hanoi/Saigon: There Is a Group Living in an Anarchist Society. What Are They Doing?"), and an outline of the process by which the soul might free itself from the shackles of society and mortality ("The Rung of Prayer," "The Rung of Love," etc.).

Were that not ambitious enough, it was also the purpose of *Paradise Now* actually to produce the social and spiritual changes it dealt with, not merely to point the way. Everyone in the theatre was meant to have a mystically transforming experience; according to the Becks, "The purpose of the play is to lead to a state of being [for audience and actors] in which nonviolent revolution is possible" [qtd in Biner 174]. *Paradise Now* thus required intense audience involvement, and what made it the most controversial and notorious of the Living Theatre's four productions was that it invited and demanded audience participation. As Jack Gelber recounted,

> Julian and Judith wanted to show the way to a pacifist Eden, something positive, a thing of beauty. Whatever their intentions, ... parts of this open-ended ritual provoked anger, boredom, frustration, and ... orgiastic fusion of performer and audience. [22]

What lucidity the performance had was frequently buried under the number of spectators climbing onto the stage to celebrate the liberation of their souls by taking off their clothes or acting out their own private dramas.

The rebirth of the Living Theatre confounded critics. While many, particularly those associated with the experimental theatre in America, were excited by the ambitiousness of the Becks' vision and the new theatrical vocabulary they had developed, most had to agree with Robert Brustein that the company "had virtually abandoned all desire to create artistic imitations" [*Third* xv]; that is, that they were not even trying to do what theatre traditionally did. Eric Bentley, while acknowledging that "The LT represents the most resolute attempts during the past 20 years to create a theater which would be a radical alternative to Broadway and Off Broadway," concluded that its efforts "finally evaporate in sound and fury signifying nothing," and argued that the company's simplistic politics led it to lose sight of the basic nature of theatre, substituting

Photo: Fred W. McDarrah

The Living Theatre, 1968
Paradise Now: "The Vision of the Death and
Resurrection of the American Indian"

"exhibitionism and voyeurism" for the proper actor-audience relationship [1].

There was also a deeper concern, best expressed by Brustein, who had been one of the Becks' strongest defenders four years earlier and who, as Dean of the Yale Drama School, hosted the first stop on their tour. He recognized that the company's "full-scale assault upon any separation whatever between the spectator and the stage" was a logical extension of explorations the Becks had begun ten years earlier in *The Connection,* but he was disturbed by the use to which they were putting their new mastery of this approach. Their "remarkable capacity to manipulate minds" was "extremely irresponsible" because it was directed at a predominantly young and unsophisticated audience unprepared to defend itself.

While preaching anarchism, the company was tightly controlled and doctrinaire, both artistically and politically. "In spite of all the invitations to participate in free theatre . . . no spectator was ever allowed to violate the pattern of manipulated consent" or the determined order of events onstage. "It was, finally, not a vision of human freedom that one took away from *Paradise Now* but rather vague, disturbing memories of the youth rallies in Hitler's Nuremberg" [*Third* xiv–xvii]. Walter Kerr added, "All that is being offered is a limited *illusion* of participating — and this in a theater formally dedicated to the destruction of illusion.... This is not participation, it is paternalism" [55–56].

In the year of Woodstock, campus riots and the Chicago Democratic Convention, the line between theatrical performance and real life was sometimes blurred, as was the line between anarchy and demagoguery. But the failure of the revolution to take place does not reduce the 1968 version of the Living Theatre to the status of a curious but irrelevant historical footnote. The Living Theatre tour was very significant to American theatre history; it influenced many young artists and brought into focus the work that others had been doing.

There were many experimental theatre companies in America before the Living Theatre tour, and more afterward, and their styles and productions took many forms. But the Living Theatre's work, while not necessarily closely resembling all the others, embodied elements common to all in a particularly visible package. In the strange, disturbing, and imperfect productions of the Living Theatre, the scope and purpose of much of America's alternative theatre was crystallized.

(There were, of course, European antecedents and parallels to much of the American experimentation, some of which were direct influences: the French director Antonin Artaud's concept of a Theatre of Cruelty in which all the theatre's weapons would be used to subvert or break down the audience's presumed resistance to new ideas; the open theatricality and epic staging of the Germans Erwin Piscator and Bertolt Brecht; Polish director Jerzy Grotowski's experiments with myth and ritual; Peter Brook's imaginative Royal Shakespeare Company productions, especially of Peter Weiss's *Marat/Sade*.)

What the 1968–1969 Living Theatre tour made clear was that the experimental wing of Off Off-Broadway and its equivalents across the country were being shaped by four basic forces whose effects would eventually be felt in the most conservative and establishment theatres. The first of these was a de-emphasis of the text as the basis for theatrical creation. More conservative directors might think it their function to present an author's vision as effectively and transparently as possible or, at most, to filter the author's ideas through their own sensibility to create a collaborative product. But many young directors of the 1960s began to see the text as a barely necessary evil, the raw skeleton of a theatrical work it was their job to create.

Actors were encouraged to improvise on themes suggested by the text, and such improvisations might supplement or replace the written dialogue. Directors invented new business or called for new and perhaps incongruous readings. Speeches might be reassigned, the order of scenes changed, or music or dance interpolated. As Robert Brustein complained about the work of Off Off-Broadway director Tom O'Horgan, "What has traditionally provided form and intelligence in the theatre — namely, the script — has become largely a springboard scenario for an entirely new work" [*Third* 70].

Judith Malina's version of *Antigone* was essentially a stripped-down and politically simplified version of the original story, but the Performance Group's *Dionysus in 69* was a total reworking of Euripides' *The Bacchae*. Much of the original text was simply cut, and the rest was mixed with contemporary dialogue. Actors moved in and out of character, frequently commenting on the action in their own voices; and improvisation and audience involvement made every performance different.

In the Open Theatre, the Firehouse Theater, and some other companies, the dramatist could be reduced to little more than stenographer, perhaps suggesting the basic themes of a play and then writing down and organizing the results of the actors' improvisations. Megan Terry's *Viet Rock* (1966) developed out of a series of Open Theatre discussions and improvisations based on news reports of the Vietnam War. Terry participated in the workshops and then wrote a script based on the results. Jean-Claude van Itallie, "author" of the Open Theatre's *The Serpent* (1968), actually entered the creative process some months after the company had been improvising on biblical themes, and combined some of their results with new scenes of his own.

(Such collaboration had its dangers; Megan Terry's version of *Viet Rock* differed in tone from director Joseph Chaikin's sense of the work, and the resulting dispute, which Terry won, seriously weakened the company. Robert Pasolli reported that

> The row ... had opened a rift which divided the troupe .... Chaikin's refusal to be involved with *Viet Rock* after the [first] performances had made some of the actors sensitive about their own involvement, and had wounded Miss Terry .... Most of the *Viet Rock* cast considered themselves authors also. They were especially sensitive to changes. [79–80]

Van Itallie had less of a problem, because he accepted that the definitive text was not his manuscript but the final product of rehearsals and performances.)

The inevitable next step was to do away with the author altogether:

a director or company member might suggest a theme or subject, and the company created a theatrical expression of it. The Performance Group's *Commune* (1970) combined bits and pieces of news stories, improvisations, and printed texts; the Bread and Puppet Theatre and the Pageant Players regularly created street plays out of workshops and on-the-spot improvisations.

In its purest form the "play" was contentless action, like the Living Theatre's *Mysteries*, in which the actors essentially just did things that actors do — moved or didn't move, made sounds or were silent — as ends in themselves. Some of the exercises in *Mysteries* were in fact developed by the Open Theatre and borrowed by the Becks from their former company member Joseph Chaikin. Exercises were so much a part of the Open Theatre's work that performance sometimes seemed like an intrusion; the company, like Andre Gregory's Manhattan Project, could go for years without feeling the need to encounter an actual audience.

Implicit in the de-emphasis of the text was the second element that much of the American experimental theatre had in common: a mistrust of logic and rationality and of their tool, language, and an inclination to reach the audience through nonrational, nonverbal means. Dance, mime, music, ritualized movement, and the direct expression of the passions became important tools for many directors and companies. Arthur Sainer, playwright and critic who worked with several radical theatre companies, later explained:

> We began to understand in the 60s that the words in plays, that the physical beings in plays, that the events in plays were too often evasions, too often artifices that had to do not with truths but with semblances. At best they were about something rather than some thing; they were ideas describing experiences rather than the experiences. [115]

John Tytell wrote of the Living Theatre that they "wanted to create a revolutionary consciousness in which an audience does not merely or passively observe but enacts its destiny" [227]. The same desire to make the theatrical moment a direct experience, rather than the depiction or description of an experience, led others to a variety of experiments.

For some companies it meant street theatre: enacting events in public spaces, frequently without warning, so that passers-by were forced to deal with the moment without knowing whether it was "real." For others it meant blending reality and fiction, or involving members of the audience directly in the action. Elements of mystic or religious ritual and ceremony were explored and incorporated into performance, in part because they represented an essentially theatrical mode that was not contaminated by literary artifice, and in part because chanting, repetition and stylized movement might affect an audience's emotions directly without being filtered through conscious thought processes.

The central event of the Performance Group's *Dionysus in 69* was its enactment of the birth of the god Dionysus. The members of the company formed a tunnel with their bodies — a "birth canal" that writhed and contracted as the naked actor playing the god was pushed through it. The important point is that this was not just a clever bit of staging; for the play to work, audience and actors were supposed to experience this as an actual rebirth into godhood. Similarly, those members of the *Paradise Now* audience who responded to the "rites" of group swaying or endlessly repeated gestures by coming onstage to join in were presumably "understanding" the play better and more purely than those who stayed in their seats and tried to figure out what it meant.

The Living Theatre's *Frankenstein* began with the company seated on the stage meditating; the program explained that they were trying to levitate the actress in the center. If they succeeded, the performance would end; if they failed, they would go on with the play. It was essential that the audience understood that the company actually believed that the ritual might work some night and, moreover, that if it did they would calmly leave the stage, confident that the magical moment had made the rest of the script superfluous.

The third force driving these experiments was a desire to break down the barriers — physical, rational, and emotional — between actors and audiences. On the simplest level this meant finding new playing spaces. Thrust stages and theatre-in-the-round had already begun the job of breaking through the "fourth wall" of the proscenium stage, and many low-budget companies worked in makeshift spaces with no clear demarcation between stage and auditorium.

Many experimental companies carried this process further, bringing the actors out into the house or the audience onstage, as the Living Theatre did. Some directors created "environmental" stagings that completely blurred the distinction between playing and seating areas, as the audience sat or stood wherever they chose to in the undifferentiated space, and the performance took place between and around them. Others required the audience to move around the space or among several rooms to follow the action.

Attempts were made to incorporate the audience into the world of the play by violating the assumed line between reality and fiction. As early as 1959 actors in the Living Theatre's *The Connection* stayed in character as they mingled with the audience during intermission; in Tom O'Horgan's LaMama production of Paul Foster's *Tom Paine* (1967) the actors interrupted the play to discuss current events with the audience; in *Dionysus in 69* the actors repeatedly stepped out of character to speak in their own voices about their reactions to the play they were performing.

The ultimate step involved absorbing the audience into the performance, either passively—actors might talk to them individually, touch them, argue with them—or actively—audience members would be allowed or invited (or required) to join in the action, as in *Paradise Now*, or to instigate it, as in the Pageant Players' *Dream Play*, in which audience members related dreams from which the players improvised actions. In 1969 the Company Theatre in Los Angeles offered *The James Joyce Memorial Liquid Theatre*, a "play" made up entirely of direct audience involvement: theatregoers were led one by one through a maze in which members of the company touched, hugged, and whispered to them, and encouraged them to touch, hug, and share meaningful experiences with each other.

As Eric Bentley lamented about the Living Theatre, such experiments in the name of what he called "the cult of intimacy" threatened to stretch the definition of theatre beyond all recognition, but the experimenters saw potential that could be defended in traditional terms:

> As the play breaks down many of the barriers between life and art, the spectator may find out something about his life through his physical entrance into art. If in *Lear* he learns some exalted and terrible truths about the human condition, in the new theatre he may learn something of value about his personal self in a given moment in history. [Sainer 79]

The fourth common element of the alternative theatre movement was self-conscious theatricality, a willingness to break down the illusion of a created reality in the play and to exploit the possibilities of admitting openly that this was a performance. This impulse was closely related to the desire to use every tool possible to affect the audience and to the attempts to reduce the distance between play and audience. If actors admitted to being actors, perhaps by changing into costume in full view of the audience or by using stylized nonrepresentational costumes and props, the audience would have to collaborate in the imaginative process and would thus be drawn into the work. Music, dance, film, masks, splitting of roles between two or more actors, and special effects of sound or lighting were all attempts to reach the audience on levels other than the conscious and rational.

The American director who explored the possibilities of open theatricality most extensively and visibly in the 1960s was Tom O'Horgan. In his several productions at LaMama and his subsequent work Off- and on Broadway, he turned plays into openly theatrical events that gained much of their power through breaking with the illusion of representational acting and staging. Rochelle Owens's play *Futz* (1967) is a satiric allegory in which a farmer's carnal love for a pig, and his neighbors' reactions to it, comment on society's fear and repression of open sexuality. O'Horgan provided physical expression of the text's ideas and emotions through film, mime, music, and dance, turning the villagers into a many-headed chorus of interchangeable roles so that they functioned as Society rather than as individuals.

Grotesque exaggeration was a favorite tool of O'Horgan's; if a speech implied anger, the actor played in a violent rage; and repressed lust manifested itself in bumps and grinds. While O'Horgan's grand style, and similar experiments by others, represented the first real alternative to the realistic Kazan-Quintero school of directing, it was not to everyone's taste. Robert Brustein called O'Horgan "The Busby Berkeley of Off Off-Broadway," complaining that he buried any play he directed under a mannered style that had "a certain ephemeral charm but [was] essentially mindless and meaningless" [*Third* 69–70].

O'Horgan's production of the rock musical *Hair* brought his methods to Broadway in 1968. As originally presented as the New York Shakespeare Festival's first production at the Public Theater, *Hair*, for all its novelty, was actually a rather conventional musical with a plot and subplots about its hippie characters and their relationships with parents and other authority figures. The play moved from the Public to a brief Off-Broadway run and was then redirected for Broadway by O'Horgan.

He threw out the entire script by Gerome Ragni and James Rado, creating a play that was an uninterrupted sequence of songs, and then staged the songs so imaginatively that they communicated the play's spirit and ideas by themselves. (When *Hair* was filmed in 1978 a wholly new book, with only general similarities to the original, was written to tie the songs together.) Singers appeared in the aisles, popped out of trap doors, climbed the walls, and hung from the proscenium arch. They

Hair

openly used hand microphones, making no attempt to disguise the fact that this was a performance, not reality. At one notorious moment some of them took off their clothes while O'Horgan mocked the prurience of those who came just for that scene by dimming the lights.

In Julian Barry's *Lenny* (1971), the action switched rapidly between Lenny Bruce's nightclub act, events in his life, and his fantasies. O'Horgan compounded the complexity by deliberately mixing stage metaphors: a nightclub routine might be acted out by supporting players rather than narrated by Bruce, while an actual event would suddenly take on fantasy proportions through an incongruity of costuming or the introduction of direct audience address, cartoon-like props, or giant puppets.

In the Broadway production of *Jesus Christ Superstar* (1971), O'Horgan's performers were lowered from the rafters or carried aloft on rising platforms, they wore exaggerated costumes and wielded huge symbolic props, and the stage floor was raised hydraulically to an almost vertical wall to block Judas's escape. In a tongue-in-cheek self-quotation O'Horgan gave his singers hand microphones but thinly disguised their cords as ropes and vines, implicitly thumbing his nose at those purists who would question microphone cords in biblical Palestine.

These four elements—de-emphasis of text, exploration of nonverbal and nonrational communication, attempts to break down the barriers between play and audience, and open utilization of the technology and artifice of the theatre — did not control the work of every alternative theatre of the 1960s; many were devoted to the presentation of traditional plays. But they were all present to some degree and in some proportion in the independently worked-out styles and philosophies of most of those companies and artists who saw themselves as developing new styles or reinventing the theatrical experience. The period of greatest experimentation spanned the mid-1960s to the early 1970s, when the pendulum began to move back toward traditional text-based production,but its influence eventually affected all but the most rigidly conventional theatres.

A sizable portion of a generation of American actors spent their formative years creating nontraditional theatre, and while this unquestionably released abilities in them that they might otherwise not have developed, it also delayed or prevented their mastery of some of the more conventional skills. Richard Gilman's indictment of the Living Theatre — "Whatever else it is the Living Theatre is unbelievably untalented in the rudimentary processes of acting — speech, characterization, the assumption of new, invented being" [30] — could be applied, perhaps with less outrage, to the radical theatre in general, because those skills were considered superfluous and contrary to the nature of play being produced.

It is less easy to measure the effect of the period on young American playwrights. There were plenty of alternative and mainstream theatres still devoted to the dramatization of the written word. The number of writers corrupted or discouraged by exposure to companies that did not respect the text is probably matched or exceeded by the number who were inspired to expand their dramatic vocabulary and attempt new styles and techniques as a result of exposure to radical productions. Sam Shepard, for instance, did not write exclusively for the most experimental companies, but without their example he might not have felt confident in exploring his own fascination with ritual and magic as dramatic tools.

The alternative theatre of the 1960s, from the new playwright workshops to the wildest experiments of the radical companies, had a liberating and expansive effect on the mainstream American theatre. Even though some of the group creations and Theatre of Cruelty productions may have been artistic dead ends, they helped expand the theatrical vocabulary, and more traditional (and perhaps more skilled) directors, designers, and performers have been able to incorporate some elements of the experiments into their work.

Many of the Open Theatre-Living Theatre rehearsal exercises have become standard in companies of all sorts attempting to develop an ensemble unity and style. Myth, ritualized action, and collaborative improvisation remain part of the creative process for writers from Sam Shepard and Elizabeth Swados in the 1970s to Tony Kushner in the 1990s. The Broadway musical *A Chorus Line* (1975) was created Off Off-Broadway in a series of workshops, discussions, and improvisational sessions during which the personal experiences of several actual Broadway dancers were combined and developed into a script. Harold Prince, the very creative director of visually stunning Broadway musicals, has built on the precedents of Tom O'Horgan's Broadway work. The theatrical vocabulary — the repertoire of what was known to be possible on a stage — has been substantially enlarged, allowing new options and new applications.

☆

The waning of the experimental fervor of the late 1960s had much to do with the general disintegration of the counterculture, and much to do with the aging of the practitioners; it is less fun to be a starving experimental artist at thirty than it is at twenty. Some young writers, directors, and performers retreated into the mainstream and some left the theatre. Some of their inventive energy found its way into other arenas, as new generations of radical young artists who might earlier have entered the theatre chose instead to explore film, video, performance art, and even stand-up comedy. And while companies like Mabou Mines and the Wooster Group in New York, Theatre X in Milwaukee and the San Francisco Mime Troupe continued to operate and evolve into the 1990s, they found themselves more and more marginalized and, in some cases, dated.

The Living Theatre itself was unable to sustain the accomplishments of 1968 or to move significantly beyond them. The American tour was a financial failure, owing in part to the ineptitude of the inexperienced tour organizers. Much of the company quit on the return to Europe in 1969, leaving the Becks with a small core who followed them the next year to Brazil, where attempts to politicize the masses though street theatre only led to alternating periods of poverty and imprisonment.

They returned to America in 1972 for four years, during which their most significant experience was a $22,000 Mellon Foundation grant to work in Pittsburgh. Judith Malina speaks with pride about when "we went to Pittsburgh when the steel industry was closing up and did a play about that situation, because we love to be where change is occurring so we can get our input into the discourse" [Interview]. But Tytell reports that they spent most of their time developing and rehearsing their Pittsburgh play, and actually gave very few performances; and Gelber adds that "the performances of *Money Tower* at the gates of the great steel companies were greeted with indifference" [27].

That was to be the pattern for the next two decades: new productions added to the repertoire almost every year (though they were still doing *Mysteries* in 1996), often eliciting the criticism that they were stuck stylistically in 1968; continued sincere commitment by the leaders (Julian Beck died in 1985, and Hanon Reznikov joined Judith Malina as co-Artistic Director); and a series of residencies, in Europe and America, which they recall as triumphs but which the record shows to have been financially precarious, critically disparaged, and culturally and politically marginal.

In 1996 they were again performing street theatre, staging vigils in Times Square whenever a prisoner was to be executed anywhere in America:

> It's about the person being killed, and then we make an appeal for a stay, which it's too late for, alas; and then in the middle of the play, in a very Artaudian reality, the protagonist of the play is actually executed. And then we do a weeping scene,... and then we go up to people who are in the circle that has gathered around us, and we touch them and we say, "I swear to you that I will never kill you. Now, could you promise me the same?" [Malina interview]

Ever the optimist, Malina can say, "There are also people who pass by and see our banners and say, 'Ah, let him fry.' But those people have been affected by the experience."

> I feel very much that we're moving forward at a very good rate because right now I have a wonderful company. We just had a terrific season in Europe.... The point is not whether you get a good review. The point is whether you stir up something, whether people talk about it, whether interest is aroused. [Interview]

☆

Meanwhile, Off Off-Broadway and its cousins around the country also continued and evolved. With the experimental branch withering away, two main strands of fringe theatre became apparent in the 1970s. The larger but less interesting of the two was the pre-commercial use of Off Off-Broadway as an artist-subsidized place-to-be-seen. Actors worked for nothing in the hope of being discovered and cast elsewhere. Beginning playwrights subsidized small-scale productions of their plays and invited producers and investors.

It was not long before the commercial theatre also saw the possibilities in this inexpensive tryout arena. With the up-front cost of even a simple play approaching a million dollars on Broadway and perhaps half that Off-Broadway, some commercial producers tried test runs of new scripts Off Off-Broadway before making fuller commitments. Inspired by the experience of *A Chorus Line*, and with the traditional pre-Broadway tryout tour also a victim of economics, producers of musicals began using Off Off-Broadway workshops as part of their development process. In effect, Off Off-Broadway came to play the role in the New York theatre that new play programs and works-in-progress readings did in the regional theatre.

Actors' Equity, alarmed by the sight of its members acting without pay, attempted repeatedly to block or control the proliferation of Off Off-Broadway showcases, only to be resisted by the very actors it was trying to protect. Outright bans on free performances having failed, Equity formulated a code in 1970 that allowed its members to work without pay only in productions that were obviously not making anyone else rich: they had to play in tiny houses, charge no admission, and run no more than ten performances. In 1974, actors desperate for work and for the chance to be discovered forced Equity to further liberalize these rules, and in 1975 and again in 1978 the union's membership voted down regulations its leadership proposed.

While never fully giving up on the pay question, Equity shifted its attention to protecting an actor's stake in a workshop that might be picked up by a commercial producer or not-for-profit theatre, particularly with plays such as *A Chorus Line*, whose original actors contributed significantly to the creative process. (The original cast of *A Chorus Line* did receive a portion of the play's profits, but Equity did not want to rely on the honor and generosity of other producers.) Unexpectedly, opposition to Equity came, not from producers, but from playwrights, who felt that the union's attempt to protect its actors was threatening their well-being. The demand that a showcase cast be given either first option on the roles in subsequent productions or a compensatory cash payment seemed innocuous until dramatists saw the extra costs discouraging producers from picking up their plays. The proposal that actors be paid for their workshop services with a percentage of all the play's future profits led some playwrights to counter ironically that an actor who got his start in a showcase owed the playwright a percentage of his lifetime earnings.

Boycotts, a 1980 restraint-of-trade lawsuit by the dramatists (settled out of court with the dropping of the proposed lien on future royalties), repeated attempts by Equity to find an acceptable package, and repeated rebellions by the Equity membership (who wanted, above all, to work and have the chance to be discovered), haunted Off Off-Broadway through the 1980s, testifying to the extent to which the alternative theatre had become a step on the ladder to mainstream commercial fame and fortune.

☆

About this time the distinction between Off- and Off Off-Broadway began to blur; and the rest of this chapter is as much a continuation of Chapter Two as of this one. While Off Off-Broadway productions were likely to have lower budgets and play in smaller theatres, the only real distinction was legal and contractual: both in New York and around the country, Equity and the various craft unions developed different contracts and pay scales dependent on such arbitrary distinctions as the number of seats in the house.

A successful Off Off-Broadway production could become Off-Broadway literally overnight, by moving to a larger theatre and paying everyone more. The Off Off-Broadway Circle Repertory Company officially became an Off-Broadway company in 1976, and the Off-Broadway Roundabout Theatre Company declared itself a Broadway operation in 1990 (primarily to make its shows eligible for Tony awards) simply by signing the appropriate union contracts. In each case, most of their subscribers could be excused for hardly noticing. Some companies, notably the New York Shakespeare Festival and the Manhattan Theatre Club, moved freely between categories or operated in different categories simultaneously.

And it was in such companies that the second important branch of Off Off-Broadway took shape. Some of the strongest of the early Off Off-Broadway companies — the Performance Group, the Judson Poets' Theatre, the Chelsea Theater Center, among others — continued to operate in the 1970s, and in the constant stream of new companies and theatres, several maintained the commitment to new plays or new production styles that had been Off Off-Broadway's original generating force, while bringing to it a new structure and permanence.

In a development that nicely encapsulated some of the revolutions taking place elsewhere in the American theatre, Off Off-Broadway became the not-for-profit theatre movement's outpost in New York. As Marshall W. Mason of the Circle Repertory Company said in 1976, "As a full-sized non-commercial resident theatre we probably have more in common with theatres around the country than with other groups in New York" [Interview]; while *The New York Times* credited the success of the Manhattan Theatre Club to the fact that artistic director Lynne Meadow "pretends she is running a regional theater in a one-theater city" [Gussow c11].

Some seeds were already there. Almost from its start, the New York Shakespeare Festival had been structured to draw on civic and philanthropic sources for its operating funds, and the Phoenix Theatre and the Circle in the Square had quickly redefined themselves as not-for-profit organizations. But the new Off Off-Broadway companies of the 1970s and 1980s were more similar to theatres in, say, Houston or San Francisco than to their New York predecessors.

Like resident theatres around the country they were created from the start as institutional not-for-profit organizations, designed to offer seasons rather than individual plays, and budgeted to make only a portion of their expenses at the box office, the rest to come from outside subsidy. Like many regional theatres, they tended to be the creation of a single forceful producer-director, and to reflect that person's artistic vision in their work.

If few had resident acting companies, many had core groups of actors who worked with them repeatedly: the Shakespeare Festival's unofficial company included at various times Tom Aldridge, Raul Julia, Kevin Kline, Mandy Patinkin, Paul Sorvino, and Jane White; while Manhattan Theatre Club audiences frequently saw Christine Baranski, Joanna Gleason, Anthony Heald, and Nathan Lane. The Circle in the Square, still under the direction of Theodore Mann, was able to call on its famous alumni to make guest appearances when finances were tight.

Only a couple of these companies were able to move into purpose-built new theatres (as was becoming almost commonplace around the country), but all were formed with the assumption of permanence or at least continuity. And if the same legal fictions that created the contractual distinctions between Broadway and Off-Broadway relegated most of these companies (because of their small theatres) to Off Off-Broadway status, they were increasingly at the core of the new Off-Broadway. In the words of Michael Feingold, chief theatre critic of *The Village Voice*,

> Off Off-Broadway, that started as a kind of wildcat movement of artists who weren't being recognized by the mainstream theatre, has become a set of establishment theatres that either are or feed directly into the mainstream. In the absence of Broadway plays, the Manhattan Theatre Club, the Public Theatre, Playwrights Horizons [and others] are where the New York audience goes for the plays — the serious plays and deep-meaning comedies — that it isn't getting uptown. [Interview]

These new regional theatres included the Circle Repertory Company, founded in 1969 by four Off Off-Broadway veterans: director Marshall W. Mason, playwright Lanford Wilson, and actors Rob Thirkield and Tanya Berezin. The Circle Rep was conceived from the start as a permanent company that would work together to develop an ensemble style and professionalism to serve new American playwrights. Under Mason's artistic direction the company discovered its strengths in

Photo: Martha Swope

Marshall W. Mason

what Mason called "lyrical naturalism," the honestly emotive presentation of realistic drama with a touch of poetry.

Lanford Wilson helped set the house style through such plays as *The Hot l Baltimore* (1973), *The Mound Builders* (1975), and *Talley's Folly* (1979), and acknowledged that the opportunity to write for actors he knew and a director he trusted helped him to grow as a dramatist. Other early Circle Rep successes included Mark Medoff's *When You Comin' Back, Red Ryder?* (1973) and Edward J. Moore's *The Sea Horse* (1974), both, like Wilson's work, Chekhovian mood pieces dependent upon the sustained ensemble performances that were the company's hallmark.

Playwrights Horizons, founded by Robert Moss in 1971, devoted itself to the developmental process; as Tim Sanford, a later Artistic Director, explained in 1996,

> We take unsolicited scripts and try to develop relationships with writers. We are looking for playwrights, not plays, and relationships with playwrights, not products to produce. You have to understand how playwrights develop. They develop over time, not overnight, and they develop through productions. [Interview]

Through such long-term relationships, Playwrights Horizons was able to guide Alfred Uhry and Wendy Wasserstein, among others, to polished versions of such prize-winning plays as *Driving Miss Daisy* (1987) and *The Heidi Chronicles* (1989) respectively; and also helped established Broadway writers such as Stephen Sondheim (*Sunday in the Park With George*, 1983; *Assassins*, 1991) explore new modes and styles, through workshops and staged readings.

The Hudson Guild (actually founded in 1922, but reorganized as a new play workshop in 1977) was particularly hospitable to realistic plays with strong acting roles, a house style that attracted many established performers and directors to the opportunity to participate in developing new plays; among its early successes were Ernest Thompson's *On Golden Pond* (1978) and Hugh Leonard's *Da* (1978).

The Manhattan Theatre Club was founded in 1969 by a group of well-to-do New Yorkers hoping to establish a convenient showplace in their affluent neighborhood. After a couple of false starts, they hired Lynne Meadow as Artistic Director in 1972, and she began an ambitious program of developing new work and new writers. As she wrote in her "Statement of Purpose" at the time:

> The MTC offers the only local theatre center in which the audience can observe and participate in the evolution of theatrical activity

from staged readings to experimental workshops to full productions. [qtd in Pereira 41]

As happened in some regional theatres where the board and the
building preceded the artistic director, Meadow found her vision for the
theatre coming in conflict with that of some of its founders; and there
was an uncomfortable period before she (and her supporters on the
board) won out. Among the many productions developed at the MTC
are the musical *Ain't Misbehavin'* (1977) and the plays of Terrence
McNally's comeback: *It's Only a Play* (1986), *Frankie and Johnny in the
Clair de Lune* (1987), *The Lisbon Traviata* (1989), *Lips Together, Teeth
Apart* (1991), and *Love! Valour! Compassion!* (1994).

The MTC also produced the New York premieres of a number of
regional theatre and London successes, among them Beth Henley's
Crimes of the Heart (1981), Alan Ayckbourn's *Woman in Mind* (1994), and
several plays by Athol Fugard. Many of these plays transferred to commercial Off- and on Broadway runs; and starting in the 1980s the club
took an active part in moving its plays to other venues, further blurring
the distinctions, not only between Off- and Off Off-Broadway, but between the non-for-profit companies and Broadway.

Other theatres have specific emphases or agendas. In the Off Off-
Broadway tradition of theatre growing out of the work of social agen-
cies, the New Federal Theatre began in the federally-sponsored
Mobilization for Youth in 1970 and found its home in the Henry Street
Settlement in New York's Lower East Side. Specializing in black drama,
the New Federal introduced plays by Ed Bullins (*The Taking of Miss
Janie*, 1974), Ntozake Shange (*For Colored Girls...*, 1975), and several
South African playwrights, while giving work to hundreds of African-
American actors, including Morgan Freeman, Phylicia Rashad, and
Denzel Washington — in the words of founder and Artistic Director
Woodie King, "filling a gap that traditional theatres do not fill. We are
continually presenting plays for a black audience,...to see a reaffirma-
tion of who they are" [Interview].

The Women's Project began in 1978 as a season of plays by women
at the American Place Theatre, and evolved into an ongoing program
there. Nine years later it split off as a separate not-for-profit company,
continuing to offer readings and full productions of plays written and directed by women, among them *A...My Name is Alice* by Joan Micklin
Silver and Julianne Boyd 1983) and *Why We Have a Body* by Claire
Chafee (1994). "We don't have an agenda of feminist theatre," explains

founder and Artistic Director Julia Miles. "We just want to see more women participating in the theatre" [Interview]. The Signature Theatre took the unique course of devoting each season to a single American playwright, offering retrospectives that, in the cases of Edward Albee and Horton Foote, contributed to a general reappraisal and revival of interest in the writers.

These companies and others, along with the older Shakespeare Festival, Circle in the Square, American Place, and LaMama, helped change the financial and institutional face of New York City theatre. Like resident theatres around the country, New York's institutional theatres were at least partly independent of marketplace pressures, being supported to a large degree by foundation and government grants (although the Shakespeare Festival relied more on private benefactors and on the revenues from commercial productions; it lived for a decade largely on the multimillion dollar profits of *A Chorus Line*).

With the reduced labor costs that came with their Off- or Off Off-Broadway contractual status, and with permanent organizations and staffs, the institutional theatres were able to stretch their budgets remarkably. In 1978, for example, when a single Broadway musical could cost $1,500,000 to mount, the Shakespeare Festival staged more than twenty productions on a budget of $7.4 million, while the Circle Rep put on seven plays and a series of staged readings on a total budget of $520,000. In 1981 the association of small theatres in New York recognized the evolution by changing its name from the Off Off-Broadway Alliance to the Alliance of Resident Theatres/New York; and by the early 1990s there were more than 180 not-for-profit theatres and theatre companies in the city.

In the early 1970s the City of New York, to protect the Broadway theatre district from being engulfed by a wave of new office construction, gave developers zoning variances (essentially the right to build higher than the law normally allowed) if they incorporated new theatres into their buildings. Four new theatres, two "Broadway" houses (the Uris, later renamed the Gershwin, and the Minskoff) and two smaller homes, for the Circle in the Square and the American Place Theatre, resulted before the construction boom ended. (Another new Broadway house, the Marquis, would appear in the 1980s as part of a new hotel whose construction had required the demolition of three older theatres. The 1990s saw long-delayed plans to restore some of the rundown Forty-second Street movie houses finally come to fruition, beginning with the re-opening of the New Victory and the Walt Disney Company's refurbishment of the original home of the *Ziegfeld Follies*, the New Amsterdam Theatre.)

Also during the 1970s several commercial theatre developers and institutional companies took over a string of rundown buildings a few blocks west of Broadway on Forty-second Street and gradually converted them into theatres, giving Off- and Off Off-Broadway a presence very close to the traditional theatre center. Geography and environment do have some commercial significance, and new homes in the Broadway area increased all these theatres' visibility and audiences. Theodore Mann felt at the time that the Circle in the Square had gone as far as it could go downtown, as he explained in 1996:

> We were ready to move uptown, because we felt the Off-Broadway movement had petered out.... We felt the mood had changed, the appetite had changed, and that what we were doing would probably be better on Broadway.... We had more flexibility in terms of the actors, designers and directors we could attract. [Interview]

He also sensed that the young, artistically adventurous audiences that Off-Broadway had played to in the 1950s and 1960s were now more likely to be found uptown:

> I think audience taste improved by virtue of what Off-Broadway did all those years since the 1950s.... The audiences that we nurtured Off-Broadway [were] now potential Broadway ticket buyers. [Interview]

Further blurring any distinctions among New York's commercial and non-commercial theatres was the increasingly common practice of moving a successful play from its limited run in a subscription season to an open-ended commercial run elsewhere. The Circle Rep's productions of Lanford Wilson's *The Hot l Baltimore* (1973) and Sam Shepard's *Fool For Love* (1983), for example, continued to play in other theatres while the regular seasons went on. At the New York Shakespeare Festival, the Broadway and national successes of *Hair* (1968), *Two Gentlemen of Verona* (1971), *A Chorus Line* (1975) and *The Mystery of Edwin Drood* (1985) not only underwrote whole seasons at the Public, but also supported the transfer to Broadway of less commercial plays, among them David Rabe's *Sticks and Bones* (1971), Jason Miller's *That Championship Season* (1972) and Ntozake Shange's *For Colored Girls Who Have Considered Suicide/When the Rainbow is Enuf* (1976).

After commercial producers moved such Manhattan Theatre Club projects as *Ain't Misbehavin'* and *Crimes of the Heart* to Broadway while other equally meritorious plays were not picked up, the Club decided that continued support was part of its commitment to the work. Executive Producer Barry Grove explains,

> We made the decision that if the play was going to have an extended life, if it was going to pay artists royalties, if it was going to bring visibility [to the MTC], if there was going to be a payoff for the people who had sacrificed at the front end, it was only going to be because we made it happen. [Interview]

The Manhattan Theatre Club developed a variety of organizational and funding strategies, including a wholly-owned for-profit subsidiary that could legally go into partnerships with commercial producers, designed to facilitate the movement of its subscription-series successes to extended runs on or Off-Broadway.

So the structure with which Off-Broadway had begun, low-budget commercial productions of plays unsuited (for one reason or another) to Broadway, still had a place in the mix. According to producer and theatre-owner Eric Krebs, "Off-Broadway houses are the only places where a certain scale of show and style of show can possibly have a chance of succeeding" [Interview]. Ben Sprecher, another producer-owner, adds, "What used to occupy the mainstay of the Broadway commercial theatre, which was plays, has now been taken over by Off-Broadway commercial theatres" [Interview]. And while both acknowledge that a large number of commercial Off-Broadway shows are transfers from not-for-profit theatres, both rankle at the suggestion that Off-Broadway producing is simply a matter of booking shows created elsewhere. "Most projects I really produce I find through some way on my own or I develop as an idea on my own," says Krebs, going on to describe how a taste for musical revues led him to contact a composer and lyricist and work with them on a new show. Sprecher describes his involvement with a project in progress:

> [The play] was commissioned by the Seattle Repertory Theatre five years ago. They did a production of it which I never saw, which had a review in *Variety* which was very positive. From that review I called the author and got the script.... And we set out on a course where I brought in a director and we rewrote the play over the course of two years. When that play finally opens, are you going to say it's just a transfer? [Interview]

Meanwhile, other line-blurring continued. LaMama and the New York Shakespeare Festival repeatedly lent or leased their stages to smaller or homeless companies, happily lending some of their prestige and ability to draw audiences as well; among the Shakespeare Festival's many adoptees were the Riverside Church production of Miguel Pinero's *Short Eyes* (1974), the Manhattan Theatre Club staging of David Rudkin's *Ashes* (1977), and whole seasons of the Manhattan Project and the New Federal Theatre.

Commercial producers routinely tried out new productions in inexpensive Off Off-Broadway workshops before moving them to larger theatres, while others marketed their plays by renting the mailing lists of not-for-profit companies, offering subscribers discounts to an Off-Broadway or even Broadway show. Through a cooperative arrangement with the commercial producers, the Manhattan Theatre Club made the first few weeks of the Broadway run of August Wilson's *Seven Guitars* (1996) part of its subscription season. A theatregoer could be excused for not knowing—or caring—whether a particular show was technically on, Off- or Off Off-Broadway; commercial, not-for-profit, or some inventive amalgam of the two.

☆

Off Off-Broadway, and the alternative theatre in general, thus joined in the partial liberation from the marketplace that the regional theatre had begun in the 1960s. The Ford Foundation made its first alternative theatre grants in 1968 and continued to support LaMama, the Open Theatre, and several other companies through the next decade, and the Rockefeller Foundation and National Endowment for the Arts, with their prejudices in favor of new artists and smaller companies, were important funding sources.

Most Off Off-Broadway companies and artists were eligible for support from the New York State Council for the Arts, and many of their equivalents elsewhere in the country also benefitted from state and city grants. Many talented young dramatists were able to write for the noncommercial theatre and still pay the rent as a result of fellowships from Ford, Guggenheim, Rockefeller, or the National Endowment. The Theatre Development Fund, which had been formed to support the Broadway theatre, moved into Off Off-Broadway with a discount voucher program in 1972, and aided in the introduction of similar programs in Boston, Chicago, and Minneapolis.

Across the country charitable foundations began to support smaller companies as well as the more established resident theatres, with the Rockefeller Fund and the National Endowment particularly generous to promising younger theatres. The Ford-sponsored Theatre Communications Group, which had limited its support to thirteen larger resident companies, was redefined in 1972 to include smaller and experimental theatres, and by the 1990s had more than 325 member companies benefiting from its casting and referral services, subscription and management assistance, and other practical and moral support. The Shubert Foundation, with a vested interest in supporting new plays that might eventually find their way into the commercial theatre, became an important contributor, as *Variety* reported in 1996:

> Grants are awarded to companies as small as the Arkansas Repertory Theater ($5,000 in 1995) and as large as Lincoln Center Theater ($250,000). Most of the nation's nonprofs have been on the Foundation's roster at one point or another, with most receiving grants year after year. [Evans 73]

The hundreds of Off Off-Broadway companies, combined with the dozens of established regional resident theatres and their hundreds of satellite alternative companies, meant a many-times-over multiplication of the outlets available to new playwrights. For the first time in a century a beginning or developing dramatist was at least as likely to be produced outside New York City as in, and the most prolific and successful young writers moved back and forth between New York and other cities, between established and alternative companies, and between the commercial and noncommercial theatre.

Lanford Wilson, for example, began at Off Off-Broadway's Caffe Cino and LaMama and returned to the Circle Repertory Company and Off-Broadway and Broadway successes, but in between he also had plays premiered at the Studio Arena in Buffalo, the Washington Theater Club, the O'Neill Center in Connecticut, and the Los Angeles Center Theatre Group. Rochelle Owens had premieres in Minneapolis and Philadelphia as well as New York; Jean-Claude van Itallie in Atlanta, Minneapolis, and Los Angeles; David Mamet in Chicago; and Sam Shepard virtually everywhere: the Theatre Company of Boston, the San Francisco Magic Theatre, the Firehouse Theater of Minneapolis, and the Center Theatre Group in Los Angeles, as well as London, Edinburgh, and New York.

Even more significantly, this structural change in the American theatre led to a change in the understanding of the creative process, and a resulting enrichment of the opportunities offered to playwrights. In the pattern that had always been the norm, a dramatist fortunate enough to find a commercial producer delivered a more-or-less finished script subject only to the inevitable rewriting and polishing of the rehearsal and tryout periods. Playwrights of the 1970s and after were allowed to go through a many-stepped process of discovering and refining their work.

A play's first appearance might be as an admitted rough draft in a reading at, say, the O'Neill Center, after which the author could use what was exposed about its strengths and weaknesses and rework it for months or longer before it again saw light, perhaps at a work-in-progress staging at a small regional or Off Off-Broadway theatre. More rewriting might then lead to a full production at a noncommercial theatre, then (perhaps with more rewriting) at another, and then (again with opportunities to polish) perhaps a commercial production.

Various innovators could be given the credit for this elemental change in the definition of what playwriting is: Ralph Cook of Theatre Genesis, Edward Albee of the Playwrights Unit, George White and Lloyd Richards of the O'Neill Center—even Margo Jones, whose Theatre '47 featured an early William Inge script that would be reworked over a decade into *The Dark at the Top of the Stairs*. The point is that the creation of a new play was now seen as a process, not the simple delivery of a finished product; and the new structure of the American theatre made this process available as it had never been before, so that by the mid-1980s it was the norm rather than the exception.

August Wilson's *Joe Turner's Come and Gone*, for example, began its stage life with workshops at the Off Off-Broadway New Dramatists in 1983 and 1984 and a staged reading at the O'Neill Center in 1984. Its first full staging was at the Yale Repertory Company in 1986, followed by productions in Boston, Seattle, and Washington, and finally a Broadway run in 1988. All of Wilson's plays have taken a similar journey, with the author exploiting the opportunity to rewrite and refine at each step in the process; and even such established Broadway writers and composers as Neil Simon and Stephen Sondheim have adapted their creative methods to benefit from this new structure.

Aside from the central benefit of giving authors the opportunity to test their plays before audiences and learn from their responses (and those of the actors and directors), this new development process gave audiences around the country the chance to participate in the creative adventure, and thus increased their sophistication and their involvement in their local theatres. And it also gave playwrights new opportunities to fail; for every play that took the entire journey from rough draft to

Broadway hit, there were dozens that found their natural level some-where along the way—and to do so was in no way a disgrace. A suc-cessful run at a not-for-profit theatre was an end in itself; and even an unsuccessful workshop reading was a relatively inexpensive and unem-barrassing way for a writer to learn his or her craft.

☆

Inevitably, with hundreds of new-play-producing theatres and prob-ably thousands of newly produced playwrights, there was a great deal of dross. Even among the legitimately talented young writers, many lost interest in the theatre, many had only one or two plays in them, and many never progressed beyond the "promising" stage. Perhaps two dozen of the new dramatists produced by the regional and alternative theatres since the 1960s stand out, either for a substantial body of im-pressive work, for one or two successes, or as the best representatives of a particular movement or subgroup; and of these, five or six seem to have some claim to placement in the top rank of American dramatists.

Sam Shepard emerged from the experimental wing of the alternative theatre movement of the 1960s, adapting its techniques to serve his in-dividual vision. Shepard's early plays incorporate elements of myth, magic, and the supernatural into a private symbolism that is sometimes obscure and plots that sometimes defy linear, rational explanation. Two themes that would continue to be central to his work are evident even at this stage: the faith that magic exists as part of the real world and is ig-nored or rejected only at great peril, and the conviction that America's salvation as a culture lies in the appreciation of and reintegration with the highest values of its past.

The recurring pattern in the early plays is of characters who either reject or toy irresponsibly with magic and tradition, and suffer as a re-sult. In *Chicago* (1965), *Icarus's Mother* (1965), *Red Cross* (1966), and oth-ers of the period, characters frightened by a reality they feel unable to cope with retreat into fantasies that prove to be no more comforting. In *Fourteen Hundred Thousand* (1966) a group of yuppies are overwhelmed by the task of building a simple bookcase for books they don't read any-way, while the musicians of *Cowboy Mouth* (1971) dream of a rock-and-roll savior while missing his magical appearance in their midst. In *La Tourista* (1967), *Operation Sidewinder* (1970), *Back Bog Beast Bait* (1971), and others he presents religion, superstition, and mysticism as more au-thentic and useful than cynical rationalism; *Operation Sidewinder* imag-ines an Air Force computer built in the shape of a giant rattlesnake (in itself a striking image of the dangers of dehumanized technology) that turns out to be the missing element needed in an Apache ritual that brings on the apocalypse.

As that last example suggests, one of Shepard's favorite devices during this period is the mixed metaphor. In *The Unseen Hand* (1969) a visitor from another galaxy seeks help from nineteenth-century cowboys in twentieth-century California; in *Shaved Splits* (1970) reality, pornographic fantasies, and revolutionary dreams flow together; in *Mad Dog Blues* (1971) living people interact with historical figures, movie icons, and characters out of myth and legend. *The Tooth of Crime* (1972) presents its characters as simultaneously cowboys, rock singers, motorcycle gang members, and pawns in some interstellar game, and challenges the audience to sort out the overlapping vocabularies and reach the core vision of a world in which tradition and history are being blindly rejected.

Shepard's later plays, starting around the mid-1970s, are generally more realistic in surface technique, but with the same perception of a reality that includes the supernatural and of a present defined by its failures to come to grips with the past. In *Curse of the Starving Class* (1977) what a family hungers for is not food but a sense of purpose and connection; in *True West* (1980) two brothers attempting to write a cowboy

Photo: Ron Blanchette

Sam Shepard

film find the myth they have dipped into more real than their actual lives. In *Fool for Love* (1983) the obsessive love-hate bond between a man and a woman is an image of the inevitable failure of any attempt to harness the infinite passions of which we are capable; and *A Lie of the Mind* (1985) uses one character's brain damage as a symbol of all the other characters' disassociation from self and other, while demonstrating that fantasy and even madness can be surer paths to contentment than reason.

Shepard's *Buried Child* (1978), arguably the best American play of the 1970s, shows an all-American farm family, clearly representative of the culture at large, decayed and degenerated into a sterile parody of itself. At some time in the past an illegitimate, possibly incestuous child was born, and to deny that blot on its exalted image of itself the family killed it and tried to erase all memory and record. Shepard doesn't force the metaphoric resonances, but the American culture's inability to deal with the moral ambiguities of its past is clearly invoked.

When the literal uncovering of the secret magically revitalizes the farm, whose barren soil suddenly starts producing vegetables in fantastic variety and abundance, the play's warning is clear: hope for the national future can only come through the unreserved acceptance of the

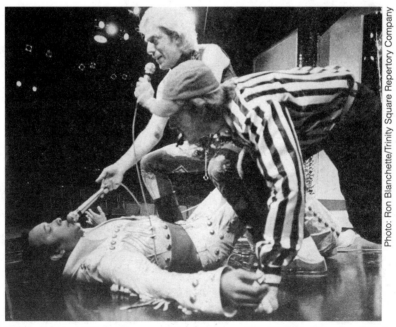

Photo: Ron Blanchette/Trinity Square Repertory Company

Ed Hall, James Eichelberger, and Bruce McGill in *Tooth of Crime*

Photo: Ron Blanchette/Magic Theatre, San Francisco

Buried Child

past, even the shameful past. (As further evidence of the new perception of play writing as process rather than product, Shepard revised both *Buried Child* and *The Tooth of Crime* for 1996 revivals. As further evidence of Broadway's displacement from the center of American theatre, the 1996 *Buried Child* was Shepard's first Broadway production.)

Lanford Wilson's vision is quieter and more comfortable than Shepard's, and is the basis for a body of work that tends to be peacefully evocative and elegiac in tone, which may be part of the reason why several of his plays were produced on Broadway. Like Shepard, Wilson began in the Off Off-Broadway of the mid-1960s; his *The Madness of Lady Bright* (1964), a sympathetic picture of an aging homosexual, was the Caffe Cino's first hit. Like Shepard, he took advantage of some of the period's experiments in performance and production styles to expand his artistic vocabulary; in his case the most profitable input came from explorations of choric speaking and of the rapid doubling and redoubling of many roles by a few actors. Some of his early plays, such as *The Rimers of Eldritch* (1966), achieve a cinematic fluidity by having a small cast move back and forth among several roles in a series of very brief scenes; while *Balm in Gilead* (1965), set in a busy all-night coffee shop, uses a large cast and the overlapping dialogue of several simultaneous conversations to almost musical effect.

Wilson's association with the Circle Repertory Company in the 1970s helped him develop these explorations into a mature style and vision typified by the orchestration of large casts of characters, each of whom is following his or her private drama, and by a message not terribly different from Shepard's. "We change so quickly, we in America," he said in 1980. "I guess I might be saying something like, 'Look at what you're throwing away, before you throw it away'" [qtd in Berkvist 33]. *The Hot l Baltimore* (1973) is an almost plotless picture of life in a rundown hotel (the title suggests a neon sign with a letter burned out) that gradually leads us to appreciate the warm, functioning community of its residents; with unstrained metaphor it suggests the beauty at risk in America's national compulsions for progress and standardization, while also reminding us that lives are shaped by small events more than by large ones. The same thoughts color *The Mound Builders* (1975), in which petty jealousies and small dishonesties among a group of archaeologists undo all their attempts to save the past.

In *Fifth of July* (1978) an embittered paraplegic Vietnam veteran returns to his family's Missouri farm with the intention of selling it, a decision that is part of a pattern in his life of fearing responsibility. But the

Photo: Ron Blanchette/Circle Repertory Company

Lanford Wilson

house is filled with friends and relatives, all attempting to sort out their own complex emotional lives, and watching each of them struggle for security or identity guides him to the discovery that his own answers lie in home, roots, and commitment. Like several of Wilson's plays, *Fifth of July* invites comparison to Chekhov in its quietly elegiac tone, its manipulation of multiple plots, and its recognition that small things, like the planting of a garden, can carry in them life-changing decisions.

That Wilson does not depend on large casts was proven by *Talley's Folly* (1979), which achieves the same Chekhovian tone while watching two emotionally damaged people tentatively feel their way toward happiness together, and by *Redwood Curtain* (1992), in which a half-American Vietnamese girl seeking her father and a mentally and emotionally lost veteran make brief contact that solves neither's problems but brings both a little closer to peace. In between came *Angels Fall* (1982), another group picture, this time of various characters accidentally thrown together, each searching for a lost sense of purpose and each helped by the juxtaposition to find it; and *Burn This* (1987), a venture into Sam Shepard and David Mamet territory, in which a mismatched couple are swept away by a dangerous passion each fears but neither can resist.

The most common settings and subjects of twentieth-century American drama have been domestic, so much so that an impoverished repertory company could do several seasons of American plays from the 1930s to the 1990s with a single living room set. One striking exception to this rule is David Mamet, whose plays are more likely to be set in workplaces and in public arenas like restaurants and bars. Mamet is interested in the public roles people must put on in such places, and in the ways such roles affect or displace their real identities.

In *Sexual Perversity in Chicago* (1974) swinging singles find that the gender roles of the dating game actually block any possibility of romance; in *The Duck Variations* (1974) two old men talking nonsense on a park bench are totally satisfied by the imitation of communication. *American Buffalo* (1977) shows small-time criminals trying to plot a robbery, only to find themselves constantly sidetracked by the need to establish and maintain the images of competence and dignity they present to each other, and by the minutia of etiquette and logistics their roles force on them.

Mamet's *Glengarry Glen Ross* (1984) focuses on the world of high-pressure salesmen and discovers that their sense of their own identity and manhood is so defined by their work that they can never stop selling, even to each other or to themselves, and *Speed-the-Plow* (1988) discovers something similar about Hollywood producers and screenwriters, though with a lighter, more ironically amused tone: to allow themselves the constant back-stabbing and money-grubbing that are part of their

Photo: Ron Blanchette/Circle Repertory Company

Zane Lansky and Conchata Ferrell in *The Hot l Baltimore*

Photo: Trinity Square Repertory Company

**Richard Jenkins, Norman Smith and Peter Gerety
in *American Buffalo***

lives, they enter into an unspoken compact to assure each other, and themselves, that they are artists.

Oleanna (1993) watches the spectre of sexual harassment drive a male professor and female student into disastrously polarized positions; the play is both an Arthur Miller-like attack on a new kind of McCarthyism and — as Mamet guides us to see that the professor is innocent of the specific charges laid against him but guilty of other, subtler manipulations — a sophisticated study of gender and power politics. *Cryptogram* (1995) is one of Mamet's few domestic plays, quietly demonstrating that the attempt by adults to hide emotional tensions from a young boy only creates an artificiality that affects him more deeply and painfully than the truth would. Mamet, like Shepard and Wilson, developed his craft through close association with low-budget alternative theatre companies, but his career is more clearly a direct product of the geographical change in the American theatre scene, since most of his early work was first produced in Chicago, at such new venues as the North Light Theatre, which he helped found.

The most important playwright to appear in the 1980s is August Wilson, an African-American who has taken on the challenge of chronicling the black American experience in the twentieth century in a series of plays, one for each decade. *Ma Rainey's Black Bottom* (1984), for example, uses the experience of blues musicians in the 1920s to demonstrate that, early in the century when there was no hint of the economic and social changes to come, it seemed that all that was of value in black culture was either dying or being stolen by whites. Wilson's 1950s play, *Fences* (1987), looks at America just before the civil rights revolution and discovers the first African-American generation to have achieved a tenuous hold on middle class security almost cracking under the fear of losing it.

The 1930s play, *The Piano Lesson* (1990), uses two powerful symbols — a family heirloom carved with the faces of slave ancestors, and the opportunity to buy the plantation that once owned those ancestors — to capture the moment in black history when it seemed a choice had to be made between a past and a future. As mentioned earlier, Wilson has made particularly fruitful use of the workshop and staged reading process, with each of his plays going through several years of development before the final versions represented by the dates given here.

Among other interesting dramatists, David Rabe would appear to be a prime example of a writer with one thing to say, which he says very well, but beyond which he cannot go. In three plays presented by the New York Shakespeare Festival — *The Basic Training of Pavlo Hummel* (1971), *Sticks and Bones* (1971), and *Streamers* (1976) — Rabe made the imaginative leap of examining the Vietnam War through plays set pri-

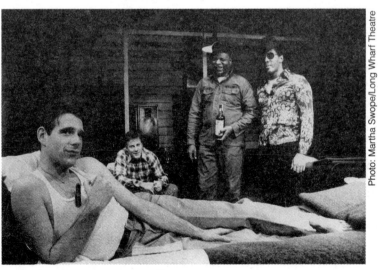

Photo: Martha Swope/Long Wharf Theatre

Streamers

marily or wholly in America, and thus dramatized the war's damaging effect on the national spirit more eloquently than any writer in any genre, but subsequent plays on other themes have been less successful.

At the center of Wendy Wasserstein's body of work is a series of plays capturing the experience of her generation of American women, those who have lived through the modern feminist revolution and have had to deal with its complex promises and demands. In *Uncommon Women and Others* (1977) college students of the early 1970s are given mixed signals about their opportunities and obligations; in *Isn't It Romantic* (1981), young women find the feminist goal of career, marriage, family, and fulfillment impossible to achieve; in *The Heidi Chronicles* (1987), a seemingly successful woman in her forties realizes how much more remains to be accomplished; in *The Sisters Rosensweig* (1993), mature women accept the results of the life choices they made and continue to make.

Terrence McNally's early work included Off Off-Broadway antiwar plays in the 1960s and a successful Broadway farce, *The Ritz*, in 1975. But he came into his real powers a decade later with plays of keen but charitable social insight: into modern romance in *Frankie and Johnny in the Clair de Lune* (1988); into homosexual mores in *The Lisbon Traviata* (1989); and, in *Lips Together, Teeth Apart* (1991) and *Love! Valour! Compassion!* (1994), into the ways both straight and gay life are affected by AIDS and other pressures at the century's end. And on the basis of two remarkably powerful plays, actually the two halves of one large work, *Angels in America* (1993), Tony Kushner became the most discussed new dramatist of the 1990s. Described by the author as "A Gay Fantasia on National Themes," the two plays mix fictional characters, historical figures, and fantasy sequences to turn the homosexual experience in the age of AIDS into a metaphor for the failures of America's past and the hopes for its future. Like almost every other play mentioned in this section, Kushner's work was developed over a period of years through workshops and preliminary productions.

Of course, dozens of other dramatists who got their start in the alternative theatre have produced single plays or a body of work of some merit, and the plays of Israel Horovitz (*The Indian Wants the Bronx*, 1964), Tom Eyen (*The White Whore and the Bit Player*, 1964), Jean-Claude van Itallie (*America Hurrah*, 1966), Ed Bullins (*In the Wine Time*, 1968), Robert Patrick (*Kennedy's Children*, 1973), Beth Henley (*Crimes of the Heart*, 1979), Harvey Fierstein (*Torch Song Trilogy*, 1981), John Guare (*Six Degrees of Separation*, 1990), and others have moved from Off Off-

Broadway or regional workshops to become staples of the American repertoire.

By the 1990s all these writers had been produced on Broadway or in major resident theatres, and Shepard or Mamet or Guare might well be considered "establishment" writers by a younger generation. The mainstream American theatre, which had been forced to expand in the late 1950s when Off-Broadway introduced new artists and new styles, and to expand again in the late 1960s when resident theatres introduced new audiences and new organizational and financial structures, had expanded once again to recognize the talent and authority of new writers and theatrical artists with new dramatic and theatrical vocabularies.

To be sure, the history of the alternative theatre was no more bump-free than that of the mainstream. Small shoestring-budget companies were subject to the same pressures that affected larger noncommercial theatres, often with more painful results. After all, the loss of an expected $10,000 grant can be a significant inconvenience to a theatre with a multimillion dollar budget, but it can threaten the survival of a smaller group. Even more than the larger theatres, alternative companies tended to be driven by the vision and commitment of their founders, and to suffer identity crises when those leaders left.

Some, like the more experimental groups of the 1960s, were the product of a particular time and place, and died when the *zeitgeist* no longer supported them; others found themselves evolving in unexpected ways. The San Francisco Mime Troupe, for example, was born in a combination of guerrilla street theatre and updated *commedia dell-arte*; when that style lost its ability to shock or attract audiences, the company wound up exploring the most conventional of forms, musicals and broad nineteenth-century melodramas, slipping social messages subversively into the crowd-pleasers. Even so, director Dan Chumley complained in 1990, "We're the most established antiestablishment theatre in the country and yet we can barely stay alive" [qtd in Berson 71]. The Women's Project, on the other hand, had expected to be temporary; founder and Artistic Director Julia Miles was a bit surprised to find it still needed two decades later, when surveys showed that under 20 percent of new produced plays were by women:

> I'm interested in getting some parity for woman playwrights. I didn't know it would take so long, frankly, because what I said was that as soon as there's some sort of parity — maybe 40 percent — we would

no longer exist as the Women's Project because there wouldn't be any need for us. [Interview]

And success, when it came, could bring its own problems. Companies that had been generated by a "Hey, kids, let's put on a show!" youthful enthusiasm found themselves midsized corporations with seven-figure budgets; twenty-year-old actors found themselves thirty-year-old administrators; and young idealists who saw themselves as alternatives to the establishment woke up one morning to find themselves very central parts of the establishment.

It would be hard, for example, to imagine a more typical small company than Chicago's Steppenwolf Theatre in 1976; even the name, harking back to a cult novel of the 1960s, defined it as young and alternative. Its actors, many of them fresh out of college, included Joan Allen, John Malkovich, Laurie Metcalf, and Gary Sinise — and that list alone bears witness to the complexities of success. As each of those talented actors (and others) moved on into the commercial realm, the company had to keep reinventing itself and rediscovering the kind of energy that had created it. Meanwhile, in less than two decades Steppenwolf's annual budget went from practically nothing to $4.5 million; it moved repeatedly, from a suburban basement to various makeshift and borrowed spaces to its own seven million dollar new theatre building; and it found itself as much a part of the Chicago theatre establishment as the Goodman.

In New York the Manhattan Theatre Club, which had defined itself as a developer of new plays and playwrights, discovered within five years that success made the ideal less sustainable.

> Owing to increased budgets, growing production costs, heightened prominence, and an associated change in the nature of its audience, ...the Club was now beginning to show signs of shifting toward greater conservatism. [Pereira 97]

The balance of the repertoire gradually shifted away from new writers, and in 1983 the MTC stopped accepting unsolicited scripts.

> Beginning in the mid-1980s and continuing through the 1990s the Manhattan Theatre Club evidenced a growing propensity towards using the work of familiar, established playwrights, ... imports, or ... a new play by a more mature, accomplished writer. [Pereira 324]

These were problems that many less successful theatres could rightly envy, but they *were* problems. In cases like Steppenwolf's, control had to shift from the founding artists to a second generation of administrators; new actors and directors had to choose between carrying on the production styles that had created the theatre's reputation and finding their own; and the company constantly had to live up to the audience expectations generated by the now-movie-star founders. If the MTC and Steppenwolf—and other successful companies that began as alternatives—survived their growing pains relatively unscathed, they were irreversibly different sorts of theatres with different challenges ahead of them.

The difficulties of growth and the fragility of success are illustrated in the experience of New York's Circle Repertory Company. Founded in 1969 by young artists with a shared vision and ambition, it produced high quality theatre for more than two decades, as it grew from a marginal Off Off-Broadway company to one of the backbones of the new Off-Broadway. But, according to Michael Feingold of the *Village Voice*,

> It started taking in younger generations, and it became a little rigid. Some of the younger writers became Lanford [Wilson] and Marshall [W. Mason] clones. This is a danger, you see. The instinct is to choose people who reinforce your self-image rather than people who challenge and revitalize it. [Interview]

One of the company's strengths, the development of a clear house style, turned out to be partly a trap. "It went into a sort of holding pattern," adds Feingold. "It wasn't generating anything new."

When Marshall W. Mason resigned as artistic director in 1987, the transition to co-founder Tanya Berezin was seemingly smooth. But the qualities that make successful company founders are not necessarily those needed by the administrators of ongoing establishments with $2 million annual budgets; and a series of managing directors had to deal with mounting deficits and unending financial problems, which may have led to an unwise gamble:

> Circle Rep was ultimately destroyed by its own ambitions.... When the company mounted Wilson's "Redwood Curtain" directly on Broadway [in 1993], the flop caused an ideological and financial crisis from which it never recovered. [Gerard 69]

In 1995 the Circle Rep's Board of Directors replaced Berezin, leading remaining founding members Mason and Lanford Wilson to quit; and the new management, Austin Pendleton, Lynne Thigpen, and Milan Stitt, was faced with the unenviable tasks of raising money, maintaining artistic standards, and carving out a new identity for the theatre. They did not have much opportunity; in 1996, after another money-losing season, the Circle Rep closed.

A year earlier, Chicago's Body Politic had ceased operations, and two other veteran Chicago alternative companies, Wisdom Bridge and Remains Theatre, lay dormant. In 1996, after several money- and subscriber-losing years, the venerable Circle in the Square declared bankruptcy.

> The Circle flourished up until 1993 and then we had a deficit problem. [A string of expensive and badly-received productions] was a big loss to us.... Then we had to stay closed for a year and a half while we were trying to gather the money. Of course while you stay closed you're gathering more deficit. [Mann interview]

Theodore Mann "retired" and his co-Artistic Director Josephine R. Abady was fired. Gregory Mosher, formerly of Lincoln Center, and Edgar Rosenbloom, of Long Wharf, were hired to bring a new identity and stability to the theatre.

Despite a major critical success (*Stanley*, starring Antony Sher) and a membership drive which added 20,000 members, Mosher and Rosenbloom reluctantly called it quits after less than a year on the job. The theatre's board suspended operations under the weight of a crushing burden of debt which included an IRS claim of more than $2million. In the end, it wasn't about programming or ticket prices, mused Mosher: "We could get Peter Brook directing Christ and the Disciples and it still wouldn't pay off the debt...We were, in fact, about to announce an amazing season," Mosher told Playbill-Online. "And then in the middle of the night, I thought 'who are you kidding?'"

Also in 1996, two more Chicago theatres, the Organic and Touchstone, merged in order to be able to continue operations; in New York INTAR and the Women's Project merged administrations, retaining their separate artistic directors. For smaller alternative companies, even more than the larger and older noncommercial theatres, financial success was often measured in terms of survival, not security.

And yet the best did survive, and others continued to join them. Across the country, at least fifty new theatres that defined themselves as alternative in some way were founded during the 1980s: Actor's Express (Atlanta 1988), "a theatre of intuition"; Alice B. Theatre (Seattle, 1984), "A Gay and Lesbian Theatre for All People"; First Stage Milwaukee (1987), a theatre for children and young adults; Pollard Theatre (Guthrie OK, 1987), "working across disciplinary boundaries"; Theater at Lime Kiln (Lexington VA, 1984), "work that reflects the indigenous stories and music of our region"; and so on [Samuels *Profiles*]. "There's a huge flood of new Off Off-Broadway theatres," reports Feingold. "Too many for me to keep up with, doing far more complicated and varied things. Theatres you've never heard of and companies I've never heard of, and the press releases arrive in every mail" [Interview].

Just as the larger regional theatres had established themselves as ongoing parts of their communities' artistic lives, various kinds of alternative theatre were clearly here to stay. From the purely careerist vanity productions Off Off-Broadway, to the new play workshops that were now the predominant source and development place of American playwrights, to the almost-establishment companies that had taken over from the commercial theatre the job of presenting serious drama, to the few experimental groups still searching out new theatrical vocabularies, the theatrical adventure begun by Joe Cino in 1958 was now an integral part of the American theatrical structure.

5

BROADWAY:
THE GOLDEN AGE AND BEYOND: 1950-PRESENT

And what of Broadway? In the 1950s no one, with the possible exception of Margo Jones, could have predicted the changes that would take place in the landscape and structure of the American theatre in the coming decades; and theatre critic John Chapman could still casually start a sentence, "The New York theatre season—which means the American theatre season . . . " *[1951–1952 3]* And in 1950 Broadway was entering what would simultaneously be its Golden Age and its last flourish as the predominant force in American theatre.

It is now clear that the 1950s—or, on the outside, the two decades following the Second World War—were the culmination of everything Broadway had been striving for as a theatrical center. Almost fifty years of intense competition, cooperation, and symbiotic cross-fertilization had produced an artistic community of remarkably high quality and professionalism. The postwar decades saw the finest playwrights, composers, and lyricists America had produced thus far, all at the peak of their powers, being presented by expert and professional producers and staged by skilled and sensitive directors. A ten-to-twenty year period that saw the best plays of Tennessee Williams and Arthur Miller, the rediscovery of Eugene O'Neill, and the classic musicals of Rodgers and Hammerstein and of Lerner and Loewe, all in less than one square mile of one city, was certainly a Golden Age.

After so many pages devoted to institutional and not-for-profit theatre, it is worth pausing for a reminder that Broadway was an entrepreneurial commercial arena. Producers would find (or occasionally commission) a new play; raise funds from individual investors; hire artists and staff; pay for sets, costumes, theatre rental, and advertising; and sell tickets. Shows would run as long as they made money, and then close, with all involved going their separate ways to look for new projects.

As noted earlier, one of the positive products of the Broadway mo-

Broadway in the 1970s

nopoly was a group of experienced, professional producers ab
all the necessary artistic and commercial decisions with a high
skill. Of course this didn't guarantee success every time out, but it
greatly improved the odds; and one important element of the Golden
Age was the fact that a generation of particularly effective Broadway
producers was in place by 1950.

Among them were Roger L. Stevens and Robert Whitehead, who
together or separately would produce *Cat on a Hot Tin Roof, Bus Stop, The
Price*, and dozens of others (Whitehead would later be a founding director of the Repertory Theater of Lincoln Center, and Stevens Chairman
of the National Council on the Arts). Alexander H. Cohen's specialties
were import-export, producing London hits *(Beyond the Fringe)* in New
York and New York successes *(Plaza Suite, Applause)* in London, and the
repackaging of cabaret acts (Edith Piaf, Nichols and May, Victor Borge)
as Broadway shows. Kermit Bloomgarden produced such hits as *Death of
a Salesman, The Diary of Anne Frank*, and *The Music Man*. Harold Prince
was learning his trade as an assistant to George Abbott and would become one of Broadway's most active and successful producers (*Pajama
Game, West Side Story, Fiddler on the Roof*, and the musicals of Stephen
Sondheim) as well as an acclaimed director.

One producer deserves special mention. David Merrick, who began
in 1949, came into his stride in the next decade. In 1950 he obtained the
rights to Marcel Pagnol's film trilogy about love in a French seaport village and assembled a creative team (director/co-author/co-producer
Joshua Logan, co-author S. N. Behrman, composer/lyricist Harold
Rome) to produce the hit musical *Fanny*. From then on, Merrick was the
most dynamic, most successful, and most colorful Broadway producer of
the next three decades. He helped create some of Broadway's greatest
hits — *Look Back in Anger, Gypsy, Becket, Oliver!, Hello, Dolly!*, and *42nd
Street*, among literally dozens of others.

In the 1963–64 season alone Merrick produced five plays —
Anouilh's *The Rehearsal*, Brecht's *Arturo Ui*, Osborne's *Luther*, Kesey's
One Flew Over the Cuckoo's Nest, and Williams's *The Milk Train Doesn't
Stop Here Any More* — and three musicals — *110 in the Shade, Foxy*, and
Hello, Dolly! They weren't all hits but, as his biographer Howard Kissel
points out, you could leave out the biggest success among them and still
have a season others would envy: "What regional theater would not be
proud to produce a season that included Anouilh, Brecht, Kesey,
Osborne, Williams, and, perhaps, *110 in the Shade*? ... What regional
theatre could afford to do such a season?" [508]

Merrick was a businessman, not an artistic idealist, and it was to increase and protect profits that he created a tax-exempt foundation in 1959. The foundation transferred some profits from his hits into a fund that could then afford to produce a string of worthy but uncommercial ventures, such as Stein's *Marat/Sade*, Stoppard's *Rosencrantz and Guildenstern are Dead*, and several plays by John Osborne, all of which Broadway would probably otherwise have missed. Kissel argues that "In many ways the David Merrick Arts Foundation was a precursor of the not-for-profit theaters that dotted the landscape from the Seventies onward" [280]; and he notes that, ironically, "many of the plays the Foundation backed turned out to be more successful than the supposedly 'commercial' ventures" [280].

Merrick's seemingly unerring commercial sense and his audacious instinct for publicity are central to his legend. A separate volume could be devoted to Merrick anecdotes — his feuds with critics and collaborators, his publicity stunts, his tangled personal life — but one will do: in 1961 his production of the musical *Subways are for Sleeping* was generally panned by the New York newspaper critics, so Merrick found a group of ordinary citizens with the same names as the critics, and quoted their praise of the show in an ad. *Subways* ultimately lost money anyway, but the trick took its rightful place in Broadway folklore. Gossip, anecdote, colorfulness, and even the hint of chicanery were an important part of Broadway's glamorous image; and Merrick's antics may have contributed as much to Broadway by keeping that image alive as he did by giving it hit after hit. In 1966 Otis L. Guernsey, Jr. called Merrick

> an individual whose contribution to the American theater is so wide and continuous that he's in a class of achievement by himself.... Merrick has elevated and enriched the American theater with his courage, taste and healthy avarice, and in turn it has quite properly elevated and enriched him. He livens things up generally, and it's a pleasure to have him around, not only for profit but also for fun. [43]

In the 1950s directors Harold Clurman, Elia Kazan, Joshua Logan, and George Abbott were at the peak of their powers; and they were soon joined by a new generation: Jose Quintero and Alan Schneider from Off-Broadway; Jerome Robbins and Gower Champion from the realm of choreographers; Mike Nichols from the Chicago school of improvisational comedy; and, from within the Broadway community, Moss Hart and Harold Prince. (In turn, that group would subsequently be joined or displaced by others: former dancers Bob Fosse, Michael Bennett, and Tommy Tune; former actor Jerry Zaks; and leading directors from not-

for-profit theatres around the country.) The new American styles of acting, generally (if inaccurately) identified by the label of one branch,
"The Method," were exciting audiences with their power and truthful-
ness. And playwrights Tennessee Williams and Arthur Miller followed
up their early successes with a decade or more of first-rate mature work.

☆

In the fifteen years after *A Streetcar Named Desire,* Tennessee
Williams brought nine plays to Broadway, including at least two that be-
long in the first rank of his work. *Cat on a Hot Tin Roof* (1955) continues
Williams's mission of proving that social outcasts and misfits share a
common and painful humanity with those of us who function more successfully, while exploring what he later called "my own credo: the difficulties of romanticism in a predominantly cynical world" [qtd in Funke].
The play revolves around Brick Pollitt, a former athlete so trapped in a
limited definition of manhood and an idealized image of friendship that
he rejected the friend whose love for him may have been sexual, and has
been running from the guilt ever since. Williams focuses on Brick's wife
Maggie, the nervous, determined cat of the title, whose fight to save her
marriage, along with the efforts of Brick's life-embracing father, allows
the play to end with tentative hints of Brick's resurrection.

(*Cat on a Hot Tin Roof* is of historical interest for reasons beyond its
quality. Like all scripts, it underwent some rewriting during the pre-
production period, but published texts are normally the opening night
versions, keeping such revision invisible to the public. Williams insisted
on publishing his original text alongside the Broadway version, giving
general readers a first glimpse into the kinds of production-based forces
that help shape a play.)

Williams's *The Night of the Iguana* (1961) presents another broken-
spirited idealist, a defrocked minister unable to accept the impurities of
the world and of his own soul. He is led to the discovery that everyone
around him is as frightened of life as he, and that their only advantage is
a willingness to accept any aid to emotional survival. He begins the play
by rejecting an offer of marriage from an old friend because it would
compromise his principles; he ends by recognizing the need to embrace
any help, however imperfect, in keeping his demons at bay. Both *Cat* and
Iguana share *A Streetcar Named Desire*'s rich poetic language and imagery, and both present Williams's messages of compassion and acceptance with undiminished theatrical power.

While his other plays of the period are not quite as strong or evocative as Williams at his best, they carry the same messages. *Summer and Smoke* (1948), for example, celebrates life to the extent of seeing a woman's progression from sexually repressed parson's daughter to village nymphomaniac as a story of growth and salvation; it is marred only by an artificial plot structure and by too great a reliance on symbolism that in this case fails to resonate as he wished. (An alternative version of the text, written in 1948 but first produced in 1976 as *Eccentricities of a Nightingale*, eliminates many of the flaws and may deserve ranking with Williams's best.)

Sweet Bird of Youth (1959) presents a young man aptly named Chance, who has relied on good fortune and the memory of a pure romance to keep him from having to deal with reality; the play lets him grow enough to face bad luck and the destruction of his fantasy, and to accept responsibility for his actions. Williams's other plays of the 1950s are slighter or less effective, but they are all clearly the work of an important writer.

Like Williams, Arthur Miller produced his best work during the 1950s and 1960s by continuing to address his central, recurring concerns: the dramatic and moral crises that arise when the world's values come in conflict with an individual's, the moral outrage that is appropriate when such social forces violate human dignity, and the affirmation that the life of the Common Man is capable of generating the largest moral and emotional experiences. *The Crucible* (1953) uses the witch trials of seventeenth-century Massachusetts as a thinly-disguised parallel to the anti-Communist mania of the early 1950s. But the play is more than a response to a topical issue, as subsequent revivals have proven; even more than the specific evils of McCarthyism, Miller indicts any social force that can demand that an individual violate his own moral sense in order to survive. Miller's protagonist in *The Crucible* is an innocent man who is given the opportunity to tell a lie (even more insidiously, a lie that will harm no one) and live, or remain true to himself and die; and to Miller the situation itself, regardless of the outcome, is obscene.

Miller's *A View from the Bridge* (1955) explores similar emotional ground while removing the political context, and consciously reaches for tragedy. An ordinary man, overcome by a passion (an incestuous love for his niece) he cannot acknowledge, much less cope with, is driven to inform on a rival for the girl and thus violate a moral code his culture and he hold absolute, and destroys his soul in the process. If the play doesn't quite work—the gap between the small characters and the bathetically Freudian psychologizing on the one hand, and the invocations of Fate and high tragedy on the other, proves too great—Miller does succeed in making Eddie Carbone's fall as moving, real, and relevant as Willy Loman's.

Other new dramatists of the postwar years, while perhaps not reaching the stature of Williams and Miller, provided an impressive level of plays. William Inge offered a kind of domesticated Williams: misfits who were more likely to be just lonely and confused rather than grotesque, with no problem too great for love, forgiveness, and compromise to make bearable, if not necessarily to conquer. In *Come Back, Little Sheba* (1950) a middle-aged couple sadly learn to accept the fact that their youthful fantasies, ambitions, and passions will never be fulfilled. *Picnic* (1953) and *Bus Stop* (1955) both show young lovers recognizing that the great romances of fantasy and fiction are not available to them, and settling for something less-than-perfect that is the best they can get. *The Dark at the Top of the Stairs* (1959) lets a troubled family find its way through a variety of emotional crises, triumphing over none but surviving all, through an admission of mutual dependence. Inge was sometimes criticized for not exploring the emotional depths of Williams. But his benign dramatization of the little stories of little people, and his counsel that less-than-perfect might be all they can hope for, met a real emotional need in audiences of the 1950s.

Robert Anderson's plays resemble Inge's (and thus Williams's) in offering sympathy for outcasts and the emotionally damaged, and Miller's in containing a note of social comment. In *Tea and Sympathy* (1953), a boy unjustly suspected of being homosexual is offered understanding—and the opportunity to prove his manhood—by an unhappily married woman. Lorraine Hansberry's *A Raisin in the Sun* (1959), the first play by an African-American woman to be produced on Broadway, shows a black family gaining strength by standing up to racists trying to block their move to a better neighborhood.

Paddy Chayefsky, one of the first playwrights to begin in television, had some Broadway successes, notably *The Tenth Man* (1959), in which the elderly members of a Jewish congregation help renew the faith of a dead-spirited young man. Poet Archibald MacLeish's *JB* (1958) was a modern-dress version of the story of Job, while Frances Goodrich and Albert Hackett's dramatization of *The Diary of Anne Frank* (1955) and William Gibson's drama of the youth of Helen Keller, *The Miracle Worker* (1959), were works of undeniable theatrical power. And of course each season had its share of light but polished comedies, of which F. Hugh Herbert's *The Moon is Blue* (1951), John Patrick's *The Teahouse of the*

August Moon (1952), and Thornton Wilder's *The Matchmaker* (1955) stand out as particularly well-made.

But the most important theatrical development of the 1950s, from the purely literary perspective, was the rediscovery of Eugene O'Neill, the discovery of his posthumous plays, and the resulting reevaluation of his entire career. O'Neill had established himself as America's leading dramatist with his unceasing stylistic experiments in the 1920s, but he had produced very little since the mid-1930s, and by the time of his death in 1953 he was almost forgotten. As recounted in Chapter Two, the Off-Broadway revival of *The Iceman Cometh* in 1956 reawakened critical and public interest in O'Neill, and contributed to his widow Carlotta Monterey's decision to release for production a play O'Neill had written in 1940 but wanted to keep suppressed for twenty-five years after his death, *Long Day's Journey into Night*.

The play fearlessly explores the dynamics of a self-destructive family to uncover all its horrors and then, like all great tragedy, finds some grain of hope and comfort in the wreckage; and the Broadway production of 1956 made it clear that *Long Day's Journey* is as far superior to anything else O'Neill wrote in his long career as his earlier plays were to other American drama of the 1920s. Without violating his lifelong vision of the human experience as limited and fated—in this case repre-

Photo: The Homer Dickens Collection

Fredric March, Florence Eldridge, and Bradford Dillman in
Long Day's Journey into Night

sented by the belief that the experiences of our youth force patterns of behavior on us that all the free will and determination in the world cannot break—O'Neill fights his way to the discovery that acknowledging such helplessness can be the gateway to forgiveness of ourselves and others. *Long Day's Journey* was followed by other posthumous plays, *A Touch of the Poet* (1958), *Hughie* (published 1959, Broadway 1964), and *More Stately Mansions* (1967) and by revivals of earlier O'Neill plays. They weren't all masterpieces and they weren't all successes, but they confirmed O'Neill's greatness and his restoration to the highest ranking among American dramatists.

The American musical theatre also reached its zenith in the 1950s. Although the conventional, empty-headed musical comedy "for the tired businessman" continued to be produced, as it would through the coming decades, the integrated musical drama form developed by Rodgers and Hammerstein in the 1940s became the norm and the standard of achievement. Rodgers and Hammerstein themselves followed *South Pacific* with the even more ambitious *The King and I* (1951), which depicted an emotion-charged relationship between two strong individuals without allowing it to lapse into a conventional romance.

If their next three musicals—*Me and Juliet* (1953), *Pipe Dream* (1955), and *Flower Drum Song* (1958)—were less successful artistically and commercially, falling victim, to some extent, to the very high standards of their own precedents, their last collaboration was happily *The Sound of Music* (1959), old-fashioned, sentimental, and operetta-like, but filled with music and lyrics characteristic of both artists at their best, and immensely popular.

The highest achievement of the integrated musical came with Lerner and Loewe's *My Fair Lady* (1956). Their source, George Bernard Shaw's *Pygmalion*, not only gave them a story that trod the thin line between fairy tale romance and worldly cynicism, but defied the musical form by leaving no room for a conventional chorus line or even for a romance between its hero and heroine. That it could be turned into a Broadway musical at all, much less a thoroughly successful one, was evidence of how far the musical had evolved in little more than a decade.

My Fair Lady not only was a triumph of the integrated musical, but also helped to advance the genre even further. In addition to its particularly literate book, it featured an essentially unmusical hero and a nonsinging star. The particular style of *sprechstimme* that Lerner and Loewe provided for Rex Harrison was not only appropriate to the cool and undemonstrative Henry Higgins, but also integrated book and music more seamlessly than ever before, as the moment at which speaking turned into singing became virtually imperceptible. While Harrison was not the first nonsinger in a Broadway musical — Walter Huston's manner of talking his way through "September Song" in *Knickerbocker Holiday* (1938) is almost legendary — his experience and example opened the musical to other musically untrained performers whose acting skills enriched their plays: Robert Preston in *The Music Man* (1957), Richard Burton in *Camelot* (1960) and Glynis Johns in *A Little Night Music* (1973), among others.

The advances of *My Fair Lady* were matched by those of two other genre-stretching musicals. Frank Loesser's *The Most Happy Fella* (1956) was virtually an opera, with a minimum of spoken dialogue, an almost continuous musical line, and more than thirty separate songs; it was saved from any tinge of pretentiousness by Loesser's solid footing in the popular music idiom. And Leonard Bernstein and Stephen Sondheim's *West Side Story* (1957), with book by experienced playwright Arthur Laurents, translated *Romeo and Juliet* into modern dress with little loss of tragic power and with an infusion of contemporary nervous energy (generated largely by the direction and choreography of Jerome Robbins) that made up for the absence of Shakespeare's poetry. By the end of the decade even an old-fashioned musical like Jule Styne and Stephen Sondheim's *Gypsy* (1959), essentially a vehicle for star Ethel Merman, had a dramatic depth and complexity that allowed Sondheim later to judge it "one of the two or three best shows ever written [and] the last good one in the Rodgers and Hammerstein form" [qtd in Zadan 67].

☆

What brought this Golden Age to an end? It would be tempting to draw an easy conclusion from the chronology: Off-Broadway and the first regional theatres appeared just at the moment of Broadway's zenith, and one might guess that all the creative forces fled Broadway for other venues. But that's too simplistic, and also inaccurate. For a long time the alternative venues were just that — alternatives. They were not in direct competition to Broadway, but offered fare not normally available on Broadway (classics, unknown writers) to generally new (geographically or demographically) audiences. Broadway's decline, starting in the 1960s and accelerating in the following decades, came mainly from internal causes, and if the new arenas and structures of the American theatre eventually competed, they did so by filling breaches from which Broadway had already withdrawn.

It is, after all, inherent in the nature of Golden Ages to end, even without external competition. Artists weaken, move on or die; artistic peaks prove impossible to match or transcend; changes in external factors, such as economics or demographics, make what had previously succeeded no longer successful; and even the most highly-developed art forms begin to stagnate without continual change or growth. Each of these forces began to work on Broadway even as it reached its zenith.

Some of the most creative artists of 1950s Broadway either died, reduced their output, or lost their creative energies just as the Golden Age was peaking. Arthur Miller was absent from the theatre for nine years after *A View from the Bridge*, a period that included his marriage to Marilyn Monroe, for whom he wrote the film *The Misfits* (1960). He returned in 1964 with two plays produced by the new Repertory Theater of Lincoln Center, *After the Fall* and *Incident at Vichy*, and followed in 1968 with *The Price*. All three are excellent plays and represent a slight but significant change in Miller's focus, from the clash between individual and society to the ways in which the individual can find his way through moral and emotional trauma.

The central character of *After the Fall* is a man afraid to move forward in life because all the relationships of his past were marked by mutual failures and betrayals; in a resolution that recalls O'Neill's *Long Day's Journey*, he discovers that acceptance of imperfection as part of the human condition can be the key to forgiveness and hope. In *The Price* a man who has considered himself a failure is led to realize that, without guidance, support, or models to follow, he has consistently chosen the right over the profitable, so that everything admirable in his character and everything successful in his life is his own creation.

Still, only three plays, two of them in limited runs, in the course of more than a decade, left something of a gap in the serious Broadway repertoire; and Miller's rate of production remained slow in the following decades, as he took on the mantle and responsibilities of a senior statesman among American dramatists; he was, for example, very active in PEN, the international writers' association. Miller's few later plays range from the characteristically political *The Archbishop's Ceiling* (1977), in which political surveillance in an eastern European country violates not just privacy but trust and honesty among friends, to the uncharacteristically poetic *Elegy for a Lady* (1982), in which two strangers delicately find their way to a comforting intimacy. Significantly these and others, such as *The Ride Down Mount Morgan* (1991) and *The Last Yankee* (1993), either failed in New York or bypassed it completely, as Broadway became no longer able to support one of its finest writers. (Several late Miller plays premiered in London, and Miller's critical and popular reputation seemed stronger outside America than in.)

Tennessee Williams continued to write for the theatre through the 1960s and 1970s, but after *The Night of the Iguana* his special ability — to depict extreme characters and behaviors with a sensitivity that made them recognizably human and with a poetry that made them aesthetically and emotionally thrilling — seemed to evaporate. Although a new play appeared every year or two until his death in 1982, and although almost every one contained at least one scene or speech with the beauty and power of his early work, plays like *The Gnadiges Fraulein* (1966) and *The Red Devil Battery Sign* (1975) were a shambles of confused symbols, awkward plotting, and grotesques who remained grotesques instead of becoming more sympathetic.

Even in the 1950s there had been signs of limitation and danger in Williams's style. He was unquestionably the finest poet the American theatre had produced, but he was not immune to the poet's temptation to overwrite; and the powerful language and evocative symbolism of *Streetcar* and *Cat* could too easily lapse into the bathos that colors parts of *Camino Real* (1953) or the blurred symbolism that keeps *Orpheus Descending* (1957) from the top rank of his work. Williams's popular reputation at his peak was as a writer of shocking, sensationalistic plays; and, indeed, such subjects as alcoholism, drug abuse, homosexuality, venereal disease, madness, castration, and cannibalism were integral to his dramatic vocabulary. None of these elements was gratuitous; Williams was employing the gothic writer's privilege of making the sensational stand for the ordinary. But to the extent that his gothic elements called attention to themselves, they ran the risk of interfering with his messages of compassion and reassurance.

These temptations and dangers, generally kept in check while Williams was at full power, would eventually prove too strong, and seriously weaken his work for the last twenty years of his life. Williams explained later that the 1960s had been a period of almost continuous mental and emotional breakdown for him, triggered by the death of his longtime companion and lover, and exacerbated by alcohol, drugs, real or imagined physical ailments, and repeated failures in the theatre. But even after he pronounced himself recovered, his continued writing seemed more a matter of habit and compulsion than of a still vital talent, and his decline deprived the commercial theatre of one of its most exciting creative voices.

A similar loss of creative energy had earlier led to William Inge's withdrawal from the theatre, and eventually to his suicide in 1973. The frustrations of his experience at Lincoln Center contributed to Elia Kazan's leaving the theatre and devoting himself to writing and film-making. On the other hand, the commercial successes of *My Fair Lady* and *Camelot* allowed Frederick Loewe to retire happily, while Leonard Bernstein, who had been juggling several careers, chose to concentrate on being one of the world's foremost symphonic conductors.

Lorraine Hansberry died in 1965, about the same time Paddy Chayevsky left the Broadway theatre to devote himself to screenwriting. Oscar Hammerstein died in 1960; and although Richard Rodgers continued to work, alone and with various partners, none of his later musicals was as innovative or successful as his collaborations with Hart and Hammerstein. The Theatre Guild gradually reduced production, finally ceasing activity in 1976 (the name was later sold to another producer, who used it briefly in 1995). Perhaps a corresponding list of losses could be compiled for any decade, but hindsight shows that the falling-away of creative talent in the early 1960s was an important contributor to Broadway's decline.

Meanwhile, the Broadway musical was undergoing a crisis of another sort. Despite the loss of the two dominant partnerships of the 1950s, integrated musical dramas of the Rodgers and Hammerstein sort continued to be produced during the 1960s, and some, notably *Fiddler on the Roof* (1964) by Jerry Bock and Sheldon Harnick, and *Man of La Mancha* (1965) by Mitch Leigh and Joe Darion, were great popular successes. But the artistic peak that the integrated musical reached with *My Fair Lady* and *West Side Story* proved also to be an artistic dead end. There was evidently no further room for growth in the form, and as it marked time it began to stagnate. As entertaining as *Camelot*, *Fiddler*, and *La Mancha* were, there was an old-fashioned air about them, and a sense of the mechanical; self-consciously literary plots, dramatic soliloquies, and violations of convention had become as conventional as the chorus lines and strict alternations of fast and slow songs in the 1920s. In 1967 Otis L. Guernsey, Jr. noted that

> We have developed this form to the danger point of near-perfection where we can machine-make it — almost. Many of the musicals which turn up nowadays, even some of the most popular ones, are canned goods, taking some proven high-quality material from a novel or play and processing and packaging it in musical form. [60]

Indeed, that same year veteran Broadway conductor Lehman Engel published a book dissecting the integrated musical and offering instructions and formulas for its construction, demonstrating how "by-the-book" musical writing had become.

☆

It is a truth universally acknowledged, that this Broadway season (whatever year this is) is the worst ever, that fewer plays are being produced than ever before, and fewer of them are of any quality. Rising costs and union featherbedding have made the production of anything but lowest-common-denominator crowd-pleasers impossible, and rising ticket prices are scaring away what's left of the shrinking audience. The end of Broadway, and of civilization as we know it, is at hand.

One could choose any season, almost at random, from the 1920s to the 1990s and find journalists and theatre professionals bemoaning the sorry artistic and financial state of Broadway. In 1940, the season of Maxwell Anderson's *Key Largo*, Lindsay and Crouse's *Life with Father*, and William Saroyan's *The Time of Your Life*, the magazine *Theatre Arts* surveyed the Broadway community and got responses like these:

> William A. Brady, League of New York Theatres: "Playwriting seems to have become a lost art. Less than ten percent of the dramatists in the United States can submit a manuscript which is fit to rehearse."

> Mordecai Gorelik, United Scenic Artists of America: "I wish I could be more optimistic about the theatre's chance for recovery under present conditions. The cost of production, even with all kinds of sacrifices, is too great, the gamble is too risky."

> John Shubert, League of New York Theatres: "I do not think there is anything that can be done to help it. It has been kicked around so thoroughly by unions, producers and theatre owners in the face of competition supplied by Hollywood and the radio, that it is really now staggering on its last legs." [qtd in "The Theatre Takes Stock"]

And so, even in the 1950s, Broadway Cassandras could see signs that the glory days were fading, or even long gone. There were more than 260 shows in the 1927–1928 Broadway season, and only sixty-nine in 1949–1950. In a given week in 1927 forty-seven shows were running; in the 1950s and 1960s the number averaged twenty-three. Adjusted for inflation, box office receipts dropped by one-third between 1930 and 1950 and remained fiat for the next fifteen years [Moore 147–53]. In the 1950s and 1960s there were fewer than half as many theatres on Broadway as there had been in the 1920s. As veteran critic Brooks Atkinson observed about the state of Broadway in 1950,

> If the theater were a rational industry with long-range capital and management and if it were operated primarily for profit, logic would have pronounced it a failure. After the business expansion of the first two decades, and after the artistic achievements of the twenties, the Broadway theater had dropped to the level of the first years of the century. In similar circumstances, Studebaker and Packard automobiles went out of business. [428]

Of course statistics can lie, or at least mislead. There were indeed several seasons in the late 1920s when the number of new Broadway productions approached or exceeded 200, but they were as much an anomaly in the general pattern as the Roaring Twenties were in the cultural and economic history of the nation. Except for those few years the annual number during the 1920s and 1930s averaged around 125, a total that included touring shows, limited runs, and some productions that would now be labeled Off-Broadway. From 1940 to 1970 the annual totals varied notably from year to year, eventually settling in the sixty-to-eighty range. And if there were fewer shows being produced, those that got on were generally stronger; the average run for a musical more than doubled between 1927 and 1960, and the average for a play increased by 50 percent [Moore 147–52].

Memory also has a way of distorting comparisons. That golden 1927–1928 season did produce *Show Boat*, *Strange Interlude*, and *Porgy*, but it also gave the world *Lovers and Enemies* (two performances), *The First Stone* (three performances), and a total of seventy-five shows that ran less than two weeks. Burns Mantle, summarizing that season for his annual volume of Best Plays, said it "will probably be remembered in New York, should occasion arise to remember it, as one that started promisingly and failed hopelessly" [3]. Mantle's sentiments would be echoed through the years by his successors: John Chapman, "The year 1950–1951 on Broadway is not likely to distinguish itself in theatrical histories as anything in particular" [3]; Louis Kronenberger, "All in all, however, [1956–1957] was a depressingly bad season" [3]; Henry Hewes, "The deterioration of the New York climate for theatrical production became mercilessly apparent in a 1962–63 season generally regarded as the worst" [3]; and Otis L. Guernsey Jr., "This [1971–1972] was a season of gray subject matter and gray, half-realized achievement" [207], further evidence that a certain amount of woe-crying was endemic to the system.

Still, as a commercial enterprise the Broadway theatre was susceptible to the problems and pressures of the marketplace, and by the mid-
1960s at the latest, the practical and artistic effects of economics and
other external forces could no longer be denied. Production costs had
increased geometrically from 1920 on, doubling every decade. In 1950 a
typical play cost $60,000 to produce, and a musical $200,000. In 1960 a
musical could cost close to $500,000; by the early 1970s, over $1 million
(and by the 1990s, figures of six, twelve, and even twenty million were
spoken of).

Part of this increase was simple inflation, part a response to a real or
imagined audience demand for more elaborate productions, part the result of greatly increased union demands, many of which were justified
(actors' salaries had been shamefully low at the beginning of the period),
but some of which led to cries of featherbedding. Broadway myth has it
that putting a lamp onstage during a rehearsal requires members of
three unions, one to carry the lamp, one to plug it in, and one to turn
on the electricity. It is true that the musicians' union requires that a
quota of musicians be hired and paid at certain theatres even if the current play is not a musical; *A Chorus Line*, its score orchestrated for seventeen musicians, played in a theatre whose union quota was twenty-six,
so for over six thousand performances nine musicians were paid to do
nothing [Stevens 92].

Inevitably, ticket prices went up, although — contrary to the perception of ticket-buyers, who were acutely sensitive to any rise — they did
not keep pace with expenses. Top price for a musical in 1925 was about
$3.00; in 1950 it was about $6.00; fifteen years later it was $9.90, ad-
vancing to $12 in 1966 and $15 in 1969, with the lowest-price seat still
$2.00, less than the cost of a ticket to a first-run movie. (Ticket prices
didn't start to leapfrog upward until the mid-1970s, with a $17.50 top in
1975, $30 in 1980, $50 in 1985, and $75 — with a $50 balcony seat common — in 1996.)

However modest the price rises, when combined with the increasing
pattern of sold-out shows and long runs (which made casual, spur-of-
the-moment theatregoing more difficult), they began to transform the
popular perception of Broadway into that of an expense account or special occasion splurge. This is the first area in which Off-Broadway posed
a noteworthy (if statistically small) competition, as the generally
younger and less affluent Off-Broadway audiences were exactly those
who might otherwise have bought the $2.00 tickets uptown.

Meanwhile, other demographic forces were at work. The Broadway audience has always been predominantly white, middle class, and middle-aged, and the 1950s and 1960s saw that segment leave New York City in large numbers.

> During the 1960's, 900,000 of its white population had fled to the suburbs.... The affluent middle-class and upper-middle-class that faithfully patronized the Broadway theatre in the 1950's and for most of the 1960's had gone. The pace of this out-migration quickened in the first years of the 1970's. [Little *After* 18]

A drive into the city to see a show, followed by the drive home, was just sufficiently more daunting than a simple cab or subway ride; and some of those who might once have been frequent theatregoers began to relegate the experience to an occasional special adventure. (Complaints by suburbanites that theatregoing had become a late and expensive night out led the Broadway theatres to move the traditional 8:40 curtain up to 7:30 in 1971; complaints that this left little time for dinner moved it back to 8:00 a couple of years later.)

So, even without any significant artistic or audience flight to the newly-appearing alternative theatrical venues, Broadway began to change. The artistic heights of the Golden Age could not be sustained, and commercial pressures were beginning to affect the nature and quality of the work on offer. Of course this was not an overnight process, nor was it immediately apparent. As suggested earlier, Broadway was so used to hearing pessimists cry wolf that indications of actual problems could be overlooked. Still, it was difficult to ignore the growing evidence that experience and talent in a show's creators were no guarantee of profits.

In the 1962–1963 season alone, reliables S. N. Behrman, Irving Berlin, Lillian Hellman, William Inge, Garson Kanin, Sidney Kingsley, S. J. Perelman, Irwin Shaw, and Tennessee Williams all had plays fail; and in the next two decades no one would be immune: Edward Albee, Leonard Bernstein, Alan Jay Lerner, Arthur Miller, Richard Rodgers, Stephen Sondheim, even Neil Simon. Nor were big stars sufficient insurance; among those who experienced the indignity of very brief runs in the 1960s and 1970s were Yul Brynner, Carol Channing, Sandy Dennis, Kirk Douglas, Alfred Drake, Joel Grey, Tammy Grimes, Charlton Heston, Deborah Kerr, Jack Lemmon, and Al Pacino.

The rise in ticket prices contributed to Broadway's first $50 million (in gross ticket sales) season in 1964–1965, and to new highs in each of the next three years. But the euphoria disguised another trend until it became inescapable: that triumphal 1967–1968 season also saw ten out of its eleven new musicals (all but *Hair*) fail, with a total loss of well over $3 million. And though the average run of a new show was longer than ever before, that was no guarantee of financial success; for every *Fiddler on the Roof* that ran more than three thousand performances and returned its investors' money sevenfold, there was a *Rothschilds* (1970) that lasted over five hundred performances without recouping more than a quarter of its cost or, worse, a *Seesaw* (1973) that ran for almost a year and lost several hundred thousand dollars *more* than its original capitalization. (In 1996 the musical *Big* ran six months and lost $10.3 million.) Meanwhile the bubble of the mid-1960s proved short-lived; and by every commercial standard — gross sales, number of performances, number of new shows — the next several years saw a seemingly unstoppable decline.

The blame was placed everywhere: on the costs; on the unions; on the white flight from the city; on the generation gap, which alienated potential young audiences from their parents' tastes; on the "theatre party ladies," brokers who booked benefit performances and demanded only light, star-filled entertainments; on the deterioration of the Times Square area, which made some people reluctant or afraid to go there. The early 1970s saw the first of several projects, all announced with great fanfare and optimism, to "clean up" Times Square and Forty-second Street; not until the 1990s would any of them accomplish much beyond the opening press conference. (Extensive new construction around 1990, including several hotels, reinvigorated Times Square — uniquely, city ordinances actually required new buildings to be fronted with large billboards and electronic signs, to maintain the Square's garish atmosphere. Later in the decade the combination of city action and extensive private investment, including a strong commitment by the Walt Disney Company, seemed likely to succeed at last in seizing Forty-second Street back from the porn shops and drug dealers.)

And certainly at the top of anyone's list of people to blame were the critics. The relationship between the theatre and the newspaper critics, and between some specific theatre people and some specific critics, would require a book in itself to analyze. One fact was universally accepted and bemoaned: the loss of several New York newspapers to mergers and bankruptcies in the mid-1960s left the city with fewer theatre critics, one of whom had tremendous power. *Whoever* reviewed for *The New York Times* could almost singlehandedly make or break a show.

To its credit *The Times* was as concerned about this situation as the theatre community was. Arthur Gelb was editor in charge of cultural coverage (under various titles) from the mid-1960s on, and had been a reviewer before then. He explained in 1996 that *The Times*'s interest in arts coverage had a long history:

> When Adolph S. Ochs bought *The Times* in 1896, . . . he felt that an intelligent reader should be informed about the arts, and that the best critics should be engaged to inform them. The theatre, of course, was in our back yard. [Interview]

And with that history came both power and responsibility. "It took almost one hundred years to give us the power that you talk about. . . . It's the combination of the critic's talent and the power and prestige of the paper." Still,

> It is not *The Times*'s responsibility to help the theatre. *The Times*'s responsibility is to help the readers . . . . The only thing *The Times* can try to do is hire the best possible person, who loves the theatre, who understands the theatre, and who has tough standards for the theatre. [Interview]

Of the few general newspapers left in New York City in the late 1960s, only *The Times* was directed to the upscale market — that is, its readers were demographically the people most likely to go to the Broadway theatre. Put another way, the people most likely to go to the theatre all read *The Times* reviews. And, despite Gelb's disclaimers — "I see no reason why that power should frighten us as long as our critics understand the theatre, love the theatre, and write honestly about the theatre" — *The Times* did take the concern of the theatre community seriously.

In the 1960s, *The Times* recruited a second respected critic to offer an alternative review for its Sunday edition, only to find that he tended to agree with the daily reviewer rather than provide a counterpoint. The idea of the alternative Sunday writer was tried on and off in various forms in the following decades, as was increasing the use of second-string critics; and lead critics tended to have shorter tenures than earlier in the century, being allowed to move on when then antagonism against them grew too strong.

And, to be fair, virtually every *Times* critic brought to the position a genuine love of theatre, a real desire to support Broadway with praise when praise was due, and a sincere disappointment when an individual show could not earn a positive review. But that was little comfort to those whose work failed to please, when a *Times* pan could mean instant failure. Also, to be fair, some of *The Time*'s power was a self-generating myth, fortified every time a frightened producer closed a show immediately on getting a bad *Times* review. Occasionally a producer sustained by a commitment to the work, a sufficient advance sale, or faith in the audience-pleasing quality of his show held on in the face of a negative *Times* review and found other reviews and word-of-mouth providing sufficient support for a run.

Other critics, from television and radio stations and from national magazines, increased their Broadway reviewing from the 1960s on, and in the 1980s the magazine *TheatreWeek* was founded to cover Broadway. But none of the broadcast reviewers, and few of the weekly or monthly writers had sufficient authority or credibility to challenge *The Times'* power, and *TheatreWeek* ceased publication after a few years. The problem of *The Times'* make-or-break power seemed unsolvable and remained a source of pain and anger as the century neared its end. In 1996 Off-Off-Broadway's Julia Miles could still say, "It's very difficult to get the plays to an audience if they don't get a good review in *The New York Times*, and I don't think that's changed that much over all these years" [Interview].

Meanwhile, increasingly inventive and frantic attempts were made to win back the shrinking Broadway audience and attract new ones. The liquor laws were amended to allow bars in theatres starting in 1964–1965, in the hope that the prospect of a drink during intermission might make some people more willing to sit through a show. In 1967 the theatres offered a special bus service between Times Square and the East Side neighborhood of many ticket buyers; in 1972 one show offered free parking; and in 1973 another paid for a free taxi ride to or from its theatre. As mentioned, curtain times were juggled to woo suburbanites; and by the mid-1970s about half the shows on Broadway were offering Sunday matinees, popular with commuters and families, in place of the usually slow Monday night performance. Box offices began taking credit card bookings in 1972; some theatres offered dinner-theatre packages in conjunction with local restaurants in 1983; and in 1994 one producer held a mid-winter half-price sale to get his shows through the slow months.

Particularly successful were two innovations in advertising and marketing. Remarkably, no Broadway show had made significant use of television advertising until 1972, when a commercial showing excerpts from the musical *Pippin* boosted ticket sales and brought in people who had never been to a Broadway show before. Television very quickly became an important marketing tool for Broadway and proved equally effective (assuming that the commercial was skillfully made) for comedies, dramas, and musicals. And 1973 saw the opening of the TKTS (an abbreviation suggesting half of "tickets," not an acronym) Booth, a cooperative venture of the Theatre Development Fund and the League of New York Theatres at which unsold tickets were offered on the day of performance for half-price. As Phil Smith of the Shubert Organization explained,

> The whole idea of the booth was audience development, not dollars. People who never otherwise went to the theatre would suddenly see a show. We were making theatre accessible. You could go on impulse . . . It was important to get a new audience that had never been to the theatre, get them into the habit. [qtd in Stevens 171]

By 1980 the TKTS Booth was selling more than 1.5 million tickets a year, well over 15 percent of the Broadway total, and the Fund's studies indicated that the majority of its customers would not have bought full-price tickets otherwise. What's more, since the shows available through TKTS were not announced in advance, the hundreds of people who lined up each day were generally motivated by a love of theatre and a willingness to see one of several possibilities — a far cry from the traditional theatregoers who sent in their mail order months in advance or

Photo: New York Convention and Visitors Bureau

TKTS Booth, Duffy Square

paid scalper's prices to see a specific show from a specific seat on a specific night. And, while money was not the primary goal, TKTS enabled many sagging shows to survive slow weeks or extend their runs; more than 20 percent of *A Chorus Line's* audience over its fifteen-year run came from TKTS [Stevens 236–37].

Sporadic attempts were made to reverse the trend of rising ticket costs. In 1971, under the banner of "Limited Gross"; in 1984, with the label of "Middle Broadway"; and in 1990, this time called "Broadway Alliance"; essentially similar projects were announced: everyone involved, from theatre owners through artists through backstage unions, would take a cut in income to allow modest productions of worthy dramas at lower ticket prices. Unfortunately almost every play produced through these programs flopped (one exception: *Love! Valour! Compassion!* in 1995), even with the lower prices.

One reason was that theatre owners offered only their least desirable houses for the experiments. Tradition, experience, and superstition had given some outlying Broadway theatres a reputation for bad luck, and the prediction became self-fulfilling as only the least influential producers and weakest shows were forced to take them. Meanwhile, box offices consistently reported that the cheapest seats were the hardest to sell; evidently, once the lowest price reached a certain level, buyers felt that they might as well splurge and sit downstairs, especially if they could do so at half-price through TKTS.

In the 1970s, about the time that the not-for-profit theatre was beginning to explore the possibilities of corporate underwriting and sponsorship, Broadway producers also looked to the business world for financial aid. The process began modestly, with individual shows engaging in cooperative advertising and marketing campaigns with New York City restaurants, hotels, or department stores. A television commercial featuring snippets of Broadway hits was the cornerstone of the state tourism board's very successful "I Love NY" campaign in the late 1970s.

Soon, advertisements and program notes for some shows began to identify "the official airline" (or car-rental company, or credit card) of the productions as part of a sponsorship deal; and hit shows discovered that the licensing and sale of sweatshirts and other souvenirs could be a significant contribution to the bottom line. In the 1990s the fast-food chain Wendy's supported a promotional tie-in of the sort more traditionally done with hit movies with revival of *The King and I*, while tapes of a revival of *Grease*, along with ticket-order instructions, were placed in the New York fleet of Budget Rent-a-car.

Corporate sponsorship was recruited to underwrite some of Broadway's outreach programs, such as free performances for schools or hospitals. Panasonic and Perrier both supported "Broadway on Broadway," the annual free performance in Times Square of excerpts from new musicals, while Yahoo! sponsored "Kids' Night Out," designed to attract younger audiences. In the 1990s resurrection of Forty-second Street, the Walt Disney Company's refurbishment of one theatre was tied to the opening of a Disney retail store next door, while the Ford Motor Company provided major financing for the renovation of another theatre, to be called The Ford Center for the Performing Arts.

It was inevitable that higher costs, a shrinking audience core, and uncertainty about how to attract new theatregoers would lead to timidity and a crisis of creative imagination on the part of Broadway producers. When even previously successful writers and performers couldn't be sure of long runs, and when even a respectable run didn't necessarily mean financial success, the search was on for the elusive "sure thing."

Increasingly wary about untried new plays and musicals, producers turned to seemingly pre-tested merchandise. There had always been a certain amount of traffic between the Broadway and London theatres, with one city's biggest hits likely to be produced in the other a year or two later. But in the late 1950s Broadway producers began hedging their bets even more by importing an entire London production — cast, director, sets, and all. In 1961–1962 and again the next season, more than half the Broadway successes were London or Continental productions, leading to complaints that New York was becoming just a stop on the post-West End touring circuit.

Anything that looked like a trend was pounced upon. When the APA-Phoenix company's Broadway seasons in the late 1960s were modestly successful, producers took this as evidence of an audience interest in older plays and began a rash of revivals. A pastiche recreation of the 1920s musical *No, No, Nanette* in 1971 signaled a supposed nostalgia craze and led to rewritings and restagings of old musicals like *Irene* (1919/1973). The multiplying costs of new musicals led to revivals of more recent vintage — *Gypsy* (1974), *My Fair Lady* (1976), *Hair* (1977), etc. — and to musicalizations of hit movies — *Promises, Promises* (1968), *Zorba* (1969), *Applause* (1970), *Sugar* (1971), etc. — in the not-always-realized hope that a pre-tested product was a safe gamble.

As Broadway's traditional audience began to contract or prove hard to woo, producers began for the first time to look beyond it. In 1967 David Merrick revived a sagging box office for the four-year-old *Hello,*

Dolly! by putting in an all-black cast led by Pearl Bailey, and the following decades saw several all-black musicals, both originals and revivals, some of which—notably *The Wiz* (1975), *Ain't Misbehavin'* (1978), *Dreamgirls* (1981), and *Bring in da Noise, Bring in da Funk* (1996)—were successes, though still to predominantly white audiences. Similarly, the success of *Hair* led to a string of rock musicals, most of which failed to lure a new young audience to Broadway; the striking exception was *Grease* (1972), which lasted out the decade playing to school groups and tourists.

☆

The convergence of two historical forces—the end of an artistic Golden Age and the new timidity of producers—was particularly felt in a severe decline in the number of new American plays produced on Broadway. The 1966–67 season included only nineteen American plays, of which barely a half-dozen were by new writers; within a decade those numbers would seem high. And here, at last, the coincident appearance of alternative theatrical venues in New York and around the country becomes significant. It was just as Broadway was beginning to feel unable to discover and develop new writers that other theatres were welcoming them, and it was inevitable that Broadway producers would look to writers who had attracted some attention elsewhere for possible commercial production.

The process began slowly and unpromisingly. As noted in Chapter Two, Off-Broadway didn't really start nourishing new playwrights until around 1960; and few of the first generation of Off-Broadway dramatists had the opportunity to develop their skills and visions before being wooed by Broadway producers, who also tended to underestimate the perceptual and philosophical generation gap between Broadway and Off-Broadway audiences. As a result, most Off-Broadway writers of the 1960s flopped in their first Broadway appearances, and only one was able to make the transfer successfully.

Edward Albee, after several commercially successful Off-Broadway one-act plays, was brought to Broadway by the same producers in 1962, with a premiere as impressive as those of Williams and Miller almost two decades earlier. *Who's Afraid of Virginia Woolf?* quickly earned a place on the highest levels of American drama with its merciless exploration of the pains of existence and the passionate defenses that we erect against them, presented through the dissection of a seemingly unsalvageable marriage.

But even Albee had difficulty sustaining his early promise; the passion and poetry of *Virginia Woolf* and, to a lesser extent, *A Delicate Balance* (1966), gave way to a cold intellectuality that may have been truer to Albee's mature vision but that was far less dramatically satisfying or commercially viable. Much of his work in the following decades was marked by unrealized ambition—the confused allegory of *Tiny Alice* (1964), in which murky intellectual puzzles are meant to represent the demands of religious faith, and the insufficiently evocative allegory of *The Lady from Dubuque* (1980), about a mysterious stranger who is some kind of angel of death—or by lifelessness—the cold, mannered picture of empty relationships in *All Over* (1971). Still, Albee was clearly a committed and talented writer; and he became, almost by default, Broadway's premier serious playwright until a pattern of critical and audience rejection led him to withdraw from the commercial theatre. (Albee returned to prominence in 1993 with *Three Tall Women*, an evocatively poetic exploration of the stages in a woman's life. It was, not incidentally, produced Off-Broadway.)

Broadway did produce one important home-grown talent in the 1960s, not an ambitiously serious dramatist from Off-Broadway or the regional theatres, but a former television gagwriter with a Midas touch. Neil Simon is—in purely financial terms—the most successful playwright in the history of the world, with (among other records) more Broadway performances of his plays in the 1960s alone than Williams, Miller, Albee, Inge, Pinter, Osborne, and Rodgers put together. Simon's first Broadway comedy was produced in 1961, and he averaged close to a play a year for the next three decades, which meant that there was rarely a season without two, and sometimes four, of his plays running simultaneously.

For the first twenty years of his career, Simon's plays were strictly formulaic, highly-crafted laugh machines. Typically, he would place two contrasting stereotypes together and let them bounce off each other; conflicts would escalate farcically, running gags would punctuate events at frequent intervals, and carefully-constructed jokes would come from every character. Rarely did the plays illuminate human psychology or behavior—the recognition in *The Odd Couple* (1965) that two divorced men rooming together would drive each other crazy just as they had their wives, or the insight in *The Sunshine Boys* (1972) that a business partnership is a kind of marriage—or offer characters who were more than mouthpieces for punchlines, but laughing audiences rarely noticed such limits.

Interestingly, after two decades of polished but mechanical comedies Simon's work did develop a new depth and warmth, as he explored a kind of William Inge world of little people finding ways to survive life's little trials through humor, in such comedy-dramas as *Brighton Beach Memoirs* (1983) and *Lost in Yonkers* (1991). Still, even in the 1960s it was undeniable that, whatever one thought about the intrinsic merit of what he did, he did it better than anyone else. As the essentially unsympathetic Stanley Kauffmann conceded, "Simon exemplifies Broadway at its current top level of operation. If there is going to be a commercial theater — and there certainly *is* going to be one of some kind — it might as well be adroitly practiced" [187].

☆

Meanwhile, Broadway producers continued to look to the newer theatrical venues for potential hits. Two of the biggest Broadway successes of 1968, *Hair* and *The Great White Hope*, had similar histories: Broadway producers saw them staged at noncommercial theatres — the New York Shakespeare Festival and the Arena Stage in Washington, respectively — and bought the rights to present them on Broadway. New York City's commercial theatre center had finally found a source for the new material it could not take the risk of developing on its own, and the relationship between Broadway and the rest of the country changed completely.

Broadway was no longer the only source of drama and musicals in America; no longer the place where plays began, to tour or be revived elsewhere only after New York had seen them. Within a very few years it would become a net buyer rather than seller, a showplace for work that began life elsewhere; and a list of the most significant Broadway playwrights from the 1970s through the 1990s would repeat names introduced in earlier chapters: Rabe, Wilson, Mamet, Shepard, Wasserstein, Kushner, et al.

Hungry for product and not content with waiting passively for an interesting new show to appear in some not-for-profit theatre, Broadway entrepreneurs began co-producing the original stagings, sometimes simply by renting the theatre and its subscription list, sometimes through the guise of grants for new play development, grants which coincidentally were spent on the new script the Broadway producer happened to bring to the theatre's attention at the same time. Sometimes the not-for-profits came to the commercial producers with a script they wanted to stage but couldn't afford; by selling an option for a potential

A Chorus Line

transfer in advance they could serve their own artistic visions. By 1974 theatre-owner and producer James M. Nederlander could say, "The regional theatres have become the tryout ground for Broadway. In other words you get a play and you try it out with [a not-for-profit theatre] and, if it's good, it moves to Broadway" [qtd in Langley *Producers* 301–2]. Two decades later, producer David Richenthal was confident that

> The not-for-profits are more than comfortable doing this, because it becomes one way they get new plays. They come to commercial producers in New York who have optioned a new play, and they get to feed their subscribers with the new play, while the producer can see the play on its feet and get an audience reaction. So it works for everybody. [Interview]

Occasionally a not-for-profit theatre took the commercial risks of a transfer itself, as the New York Shakespeare Festival did with *A Chorus Line* and others. (Typically, Joe Papp was able to hedge his bets by finding his own backers; longtime Festival supporter LuEsther Mertz donated the costs of moving several shows to Broadway.) Increasingly, as commercial producers became more and more cautious, the road to Broadway became a two-step process, a regional theatre success being revived by a not-for-profit Off-Broadway company or staged Off-Broadway by a commercial producer in a low-cost test of the New York waters before moving to Broadway. And increasingly, as costs and risks mounted, many new plays ended their journey before the final step. Even with all the pre-testing, fewer and fewer non-musicals appeared on Broadway, a commercial or not-for-profit Off-Broadway production being their only exposure in New York.

Some not-for-profit theatres struggled with the ethics of these new

Photo: Martha Swope

A Chorus Line

relationships, while others embraced and exploited them, using Broadway at least as much as it used them. Whatever misgivings there may have been were soon resolved by economic forces; as foundation funding shrank or shifted in the 1980s, the possibility of commercial transfers had to be factored into any not-for-profit theatre's finances, and the new mutual-exploitation relationship became the norm. From 1970 on, every Broadway season featured several transfers from regional theatres; and by the 1980s such borrowings, along with transfers from Off- and Off Off-Broadway and imports from London, made up the bulk of Broadway's offerings and almost all of its successes. In 1972 the Tony-winning Best Musical, *Two Gentlemen of Verona*, and the Best Play, *Sticks and Bones*, were both New York Shakespeare Festival productions; and, indeed, virtually all of the Tony and Pulitzer Prize-winning plays from 1969 on were first produced somewhere other than Broadway.

☆

Eventually this would be true even of that most purely home-grown Broadway product, the musical. First, though, some way had to be found out of the artistic cul-de-sac the integrated musical had become. One solution was to move backwards. Both Jerry Herman — *Hello, Dolly!* (1964), *Mame* (1966), *La Cage aux Folles* (1983), etc. — and the team of John Kander and Fred Ebb — *Cabaret* (1966), *Chicago* (1975), etc. — created polished and thoroughly satisfying musical entertainments that eschewed the psychological and dramatic complexities of the Rodgers and Hammerstein models and, surface details aside (*La Cage* was about a homosexual couple), might have been written in the 1930s or even the 1920s.

The other direction, exploring new shapes for the Rodgers and Hammerstein musical to evolve into, was the domain of Stephen Sondheim, who had been a protege of Oscar Hammerstein and who began at the top, collaborating with Leonard Bernstein on *West Side Story*, and then spent the next three decades experimenting and stretching the musical form. As a lyricist, Sondheim's specialty was the kind of song whose intricate rhymes and surprising imagery forced you to listen carefully; as a composer, he was willing to look beyond traditional harmonic and stanzaic structures.

Company (1970) was a coolly ironic view of big city life in which most of the songs commented on the action from outside rather than growing out of the dialogue; *Follies* (1971), a study in memory and fantasy in which past, present, and what-if appeared on stage simultaneously; *A Little Night Music* (1973), an attempt to capture the atmosphere and waltz tempo of operetta without using any of its conventions; *Pacific Overtures* (1976), a virtual opera depicting the nineteenth-century opening of Japan through Japanese eyes and Japanese stage conventions; *Sweeney Todd* (1979), a Grand Guignol opera; *Sunday in the Park With George* (1984), a multi-leveled exploration of the artistic temperament; and so on.

Just as Edward Albee was Broadway's chief serious dramatist of the 1960s and 1970s more or less by default, Sondheim was embraced, as he well deserved to be, partly because he was just about its only ambitious creator of musicals. This was true in spite of the fact that, like Albee, Sondheim was not for all tastes. A cold intellectuality colored much of his work, as it did Albee's, and repeatedly disappointed theatregoers looking to the musical for lush melodies and romantic stories. (It is not irrelevant that in his entire career Sondheim had only one hit song, the deliberately commercial "Send in the Clowns" from *A Little Night Music*.) Almost all of Sondheim's musicals won awards, critical praise, and a passionate cult following, and almost all of them lost money. It is, in fact, a tribute to crass commercial Broadway that his musicals continued to be produced by backers who recognized that quality, and not just the profit motive, had to be supported.

Meanwhile, almost unnoticed at first, two other things were happening to the Broadway musical. As early as *West Side Story* the generating and unifying force was not so much the book or the songs as the direction and choreography of Jerome Robbins; the central image of that show was the nervous energy of young people expressed in dance. When Tom O'Horgan threw out the plot of *Hair* and let the rock music and the physical appearance and antics of the cast carry the Broadway version, he created a musical whose medium was its message. Although *Grease* had a thin storyline, its real purpose was to recreate, through gentle and imaginative parody, the spirit of a mythic era of rock-and-roll innocence. Choreographer Bob Fosse gave all his musicals a signature jazzy angularity that was remembered long after their plots or even music; as composer-lyricist Stephen Schwartz complained, "People are much more likely to know that Bob Fosse directed *Pippin* than that I wrote it" [qtd in Sponberg 132]. In 1975 director-choreographer Michael Bennett turned the experiences of some Broadway dancers into a dramatic metaphor and created the decade's finest musical. *A Chorus Line* had virtually no plot — several dancers try out for a Broadway show and some are hired — but the love of dance, the excitement of theatre, and the tension of the moment were what the show was about.

Labeled variously the Concept Musical or the Theme Musical, this new form was built around a vision, as often directorial as authorial, rather than a mechanical outline or even a plot. In its most extreme form the new musical was almost indistinguishable from a concert: *Bubbling Brown Sugar* (1976) was an attempt to recreate the flavor of Harlem in the 1920s through a string of musical numbers, while *Ain't Misbehavin'* (1978) was essentially a recital of Fats Waller songs, and *Dancin'* (1978) was a program of unrelated dance numbers choreographed by Bob Fosse.

But even more traditionally structured musicals, like Sondheim's, could be driven as much by their look, their sound or their attitude as by plot and character. *Company*, for example, began life as a collection of one-act plays by George Furth, designed to showcase a versatile actress. Director Harold Prince saw the possibilities for a musical about modern urban marriages in various states of health; to provide continuity, he suggested introducing a bachelor to visit each couple in turn. The final product used about a tenth of Furth's original script in a musical, set against Boris Aronson's stark and modernistic designs, about the bachelor's own emotional crisis. According to Sondheim,

> Up until *Company* most musicals, if not all musicals, had plots. In fact, up until *Company*, I thought that musicals had to have very strong plots. One of the things that fascinated me about the chal-

Photo: Martha Swope

Larry Kert and cast in *Company*

lenge of the show was to see if a musical could be done without one . . . It dealt with the increasing difficulty of making one-to-one relationships in an increasingly dehumanized society. And one of the reasons we had it take place in front of chrome and glass and steel was that it took place in an urban society. [qtd in Zadan, 131–140]

It is ironic that the musical, the purest representative of the traditional and commercial American theatre, turned out to be the genre most affected by the alternative theatre's experiments with de-emphasizing the text in the late 1960s.

And at the same time something else was happening, a British invasion. One of the most striking things about the Broadway musical had always been how very much a Broadway product it was. Though musicals in the Broadway style were written elsewhere in the world, few were up to the Broadway standard or had the special Broadway magic; and the occasional exceptions — e.g., Anthony Newley's *Stop the World — I Want to Get Off* and Lionel Bart's *Oliver*, both from London in 1962 — were novelties more than threats to the Broadway hegemony.

And then came Andrew Lloyd Webber. Working first with lyricist Tim Rice and later with other collaborators, the British composer soon

Hal Prince and Stephen Sondheim

came to dominate the musical as no one since Rodgers and Hammerstein had. Webber and Rice's first Broadway hit was *Jesus Christ Superstar* (1971; dates in this section are all of the Broadway productions). An unscripted cycle of pop and rock songs loosely following the gospel story, it had begun life as a record album, as did their next musical, *Evita* (1979).

Although some later Lloyd Webber musicals would include dialogue and conventional plot structures, the conception of a musical as a cycle of songs held together by little more than their juxtaposition and clever staging put him right in the center of the evolution of the concept musical. *Superstar* was directed on Broadway by Tom O'Horgan, in one of the last flourishes of his daringly unorthodox style, with singers rising out of the floor or descending from the rafters; and *Evita* by Harold Prince in his most spectacularly visual mode, with the stage dominated by a giant screen on which film or onstage action was projected.

Lloyd Webber's hits thus not only destroyed the myth that only New Yorkers could really write Broadway musicals, but also contributed to a rapidly snowballing inclination by producers and directors to dress musicals in elaborate staging effects, and a resulting audience expectation of getting a lot of visual spectacle for their increasingly expensive

Broadway ticket. In Lloyd Webber's *Cats* (1982), directed by Trevor Nunn, a part of the stage rose to carry one of the singers to cat heaven; for *The Phantom of the Opera* (1988), directed by Prince, the back wall of the theatre had to be knocked out, and the building extended several inches, to make room for the stage machinery that created the Phantom's catacombs and the famous falling chandelier. *Miss Saigon* (1990, by Alain Boublil and Claude-Michel Schonberg; from Paris by way of London) featured the effect of an onstage helicopter; Lloyd Webber's *Sunset Boulevard* (1994) required an elaborate and solid set to rise in the air so another stage could appear under it; the Broadway staging of the Disney cartoon *Beauty and the Beast* (1994) featured real-life duplications of the film's magical effects.

It is little wonder that pre-opening expenses rose well above the cost of a modest movie and that ticket prices saw their biggest leaps upward during this period. And it is little wonder that the audience's relationship to the theatre changed in the process. With fewer shows being offered on Broadway, and most of those the highly-touted, direct-from-London, difficult-to-get-seats-to spectaculars, casual theatregoing was definitively a thing of the past.

There were still home-made musicals, of course, but they were no longer Broadway creations. It is a theatrical truism that musicals aren't

British Invasion

written, but rewritten. The old Broadway system, with a circuit of out-of-town tryouts and previews, allowed a musical's creators to polish or completely reconceive their show before it officially opened, but the new Broadway could not afford such luxury. Group sessions and improvisations of the sort Michael Bennett used to create *A Chorus Line* were not appropriate for every project, though several big musicals — *The Best Little Whorehouse in Texas* (1977), *Pump Boys and Dinettes* (1982), *Sunday in the Park With George* (1984), etc. — began life in very modest Off Off-Broadway showcases. By the 1970s Broadway musicals were being born (or planted for tryouts) in some of the same regional repertory theatres that were providing New York with its dramas and comedies: *Annie* (1977), from the Goodspeed Opera House; *Tommy* (1993), from the La Jolla Playhouse; *Beauty and the Beast* (1994), from Houston's Theatre Under the Stars, etc.

In 1989 an attempt was made to create a development space for new musicals on a college campus in Purchase, New York — a place where Broadway professionals could have the same luxury of works-in-progress readings and workshop stagings that playwrights were getting around the country. Unfortunately New York critics ignored the request that they stay away, and word that one of the first workshops, of Kander and Ebb's *Kiss of the Spider Woman*, was a disappointment destroyed the illusion of safe experiment and discouraged others from participating. (*Kiss* eventually made it to Broadway in revised form, and was a hit.)

Meanwhile, an unanticipated result of Broadway's reduced output and its concentration on elaborate productions that required large theatres was a lack of product for "the road," the commercial houses around the country that traditionally booked touring companies of last year's Broadway hits. In 1986 thirty-eight commercial and not-for-profit theatres specializing in musicals formed the National Alliance for Musical Theatre, to cooperate in supporting the creation of new musicals outside New York; in the next decade Alliance theatres, eventually numbering eighty-three, staged over two hundred original musicals, many of which toured to other member theatres, bypassing Broadway completely.

☆

Higher costs, more elaborate productions, shrinking or shifting audiences, a growing pattern of borrowing rather than creating new plays — the whole definition of Broadway producing was undergoing a change. In the 1950s, when plays cost $60,000 to mount, a producer could search out "angels" with as little as one thousand dollars to invest, but production budgets in the millions, for plays as well as musicals, made finding a sufficient number of small investors difficult; in 1972 Harold Prince was reduced to advertising for angels in *The Wall Street Journal.*

Eventually, the small investor became virtually obsolete. By the 1980s many Broadway shows were backed primarily by corporations, frequently foreign and frequently those in related entertainment fields — movie studios, TV networks — with a vested interest in maintaining a supply of new product. (There was precedent for this: in 1956 CBS put up the entire $350,000 cost of *My Fair Lady* to obtain the recording rights.) The Dutch conglomerate Polygram, for example, invested in musicals not primarily in hope of Broadway profits, but as a way of getting recording and film rights, while Japanese television networks could invest about what they would have had to pay for broadcast rights, and get the chance of theatrical profits as a bonus. The toy store F.A.O. Schwarz, featured prominently as a setting of the 1996 musical *Big*, invested in what amounted to a nightly advertisement for the store.

Vested interest also involved the theatre owners in production to an unprecedented degree. Broadway landlords of the past had occasionally supported shows that played their theatres, sometimes through unpublicized rent concessions. But a change in the complex financial arrangement between producers and landlords led unexpectedly to greater involvement. Traditionally, theatre rental had been a package deal: in return for a specified percentage of weekly ticket sales (usually somewhere between 25 and 30 percent), the producer got not only the use of the building, but box office staff, ushers, cleaning, etc. If the landlord's share fell below a specified amount and didn't cover his expenses, he could and usually did evict the show; a theatre owner was likely to be better off with an empty house (with its lower overheads) than with a money-losing or even marginal show.

In 1975, to attract *A Chorus Line* to one of their theatres, the Shubert Organization offered a new deal: a much lower percentage (10 percent) plus a flat fee for services.

> It became the benchmark for the arrangements theatre owners made with producers. It was a change of philosophy. All of that shared bookkeeping disappeared. The show paid its costs and the theatre paid its cost and were subsequently reimbursed for whatever those costs would be. [Bob Kamlot, *A Chorus Line* General Manager, qtd. in Stevens 154]

In theory the change was negligible, possibly even more advantageous to the producers of a hit show. What took a while to discover was an unexpected benefit for the landlords in the new arrangement: even with a weak show, their expenses would still be paid, so if a producer wanted to keep a show running at a loss, there was no reason to stop him. A front page *New York Times* story in 1993 explained how this new economics worked with a musical that had not yet turned a profit:

> The Nederlander Organization and the producer and investor Stewart Lane, who jointly own the Palace Theater, together have $1 million invested in "The Will Rogers Follies," and they are still some $400,000 short of recouping that investment; but for more than two years Mr. Lane and the Nederlanders have been collecting $20,000 to $30,000 a week from the producers for the use of the theater...And that doesn't count the nearly $100,000 it costs the producer to pay the salaries of the Nederlander employees who work in the theater. [Weber "Make" C16]

Now it was always in a landlord's interest to have his theatre occupied, and from the mid-1970s on, theatre owners became increasingly involved as investors and eventually as active producers, helping to create tenants for their properties. By the 1980s most Broadway theatres were owned or operated by three chains, Shubert, Nederlander, and Jujamcyn, and it was the rare play or musical that did not list one of those names among its investors or, indeed, as its primary producer.

Inevitably, landlords are not the same kind of producers that David Merrick and Kermit Bloomgarden were. Veteran producer Alexander H. Cohen compares his method of transferring a London hit to Broadway with a theatre owner's:

> The Shuberts do not originate projects. They look at projects. They go to London and say, "Oh, it's *Skylight* [by David Hare] — one set, three characters; that ought to do it. Let's put up the money." And they put up the money, and then the London producer, in this case the National Theatre, sends the show over, supervises it, and puts it on. [Interview]

In contrast, Cohen explains, when he saw Ronald Harwood's *Taking Sides* in London and arranged to produce it in New York, he had the author rewrite it; hired a new director and designer; recast the play, keeping only one member of the London cast; and in effect created a new production. (Both plays opened in the fall of 1996, to mixed but generally favorable reviews, and had equally short runs.)

"The Shuberts have never produced anything," says critic Michael Feingold. "They wait for people with enough capital to come in and say 'We want to put something in one of your theatres,' and their only function is to calculate whether the thing would maximize profits" [Interview]. To the extent that these criticisms are accurate, and theatre owners are more likely to be bookers than originating producers, their dominance contributed to Broadway's decline as a creative theatrical center and its evolution into a showplace for work originated elsewhere. In 1996 *The Times* concluded that "producing, the Broadway tradition of taking an original play or musical and shepherding it from the written page to the Broadway stage, has all but ceased to be a career" [Marks "Broadway" 1].

The Times article continues, "And in truth, many of the people listed as producers of Broadway shows are not producers at all. They are investors who have been granted producing credits as concessions to vanity" [34]. Some big-money individual investors remained active on Broadway, but now they got billing above the title, along with the landlords, the out-of-town theatres where the show had been tried out, the foreign corporations buying production or recording rights, and maybe even (in Alexander H. Cohen's words) "some poor bastard who produced the show and couldn't get the money without those twelve other guys." *The Times* cites one not-particularly-extreme example:

> Take the revival of 'The King and I.' ... When the original production opened in 1951, the only producers were Rodgers and Hammerstein themselves. The cost of the show was $360,000. The 1996 production ... costs $5.5 million. And the list of producers reads like the result of a Wall Street merger: 'Dodger Productions, the John F. Kennedy Center for the Performing Arts, James M. Nederlander, Perseus Productions with John Frost and the Adelaide Festival Center, in association with the Rodgers and Hammerstein Organization ....' [Marks "Broadway" 34]

☆

While all this was going on, some indicators suggested a rebirth of Broadway. After dipping in the early 1970s, gross profits rose astronomically, breaking through the $100 million mark in 1977 and reaching $406 million by 1995. Of course, most of that was the result of higher ticket prices, but some was a reflection of the fact that caution and pretesting were beginning to have an effect, and those fewer shows that were being produced on Broadway — by the mid-1980s seasonal totals hovered around thirty — were running longer. Broadway sold eleven million tickets in 1980–81, a record it never matched again, though it was still selling over nine million a year in the mid-1990s (almost twice as much, producers delighted in pointing out, as the combined attendance of all the games of all New York's professional sports teams put together). There might be fewer habitual theatregoers and more once-a-year and special-event ticket buyers in the mix, but there were clearly sufficient numbers of the second group to keep the commercial theatre viable.

And the kind of near-fantasy story that was part of the Broadway myth could still be acted out, though it was noteworthy enough for the *Wall Street Journal* to make a front page story out of it. In 1994 two first-time producers paid $4000 for the commercial rights to an Off Off-Broadway workshop production, Jonathan Larson's musical *Rent*. Eighteen months, several further workshops, additional partners, about $3 million in further investments, and the winning of the Pulitzer Prize later, the musical opened on Broadway and quickly won several Tonys.

> "Rent," Broadway's biggest artistic sensation in years, is also turning out to be a gold-plated business phenomenon . . . . If the theater stays 90% full, it will be pulling in annual revenue of close to $23.4 million . . . . Plans for a minimum of two touring companies now in the works could pull in another $55 million . . . . Hollywood studios are clamoring for the movie rights . . . . Even Bloomingdale's is minting "Rent" money [with clothes inspired by the show]. [Trachtenberg A1]

There was never any real doubt that Broadway would survive; that money, careers and stars could be made; and that audiences could be entertained. But it no longer bore very much resemblance to the Broadway of 1920 or even 1950.

Still, for the half-century that Broadway *was* the American theatre it carried its responsibility well, producing a substantial body of excellent work and several generations of first-class artists. "In a curious way, the commercial theater was less preoccupied with money than its not-for-profit successors," argues Howard Kissel, "if for no other reason than that there always seemed to be plenty of it around."

> The profits of a *Hello, Dolly!* could subsidize the losses of an *Arturo Ui*. When money was not so problematic, other values could take precedence . . . . Financial considerations aside, have the regional or cutting edge companies produced more vibrant, more substantial, more enduring works in the last thirty years than the commercial theater did, say, between 1933 and 1963? I do not think so. [508–510]

And Gregory Mosher, whose career has been in the not-for-profit the-atre, acknowledges Broadway's accomplishments even in its later years:

> The fact is that the Broadway game is much tougher, and also the standards are much higher. Let's be honest: Michael Bennett's stan-dards, Harold Prince's standards, Mike Nichols' standards — in gen-eral, the standards of the Broadway theatre are higher than those of the not-for-profit movement. There, shoot me; I've said it. The great works of the American theatre in the last 25 years, the crown-ing achievements, have often come out of the commercial the-atre. [Interview]

Chapter One ended with a census of Broadway's offerings in Janu-ary 1950. In the parallel week of 1995 there were nineteen shows on Broadway: fifteen musicals, one drama, two solo shows, and a juggling act (the absence of any comedies and at least one or two more dramas was unusual but not unprecedented). But seven of the musicals and the one play were British imports, while an eighth musical came from Canada, and most were produced by the original foreign producers who were, in effect, treating New York as a road company. The other musi-cals had all started life elsewhere in America, in theatres ranging from California to Off-Broadway, while two of the novelties had previously toured. That left one, comedian Jackie Mason's solo show (itself essen-tially a nightclub act), that was a traditional made-for-Broadway pro-duction.

For the tourist or casual theatregoer, what was offered — *Carousel, Cats, The Phantom of the Opera, Miss Saigon, Show Boat, Kiss of the Spider Woman,* and the rest — was a bounty with all the glamour and profes-sionalism the label "Broadway" suggested. Broadway, and the commer-cial arena in general, would continue to have a role in the American theatre, but it was no longer primarily as a creative force. It had evolved instead into a showcase, a central meeting place where Broadway exper-tise could contribute to the proud display of the best work of theatre artists from around America and the world.

Michael Crawford, Sarah Brightman in
The Phantom of the Opera

6

MILLENNIUM APPROACHES

The same January 1995 week cited at the end of the preceding chapter saw at least four times as many shows Off- and Off Off-Broadway as on. Meanwhile, Chicago audiences had a choice of close to fifty shows, ranging from the national company of the Broadway musical *Les Miserables* to an Off-Loop theatre's Young Playwrights Festival. Los Angeles theatres offered more than seventy-five productions, Washington fifteen. There was theatre in Phoenix, Berkeley, Sarasota, and Santa Monica; Hartford, Washington, Norfolk, and Indianapolis; Costa Mesa, Vero Beach, Highland Park, and Salt Lake City; Madison, Milwaukee, Minneapolis, and Manalapan.

There was Shakespeare in Portland, Boston, and Atlanta; Shaw in Washington and Malvern; Simon in Memphis and Austin, *The Mousetrap* in Worcester and Sanibel; *Peter Pan* in Memphis and Seattle. There was Molière in Costa Mesa, Stoppard in San Francisco, Sheridan in Washington, Sophocles in Cambridge, and Fugard in Chicago. You could see Mamet's *The Woods* in Philadelphia and Sondheim's *Into the Woods* in Palo Alto. There were world premieres in Chicago, Baltimore, Springfield, Minneapolis, Tacoma, Milwaukee, Dallas, Portland, Pittsburgh, and New York.

And that was just the first week in January, when many theatres were dark. In January as a whole, you could see *Hamlet* in Montgomery, San Diego, and Atlanta; and *I Hate Hamlet* in Rochester. Other plays by Shakespeare were offered in Palo Alto, Denver, New Haven, Chicago, Minneapolis, San Diego, Sarasota, Atlanta, Dallas, Fort Worth, and Washington. You could see *Death of a Salesman* in Troy and *Long Day's Journey into Night* in Washington. Plays by August Wilson were performed in Cleveland, Jackson, and Chicago; plays by Lanford Wilson in San Jose and Sarasota. And there were further new American plays in Douglas, Los Angeles, Costa Mesa, Wilmington, Washington, Marietta, Honolulu, Lowell, Detroit, Minneapolis, St. Louis, and Kansas City.

There were professional theatres in San Francisco, Los Angeles,

Sausalito, Berkeley, Sunnyvale, Concord, Santa Monica, Blue Lake, San Juan Bautista, Nevada City, Venice, La Jolla, Mill Valley, San Diego, Santa Monica, Sacramento, San Jose, Santa Cruz, Costa Mesa, Palo Alto, and Salinas, California. There were professional theatres in Cambridge, Stockbridge, Boston, Lowell, Newton, Lenox, Springfield, Williamstown, and Worcester, Massachusetts. There were professional theatres in Philadelphia, Bloomsburg, Cheltenham, Pittsburgh, Lancaster, Allentown, and Bethlehem, Pennsylvania. There were eight theatre companies in Seattle, nine in Atlanta, twenty-two in Washington and nine in Minneapolis/St. Paul. There were theatres in Tulsa and Guthrie, Oklahoma; Tucson, Tempe, and Phoenix, Arizona; Portland and Ashland, Oregon; Knoxville, Crossville, Memphis, Johnson City, and Nashville, Tennessee.

☆

There were some problems. In the early 1990s the National Endowment for the Arts survived another of the regularly-scheduled attempts by politicians to destroy it, but a more broadly-based political mood of austerity haunted it through the decade. This not only meant a reduction in the number and size of grants, but forced a change in the philosophy of giving. Gigi Bolt, Director of the Theatre and Musical Theatre division of the NEA, points out that the NEA's total 1995–1996 allocation, $99.5 million, was lower than its budgets of the early 1970s.

> The amount is low enough that it was clear that we would not be able to continue giving meaningful ongoing operating support. Our grants are now project-based as opposed to seasonal; it is possible that an organization will be supported one year and not the next year. So that's why we're trying to help in a more ongoing way through other avenues. We will now be focussing [a part of] our very limited funds on ... leadership initiatives, through the agency's power to convene organizations and experts in the field to help solve some of the problems that we're facing. [Interview]

State arts council budgets showed similar or even more drastic declines; New York's support of theatre dropped from $4.7 million in 1990 to $2 million in 1996. Most of the not-for-profit arts community was forced to accept the fact that government money could not be relied on as a significant element in their operational budgets — Gregory Boyd of the Alley says, "We get some money from the NEA but we've basically written that off" [Interview] — and *The New York Times* reported that "many small-theater operators have applied for government money and been turned down. Now they don't even bother" [D. Smith]. In 1997 Joy

Zinoman of Washington's Studio Theatre could say that the complications of public funding weren't worth the hassle:

> I don't like Government money.... No matter how much they talk about not interfering and not having any strings attached, you are dealing with public money and the people who administer it have to be responsive to the people. [qtd in Molotsky]

Meanwhile, the large national foundations that had helped create the not-for-profit regional theatre — Ford, Rockefeller, et al. — had all but withdrawn from arts funding.

Some theatres could not survive the reduction in subsidy and had to close down, and even some of the strongest faced serious retrenchments. Hardly any theatres could afford full-time companies any more, so both the growth opportunities for actors and the special relationship that could develop between a company and an audience were lost. In some theatres economizing took the form of reduced artistic ambitions (less Shakespeare, more three-character-one-set plays); as Robert Falls of Chicago's Goodman Theatre explains, "It's an impossibility for me to do, say, three epic works back to back, no matter how passionate I am about them, because there is simply not going to be enough money to produce them" [Interview]. The difference could be seen in numbers: at Washington's Arena Stage, the repertoire of the 1990–91 season provided 120 acting roles; in 1996–97 the same number of plays had a total cast of 70.

In others, whole programs had to be dropped. The Long Wharf Theatre painfully curtailed its new play development programs in 1990; even though Artistic Director Arvin Brown felt that "new play development is not a frivolity; it's central to what I want to see this theatre do," he was forced to give his main stage a higher priority:

> At Long Wharf we cannot mount a full season of four and five character plays. It's too limiting in terms of the repertoire; if we start finding ourselves absolutely unable to mount productions from the major periods of dramatic literature, we're going to suffer a great deal and we're going to feel it from our audience. [Interview]

In 1992 the Theatre Communication Group's annual survey of member theatres showed that the output of workshops and new play development programs had dropped 60 percent in three years, the amount of touring 40 percent [Janowitz, "Theatre Facts 92" 5]; three years later TCG reported that "the most troubling performance statistics" were further annual double-digit drops in new play readings and workshops [Samuels "Facts" 6].

Meanwhile, other problems were complicating the economic picture. From the start, regional theatres had depended on subscription buyers as the core of their audience, and had recruited that core according to principles laid down by Danny Newman: essentially, the concentration of marketing on that segment of the population (white, educated, middle-aged, affluent) that was most likely to subscribe. But, increasingly from the late 1980s on, there was evidence that the potential subscription base had been exhausted. In some cities that demographic group was shrinking; in others it was becoming less reflective of the population at large, so that theatres appealing only to that core would be marginalizing themselves out of touch with the culture.

This meant either an absolute necessity or at least an aesthetic and moral desirability of reaching out to audiences that had been comfortably ignored in palmier days. Analyzing TCG's annual survey in 1990, Barbara Janowitz warned, "The need to attract a younger, more culturally diverse and societally representative audience ... may result in alternatives to traditional subscription sales which may, in turn, prove more financially burdensome" ["Theatre Facts 89" 35]. A year later, the survey showed that "the practice of ignoring the 'fickle single-ticket buyer' in favor of the 'loyal subscriber' became outdated, as theatres placed an increasing emphasis on marketing to non-subscribers" [Janowitz, "Theatre Facts 90" 34].

The problem was that Danny Newman was right. It was very difficult and very expensive to bring new people into the theatre; a study by the President's Committee on the Arts and Humanities reported that "younger Americans are unlikely ever to attend live performances of musical and dramatic theater" [Baldinger 5]. Managements around the country found themselves spending a lot more on advertising and inventing new ways to make their product seem attractive to a class of consumer they had never really appealed to before. In New York the Roundabout Theatre scheduled singles' nights, gay and lesbian nights, and "early to bed" nights with earlier performances. In Cambridge, ART offered a matinee series for young mothers, with child care provided at the theatre. In San Diego the Old Globe advertised its play about Jackie Robinson at the Padres games. Theatres tried mini-subscriptions, student discounts, pay-what-you-can nights, local touring.

And even if the newcomer was enticed into the theatre, conversion from single-ticket buyer into repeat theatregoer wasn't guaranteed, as the New York Shakespeare Festival had learned in the 1970s:

> If someone called for A CHORUS LINE, they got on our mailing list and were told about the other shows we were doing, though ... if four phone calls came in, three were only interested in A CHORUS LINE and they had no interest in the NYSF or other productions. [Cliff Scott, NYSF ticket office, qtd in Stevens 111]

There were occasional exceptions to this rule. The Manhattan Theatre Club was able to convert single-ticket buyers to its Broadway transfer *Love! Valour! Compassion!* into contributors, as Executive Producer Barry Grove reports: "We made phone calls saying 'Did you like the show? Did you know it was produced by a nonprofit? Did you know we're tax-deductible? Would you consider making a contribution?' And we were getting contributions" [Interview].

This shift in audience composition also meant a much less predictable annual income, and therefore new difficulties in planning out a budget and an artistic season. And increased dependence on single-ticket buyers threatened to reverse one of the regional theatre's greatest accomplishments, the development of an adventurous audience open to a variety of theatrical experiences. Single-ticket buyers were impulse buyers, drawn to a specific play rather than to the idea of theatre, and that meant offering plays that they'd buy tickets to. Jon Jory of the Actors Theatre of Louisville:

> As we become more dependent on single tickets, we actually become more dependent upon audience attitudes, and what that is basically going to mean for a lot of theatres is that you're going to have to deal with audience tastes. So if you have to replace subscribers with single tickets, you're probably going to do more popular work. It limits your repertoire, but it's a fact of life. [Interview]

The need to search out new audiences had other artistic implications. The impulse (admirable at best, cynical and desperate at worst) to attract a multicultural audience with ethnic plays and performers was discussed earlier. But many theatres found that the quest for multiculturalism was difficult and full of pitfalls. In 1978 the Mark Taper Forum produced a play about Native Americans and marketed it heavily to that population. It was, according to Director of Audience Development Robert Schlosser, "a complete bust" because, as the theatre learned only later, many in the Native American community found the depiction of their rituals in a play offensive [Shirley 52]. American companies attempting Asian-oriented plays tended to devote their energies to usually-unsuccessful attempts at duplicating traditional forms and performance styles when, according to one scholar, "Asian American theaters generally produce relatively realistic, contemporary plays dealing with . . . the lives of Americans of Asian descent [and] show minimal interest in performance or production styles derived from Asia" [Sorgenfrei 49].

And even when theatres got it right, ethnic audiences were as difficult to keep as any other single-ticket buyers: as a result of a concerted effort by the Mark Taper Forum in 1992 to do Hispanic-oriented plays and market them to that community, "the percentage of Latinos among Taper ticket buyers (both subscription and single ticket) rose from 2% in 1991–92 to 20%. Most observers agree, however, that the Latino stats . . . dipped the following season" [Shirley 52]. At the Arena Stage, Artistic Director Douglas C. Wager acknowledged in 1997 that a quarter of the theatre's productions over the past several seasons "were chosen to be of interest to the black community" but that subscriptions were still down [qtd. in Weber "Birth"].

Two artistic directors who *were* generally successful at multiculturalism, Lloyd Richards of Yale and Bill Bushnell of the Los Angeles Theatre Center, make essentially the same point, that no one-shot or token ethnic productions can have any real effect. "There [must be] no sense of 'This is something special for you. Come once and see it, and you may or may not come back,'" warns Richards, and Bushnell adds, "Most people looked at it like projects — 'We're going to have our black project.' You need to understand that this is not a 'project.' This is a lifetime work" [Interviews].

In fact, the whole principle of multiculturalism began to come under re-examination in the 1990s. As the Taper's experience with Native Americans exemplified, well-meaning but ill-conceived "projects" did little to advance the cause of cross-cultural understanding, and some ethnic artists saw the whole adventure as little more than self-serving tokenism that did more harm than good:

> About a decade ago [the] Wallace [Funds] put all that money into the resident theatre movement to develop a multicultural and different audience because they felt that the traditional subscription base was getting old and dying off. . . . [A theatre] might get a million dollars to develop minority audiences. They would produce one black play for $150,000 and promote very heavily for another $100,000, and keep the $750,000 to do all the traditional things they'd always done. [King interview]

"All this did," adds King, "was try and move black writers and artists away from black theatres for short periods of time, and m extremely difficult for these black theatres to continue to produce and to build their own audiences."

In 1996 African-American playwright August Wilson addressed a conference of the Theatre Communications Group, rejecting all attempts by the mainstream theatre to offer lip service to multiculturalism. Supporting black plays in white theatres, he argued, only had the effect of denying support to black theatres. "Of the 66 LORT [i.e., largest regional] theatres, there is only one that can be considered black," he noted; and every grant a white theatre receives means one less for a black theatre.

> Black theatre doesn't share in the economics that would allow it to support its artists and supply them with meaningful avenues to develop their talent and broadcast and disseminate ideas crucial to its growth. The economics are reserved as privilege to the overwhelming abundance of institutions that preserve, promote and perpetuate white culture. [16]

Wilson's criticism was thus not merely economic, and he went on to attack one of the mainstream theatre's proudest accomplishments, the casting of actors without regard to race:

> Colorblind casting is an aberrant idea that has never had any validity.... To mount an all-black production of a *Death of a Salesman* or any other play conceived for white actors as an investigation of the human condition through the specifics of white culture is to deny us our own humanity... as black Americans. [72]

There are, of course, answers to some of King's and Wilson's charges. But the significant thing is that the charges were being made. Some of the artistic and social principles that the mainstream American theatre had taken for granted were beginning to be questioned; and as the millennium approached, Wilson's call to minority artists — "We cannot allow others to have authority over our cultural and spiritual products" [72] — would reverberate in ways yet to be discovered.

☆

Indeed, the last decade of the century saw challenges to a number of the premises on which the American theatre, particularly the regional not-for-profit theatre, had been built. Neither government subsidy nor national foundation support could be taken for granted, or even expected. Subscription audiences were shrinking, and the theatre's attempts to be socially responsible were backfiring. Even more basic assumptions and values would be questioned: the typical management structure of not-for-profit theatres, the advantages of standardization, the construction of seasons, the theatre's service to its artists, even the concept of subscription sales.

John Sullivan, Executive Director of the Theatre Communications Group, points out that the almost universal model, "which is that of an artistic director and a managing director, both reporting to a board of trustees," was the product of a time when everyone was playing on the same field:

> In its earlier years TCG played a central role in establishing models for a very new and young nonprofit theatre movement....I think that the other major force in that development was the NEA [and] the growth of a not-for-profit arts infrastructure to support the development of not-for-profit cultural institutions throughout the country. [Interview]

With the decline or collapse of the national funding infrastructure, theatres will have to look for support and definition locally. And that, Sullivan believes, is likely to lead individual theatres to find structures that fit their unique situations; and "part of our job [at TCG] is to provide our membership with as many options and new ideas as possible." Sullivan cites, for example, theatres led by designers or producers, or run as cooperatives: "each locale is a distinct ecology and the . . . theatre is going to be defined different ways in each ecology" [Interview]. Suzanne Sato of the AT&T Foundation agrees:

> We all thought there was a successful model . . . . But survivability is sort of tailor-made to each organization, and you have to determine, based on your mission, which growth model works the best for you. It's not that there's going to be a new Danny Newman [with an all-purpose solution]. [Interview]

The most vocal critic of the subscription system is Gregory Mosher, who operated under the standard model at the Goodman Theatre, but abandoned it for a membership structure (a token annual fee entitles members to priority booking and deep discounts for whichever plays in the season they choose) at Lincoln Center and then at the Circle in the Square. His primary objections are two: that subscription brings in the wrong audience, and that it commits the theatre to a stifling production schedule.

While the theory of subscription audiences is that they are making a commitment to a love of theatre and not to individual plays, Mosher argues that in practice every play in the season has some audience members who didn't particularly want that one.

> Show me the twenty thousand people who all want to see the new Fugard play, a Tennessee Williams revival, a Shaw — just name one of those seasons. . . . I can imagine an audience member who might really want to see the new Mamet play and hate the idea of seeing a revival of *Anything Goes*, and I can imagine an audience that would like to see *Anything Goes* and not the Mamet. Why should they have to see all of them? [Interview]

Howard Stein reports that the more eclectic a season is, the harder it is to please subscribers: "Bob Brustein never had a substantial [renewing] subscription audience at the Yale Rep, never. We had to get a new one every year, because people had too many events that were not entertainment for them" [Interview]. In his book on the Manhattan Theatre Club, John W. Pereira comments that "Subscription audiences are notorious for their reserve, and it is a sticking point with both artists and the management staff of subscription theatres" [240]; and quotes actress Frances Sternhagen — "The subscription audiences tend to seem reluctant to respond with much enthusiasm [but] after the subscribers' schedule is over . . . the [single ticket] audiences are much more enthusiastic" [372–3] — and playwright Donald Margulies:

> I don't want to bite the hand that feeds me, but subscribers in general tend to be very demanding . . . They grumble a great deal about the punctuality of the curtain, and the position of their seats, and the running time of a play, and the language in a play. [374]

In part, argues Mosher, that's because the system almost encourages an attitude of grumbling:

> We say to them, "Subscribe early. Renew early. You'll get better seats," as if that was the point of going to the theatre, to get better seats. . . . We lie to them in the subscription brochures. We tell them difficult and unpleasant plays are "provocative." We describe everything as "the laugh riot of two continents." [Interview]

And the problem that everyone acknowledges — "they're the same fifty-five-year-olds who have been coming to everything for the last thirty years" — is also built into the system, says Mosher, because "Common sense tells you you can attract a different audience when they don't have to shell out a check for a few hundred dollars for two subscriptions and commit to a series of dates."

August Wilson sees the subscription system as explicitly exclusionary:

> The subscription audience holds the seats of our theatres hostage to the mediocrity of its tastes .... While intentional or not, it serves to keep blacks out of the theatre .... It is an irony that the people who can most afford a full-price ticket get discounts for subscribing, while the single-ticket buyer who cannot afford a subscription is charged ... additional. [73]

Gregory Mosher's final objection to the standard subscription system is the rigid season schedule that accompanies it. Why should a theatre have to present six plays for five weeks each, when the artistic director has only three really interesting projects in mind? Why should directors and actors be locked into a limited rehearsal schedule when some plays require more time? Why should the best play in the season and the worst both have the same brief runs?

> Artists who have devoted their life savings and have worked hard to master their craft deserve circumstances where they can prepare a play properly. They deserve, when they've achieved something wonderful, not to have it cut off after two weeks because some less inspired production has to move into the theatre.

As the other quotations on these pages show, Mosher is not alone in seeing flaws in a structure that has been the backbone of the resident theatre movement since Margo Jones and Theatre '47. Mosher himself acknowledges that his solutions — the membership system and a varying schedule of open-ended runs — are not available or appropriate for everyone. According to *The New York Times*, the low-priced memberships Mosher announced in 1996 for the Circle in the Square ($37.50 a year plus $10 a ticket) would meet less than half the theatre's expenses, even at full capacity, and therefore require unusually large subsidy; and some observers questioned whether the cheap tickets would in fact bring in a different audience [Grimes B1]. Mosher's very successful membership campaign, his marketing innovations together with great critical acclaim could not rescue the theatre from its engulfing debt. He resigned in June 1997 with the theatre's future in grave doubt.

And the principle of open-ended or extended runs depends on the availability of transfer houses, something that only New York City, with its excess inventory of Broadway theatres, can guarantee; moreover, as TCG warned

> Popular box-office success can prove elusive, and theatres that begin to depend on nonsubscription extensions of regularly scheduled productions to fund their operations may leave themselves vulnera-

ble to a capricious marketplace. [Samuels "Facts" 15]

Still, as with John Sullivan's admission that the gospel TCG preached for thirty years might no longer be valid and August Wilson's challenges to the theory of multiculturalism, the fact that the questions were being asked may be more significant than the answers offered. As the post-Broadway era of the American theatre entered middle age, a midlife crisis — or, at least, a midlife period of self-examination — was not at all inappropriate.

☆

Like most crises, it was ultimately about money. It was becoming clear, perhaps belatedly, that one of the dreams on which the great explosion of theatrical activity across America had been built was not to be fulfilled. In the first discovery of the possibilities of not-for-profit corporate status, in the heady days when six- and seven-figure grants from the Ford Foundation were almost commonplace, it seemed that the American theatre had been forever liberated from the marketplace. A sea-change had taken place in the culture with the recognition that theatre was a resource worthy of subsidy; and money — from government, foundations, corporations or individuals — would always be there to fill the expected and accepted gap between ticket sales and expenses. The actual mix of sponsors might vary, and there would be the bother of all those grant applications, but the theatre's artists would be free to make art, without any real concern for money. Suzanne Sato was Managing Director of the Circle Repertory Company in the 1980s:

> Everybody knew the mantra of public/private and individual/corporate/foundation. But the sense was that the balance was always going to be there and it was just a question of building each of those chunks. Build your public, build your corporate, build your private — it was just going to be a question of how you managed growth. [Interview]

That might even have been true for a while, in the glorious 1960s and 1970s, though as early as 1974 Stephen Langley was warning that "No American arts manager should be so optimistic as to believe that private and public subsidy for the arts is inevitable" [Theatre Management 119]. But then it stopped being true, and eventually the theatre's artists were forced to recognize that it wasn't true, and that it would probably never be true again. Yes, the great sea-change had displaced Broadway as the creative center of American theatre and American drama; and yes, the culture had acknowledged that theatre usually couldn't be profit-making and needed support.

But that support was going to have to be hunted for, fought for, and occasionally lost; and that struggle was going to be a continuous one. The artistic directors of not-for-profit theatres might not have to make decisions solely on what would sell tickets. But they would have to be concerned about where the money was coming from, whether it would be enough, what strings would be attached to it, and how best to spend it — always, every day, and forever.

Bad news like that is always resisted, and it is possible to say, without harsh condemnation, that the not-for-profit theatre spent most of the 1980s in denial. As Jon Jory explains, "We have a very romantic tradition in this country that there is such a thing as art for art's sake, and there is tremendous pressure on artists not to possess the common sense necessary to deal institutionally." The examples cited in earlier chapters of talented directors appointed as artistic directors and failing at the job, and of artistic directors who made art while deficits mounted, can be understood in this light. Referring to no one specifically, Jory adds, "They've grown up to act in plays or direct plays or design plays, and they have no experience of the necessities of an institution, and then they go into an institution and are shocked" [Interview].

The same commitment to the dream of total liberation from the marketplace can be seen in the "entitlement" mentality that became apparent in some parts of the subsidized theatre in the 1980s, the expectation that money would always be forthcoming, and the petulance when it wasn't. It contributed, no doubt, to the artistic community's failure to develop an effective lobbying and public relations arm, to continually make the case for subsidy to Congress and the American people. And it was one source of the shortsightedness that led to very few theatres establishing endowment funds (that is, investing money to provide ongoing income rather than spending it immediately on the assumption that more would follow) until the late 1980s; according to TCG, as late as 1995 only two-thirds of the largest not-for-profit theatres in America had endowment funds.

And one of the most energy-wasting ways of resisting the evidence that financial concerns would always be a factor in a not-for-profit theatre's artistic life was an ongoing debate about the appropriateness and morality of any contact with the commercial theatre. As previous chapters showed, Broadway producers turned to the not-for-profits for pre-tested material as soon as it became apparent that interesting new work was being done there, and some in the commercial theatre began to see the regionals as useful try-out venues.

Unsurprisingly, some in the regional theatre had misgivings about this; in theory the not-for-profit theatre was apart from the marketplace, and any collaboration felt like contamination. As early as 1970 critic Martin Gottfried wrote

> Who would have thought that America's resident theaters — so resolutely *noncommercial*, so *artistically pure* — who would have thought that so soon after their development they would be eagerly supplying Broadway with new, and sometimes very profitable, material? ["What" 1]

And as late as 1989 Robert Brustein was complaining,

> Considering its ever-increasing reliance on Broadway for royalties and "enhancement money," the nonprofit theatre can even be said to be censoring itself. What is the celebrated "artistic deficit" but a hesitancy to produce projects considered too controversial to move to New York? ["Arts Wars" 20]

(Interestingly, the suspicion went both ways. Broadway producer Alexander H. Cohen admits that in the early years the commercial theatre thought the subsidized not-for-profits were offering unfair competition. Well into the 1990s Lincoln Center was getting the same criticism for having popular successes on Broadway, to which Gregory Mosher, Bernard Gersten, and Andre Bishop all offered the same reply: commercial producers could have produced the same revivals, star vehicles, and imports, but they didn't, so they had no right to complain when Lincoln Center did.)

But the debate was a false one from the start. Broadway money was no more tainted than the Ford Foundation's. In Arvin Brown's words,

> Theatres have in fact not been corrupted by this association with the commercial theatre. Particularly in the area of straight plays, the commercial theatre is so colorless at the moment that any possibility that they're getting into the minds and hearts of people in the regional theatres and distorting their vision is really kind of nonsense. They're sitting back and waiting to find out what it is that we're all doing, to get any thoughts at all. [Interview]

The benefits of commercial transfers far outweighed any imagined contamination. As noted previously, the New York Shakespeare Festival lived for years on the profits from *A Chorus Line*; and the more apparent it became that the not-for-profit theatre was not apart from the marketplace, the more foolish it was to turn up one's nose at marketplace money. Meanwhile commercial transfers could lead to other, "purer" financial gains, as Robert Falls of the Goodman Theatre notes: "There's no doubt that board members, trustees, corporation heads like to read that you are a success in *The New York Times*. They like to read that you've got a hit play on Broadway. That bodes well for the institution" [Interview].

On the other hand, it could be foolish to count on receiving untold riches from the commercial sector. *A Chorus Line* and the Center Theatre Group's million dollar royalty share from premiering several Neil Simon plays were almost unique. TCG's 1993 survey found only four regional theatres making more than $100,000 from commercial transfers, while twenty-five others averaged about $17,000 each. "Hitching wagons to enhancement deals...or to profit participation...with the goal of making windfall profits is a prescription for disappointment, if not financial catastrophe" [Mintz 29]. And even success had its dangers; Pereira reports that the Manhattan Theatre Club's first Broadway hit, *Ain't Misbehavin'*, led to a decline in funding from sources who assumed that the company was now rich [116].

Meanwhile it was becoming obvious to many that, as the commercial theatre came to rely on the not-for-profits for virtually all its new product, a purist who refused to collaborate would be actively hurting the art form. One of the inherent difficulties in a nationwide abundance of theatrical activity is the loss of what made the Broadway-dominated years so fertile, the close community and instant awareness of every new development.

> The commercial theater of the early post-world war era was a relatively coherent and orderly system which could bring national attention to those artists who conformed to its demands. This system is being replaced by an entropic universe of theaters which may provide a greater number of artistic opportunities but which lacks the power to bring national attention to such excellent work as it can produce. [Sponberg xxviii]

Whatever the inherent importance of Broadway, New York City is still the business and communications center of the country, and things that happen there get more national notice than events elsewhere. In 1979 Gordon Davidson told of how the success of Michael Cristofer's *The Shadow Box* at the Mark Taper Forum inspired him to recommend it to other theatres, with no success. After a Broadway run that resulted in the 1977 Tony and Pulitzer Prize, *The Shadow Box* became a staple of the regional theatre repertoire [qtd in Aaron 58]. In 1995 Robert Falls told a similar story about Scott McPherson's *Marvin's Room* [Interview]; and in 1996 Martha Lavey, Artistic Director of the Steppenwolf Theatre, concurred:

"We don't begin a production with New York in mind.... We're not in the business of producing shows in New York. But it gives us higher visibility" [qtd in S. Smith 12].

Typically, Joseph Papp was particularly adept at this art; some of the profits from his Broadway successes paid for Broadway runs for such plays as *That Championship Season, Sticks and Bones, For Colored Girls...,* *Miss Margarida's Way* and *Runaways,* not in any real hope of making money from the transfers, but to expose the Broadway audience to these plays and expose these plays to the publicity that would lead to other productions.

Lloyd Richards offers another reason why Broadway transfers should not be considered a capitulation or contamination, but rather an important part of the regional theatre's mission. He tells of a conversation with a young playwright in the early years of the O'Neill Center:

> I remember walking with [him] and he said to me, "I have a great need for this kind of a place, a place where we can work without pressure. But I also have a need to see my picture on the front page of the Sunday *Times* Arts and Entertainment section." A playwright works in solitude for years to develop something, not knowing whether the public will accept it. And what is the ultimate in acceptance for a playwright? If that sounds crass or commercial, it isn't, because it is a need for affirmation of the work. [Interview]

Arvin Brown makes a similar comment—"The playwright, who may have devoted four years of his life to the writing of a play, deserves that chance at a larger audience" [Interview]—and Tim Sanford of Off-Broadway's Playwrights Horizons sees such transfers as evidence that the originating theatre has done its job:

> Many of the writers we've had hits for have graduated in a way from Playwrights Horizons. I'd be happy if every play was received well and had a future life. That's not why we choose plays, but you want to feel, if you're producing a play, that there's an audience for it. [Interview]

And Barry Grove of the Manhattan Theatre Club sums up all these arguments. He notes that if a commercial producer transfers a not-for-profit's play, runs it for six months and loses $50,000, it's a flop. On the other hand,

> If we can pay artists greater salaries than we would otherwise be able to pay them, run the play for six months, increase the royalties dramatically to the author and director, increase the visibility of the in-

stitution, and only lose $50,000, when in our subscription season we lose more than that every week, we're a success. [Interview; similar comment from Gregory Mosher]

As Joseph Wesley Zeigler concluded as early as 1973, "It is a matter not of overthrowing Broadway's power but of using it" [*Regional* 239].

Certainly, by the 1980s the issue should have disappeared, and only the continuing fantasy that the not-for-profit theatre could and should be above crass financial concerns kept it alive. Once again, Jon Jory of the Actors Theatre of Louisville:

> Whole conversations are held about the American regional theatre as if it wasn't in the marketplace. As soon as that conversation begins, I become very quiet, because my experience of twenty-seven years of running one of these theatres is that it exists in the marketplace, and the marketplace impacts on it. [Interview]

☆

The impact of the marketplace, and the necessity of dealing with it, can be summarized in six basic facts of life in the American theatre. First, *there is never enough money.* That's a given. The noncommercial theatre, after all, was built on the assumption that income could not meet expenses; and both commercial and noncommercial theatres are subject to an artistic variant of Parkinson's Law: ambition expands to meet the funds available. If a theatre magically found itself with a surplus of funds, its directors would immediately find artistically valid ways of spending it: new workshops, new playing spaces, grander productions. And if that funding were to dry up after a few years, the results would be felt and mourned as tragic shrinkage rather than the end of a pleasant interlude. (Arvin Brown of Long Wharf: "We had reached a point, five or so years ago, where we were at our producing peak ... and I would be asked what I saw for the future, and my feeling was 'more of the same.' Once the economic crisis hit, we fell away from that ideal.")

Second, *nobody is entitled to subsidy.* In an ideal world all artists would be subsidized by a society that recognized the value of their contribution. And even in the real world, a very strong case can be made that the world, the government, the rich, the man on the street should support art. But they don't *have* to. They can be made to want to. They can be guided, cajoled, and educated until they realize a value to them in giving. And doing that guiding, cajoling, and educating is part of the artistic director's job description. The words of Robert Falls of the Goodman Theatre bear repeating:

> For the pleasure of being able to spend time in a rehearsal room with a playwright and actors, there is the responsibility to communicate to a board of directors, and therefore to the community, the necessity of my particular vision and why it needs to be supported.... That's the definition of an artistic director. [Interview]

One of the surest roads to oblivion for a not-for-profit theatre, and to dismissal for an artistic director, is the complacent assumption that the money will always be there, that sources that contributed last year will automatically return this year, and that if they choose to take their money elsewhere, there's something wrong with them.

Which leads to the third fact of life, *he who pays the piper calls the tune.* Whether "he" (or she) is the government, a foundation, a corporation, a millionaire, a single-ticket buyer, or the community at large, it's his money. He can decide whether to spend it and where to spend it, and he has the absolute right not to come back to spend more if he was disappointed last time. *All* money comes with strings attached, if only the requirement to do good work.

It is far too easy, especially in the not-for-profit realm, to fall into the trap of assuming that the buyer should want what the artist chooses to offer. The foundation that decides that homeless people need its money more than theatre artists, or the government that chooses to spend taxpayers' dollars serving wide audiences rather than elite ones (or to cut back on its spending), has a valid, legitimate position and every right to take it. The younger, ethnically diverse audiences that are hard to lure into the theatre may legitimately see the theatre as not offering them anything worth coming to. The local millionaire who has to be courted and coddled has every right in the world to expect special treatment and to be able to choose, for whatever reason, where and whether to give.

The single greatest error that the arts community made in responding to attacks on the National Endowment for the Arts was assuming that the case for subsidy was self-evident and that anyone who didn't see it was a philistine, when the fact was that a portion of the populace had real concerns — moral, social, economic — that needed to be respectfully addressed, not dismissed with contempt. Rather than ignoring or resenting the fact that donors want to have some say in how their money is spent, artists must decide whether the tune the payer wants played is one they are prepared — or able — to pipe. If so, fine; if not, it becomes an integral part of the job to win them over to another tune, or to thank them politely and go elsewhere.

Fourth, *all art, like all politics, is local.* With the clear evidence of withdrawal from the funding pool of both government and national foundations, it should be obvious that future underwriting of not-for-profit theatre will have to come from local sources. Gigi Bolt of the NEA and Ruth Mayleas, formerly of the Ford Foundation, are quick to confirm this:

> If one cannot rely for a significant portion of the budget on government and foundations, then, from the point of view of the health of the organization, the future lies very much in support from individuals and local businesses and foundations. [Bolt interview]

> There isn't any question that managements are going to have to convince their communities — and by that I don't mean just their individual subscribers and audiences, but their funding sources as well — of the value of what they do. The task will continue to be to impress on those local sources the importance of their institutions in the life of the community. [Mayleas interview]

In this context it is worth noting that some of the most financially secure theatres in America are those that assiduously and unceasingly cultivated local support. Laura McCrea of the Berkeley Repertory Theatre and Jon Jory of Louisville make essentially the same point:

> One of Berkeley Rep's strengths is the sense of ownership that the subscribers feel. It's their theatre, and that causes them to continue to support us even in difficult economic times. [qtd in "Advance or Retreat" 45]

> Communities the size of Louisville are sensitive to those institutions which they feel actually relate to the community rather than exploiting the community. [Interview]

But "local support" means more than merely passing the hat among the neighborhood millionaires. It means developing an ongoing relationship with the audience and the community, so that the community *wants* the theatre. For Lloyd Richards it's a matter of ethnic and cultural relevance: "You have to permit people to know that what's going on in that space is about them, that it is of value to them" [Interview]. For Gregory Boyd it's the continuity made possible by a resident company: "The audience immediately has a proprietary interest in the theatre because of the team, the same company of actors every season" [Interview]. Both Boyd and Jon Jory compare their communities' affection for their theatres to the support for the local football teams. Suzanne Sato of the

AT&T Foundation reminds us that developing such local support involves an implicit contract:

> I was at the Hartford Stage. That theatre sits in an extremely economically challenged region, but the community has said that Hartford Stage is important to them and they're going to insure its health. But Hartford Stage's role in that pact is to continue to deliver theatre that makes a real difference to the community, that continues to revitalize itself, that gives them a real range of challenging opportunities, that doesn't pander. The theatre has to live up to its end of the bargain. [Interview]

The term "regional theatre," John Sullivan of TCG reminds us, originally meant not-New York, but the future lies in redefining it as of-the-region.

This point is so important that it bears rephrasing as the fifth fact, *you have to please the audience.* That was so obviously true, in purely practical terms, of the commercial theatre that it was one of the first truths the noncommercial theatre was tempted to ignore. Earlier chapters documented such sad stories as the Ford Foundation's transformation of the Mummers into a professional company Oklahoma City didn't want, and the recurring failures of artistic directors who tried to impose their tastes on communities that didn't share them. Recall, too, the marginal experimental companies of the 1960s that came together for extended rehearsals, rarely deigning to share their work with an audience; in doing so, of course, they condemned themselves to perpetual marginality.

But even more mainstream theatres, with the apparently reliable cushion of subsidies and ever-renewing subscribers, could lose sight of the need to give an audience value for money; more than one artistic director interviewed for this book spoke with pleasure of failed productions that were exciting creative adventures, without giving thought to the people who paid to see those failures. "I get into a lot of quarrels about this," says Gregory Boyd of the Alley Theatre. "But the undeniable fact is that a lot of work in American not-for-profit theatres is just not very good."

The most common cause of artistic directors' dismissals and theatre companies' deaths since the 1950s has been the failure to give an audience what it wanted (or to guide an audience, carefully and gradually, into wanting what was offered). With the subsidies and subscribers no longer automatically renewing, the need to attract, hold, and please an audience is the purest example of the not-for-profits' engagement in the marketplace. "We have very generous corporations and foundations locally and nationally," acknowledges Gregory Boyd. "But basically no theatre is going to survive if it doesn't get an audience" [Interview].

And finally the reassuring sixth fact of life: *good work can be done on any budget*. Every theatre in America has had the surprise of a low-cost production becoming a hit; every director and designer, the experience of being forced by budget constraints to invent something that proved more effective and satisfying than the more expensive alternative would have been. At least as much artistic invention has been presented on bare thrust stages as on elaborately-designed computerized sets; at least as many important new plays have been born in black-box studios as on main stages; at least as much exciting work has been done in the smallest theatres across America as in the largest.

And the future? Ask any number of theatre professionals to predict the shape of the American theatre in the next century, and you will get at least that number of different replies. Here is a sampling, all from personal interviews: first, on the prospects of survival at all.

Arvin Brown, Artistic Director, Long Wharf Theatre:

> I've got to say I'm fairly scared. Going hand in hand with the burgeoning of theatre around the country in the early stages there was a concomitant rediscovery of language and an excitement not just about theatre but about the performing arts experience, and each fed the other. I feel we're in a terrifying reversal of all that, and that there is a return of an ability to classify the theatre as elitist.... I think it's fed, unfortunately, by a younger generation of people who have retreated from the performing arts, so it's not a question of reawakening a love of language and a love of complex issues and a love of depth of characterization, but starting anew and trying to bring people to something they've actually never understood.

[Six months after this interview, Brown announced his resignation and intention to devote himself to directing in film and television.]

Gregory Mosher, Artistic Director, Circle in the Square:

> There is a certain kind of theatre which is dead and just hasn't rolled over yet.... That theatre is over, the theatre that takes an audience for granted, because it's had that audience for thirty years.... They've blocked the most energized artists, the most ambitious artists, and they've blocked the most spirited audience members,

those under the age of forty. . . . I think all of these resident theatres will just end unless they manage to reinvent themselves. Maybe someone, just as Mac Lowry and the pioneers of the movement did, will create a model that will let them reinvent themselves. . . . So I've come to rejoin the battle. [Six months after this interview, Gregory Mosher announced his resignation from Circle in the Square]

Robert Falls, Artistic Director, Goodman Theatre:

I think there is going to be an attrition in the upcoming years. The incredible explosion of theatrical activity around the country, the growth of an American national theatre has peaked, and there's going to be a sort of survival of the fittest in the next ten years, where any number of theatres are going to disappear. And I'm not sure that's necessarily a bad thing. I think that theatres have lives and theatres have deaths and there's a time span that a theatre lives; and that sometimes, particularly if the community itself is not willing to support it, then it just has to go away.

Ben Cameron, Senior Program Officer, Dayton Hudson Foundation:

We're going to see fewer theatres. There will always be a churning entry level of young companies struggling to get a foothold — ironically, never having been major beneficiaries of subsidy in the first place, they're positioned to withstand financial onslaughts. The major theatres of Guthrie dimensions have enough avid supporters that they will fare reasonably well, though I would expect a reduction in production scale. The ones that are really going to be hit hardest are the midsized theatres; that's the sector in which we're going to see the greatest attrition.

Tim Sanford, Artistic Director, Playwrights Horizons:

There are days when you feel discouraged about the increasing age of the subscriber base and the artistic retrenchment. Other times I feel that we're in a golden age of playwriting that not many people know about yet, that there are so many young playwrights waiting to emerge. People have been feeling like the theatre's dying forever, and it's probably not the case.

Gregory Boyd, Artistic Director, Alley Theatre:

I'm hopeful about the future. I think we're on the verge of a real renaissance in American playwriting, and the way we can insure that is by getting younger audiences into the theatre. A young person who might write a play someday has to be able to know what the theatre is. The reason they're all writing movies or rock videos is that they know what those things are. If that kind of talent can be admitted into the theatre, as audience first, and then finding a way in companies to develop their talents, then I think we're going to see some amazing young playwrights. I see some of them now, and that's a cause for real hope.

Barry Grove, Executive Producer, Manhattan Theatre Club:

As we move into an ever more complex world of technology, with the ability to be at home and move virtually everything over our combination television-telephone-computer, we are going to need more than ever the human connection that the theatre makes, the two-boards-and-a-passion meeting of artist and audience.

Arthur Gelb, former Managing Editor, *The New York Times*:

When we go through some of the old clippings, it is fascinating to see in the late 1800s that the theatre's dying. It's always dying. But it never dies, because people will always want to see live theatre, the intimacy of the actor on that stage, the relationship of actor and audience.

And Gigi Bolt, Director, Theatre and Musical Theatre, National Endowment for the Arts:

The universe of arts institutions as they currently exist may look somewhat different some years from now. Some will no doubt be stronger, even in this environment, and many will survive, but some may not. And who survives and certainly who flourishes will almost inevitably be a result of their connection to a community.

And now some thoughts about the shape of the future, first of the Broadway theatre. (It may be the Walt Disney Company's major investments in Broadway in the 1990s that inspired the similarity of language that follows.)

Alexander H. Cohen, Broadway producer:

I think it will be Disney World. I think that eventually Broadway will become a theme park and reflect its former self with nothing but revivals of classic musicals.... I'd rather have a museum than blank space,... but the person who comes to New York from all over the world has heard about Times Square and Broadway theatre all of his life, and what does he get? *Cats.* Disney World.

Eric Krebs, Off-Broadway producer and theatre owner:

Broadway has always been commercial, but it's becoming more and more expected that you're going to do spectacular production-oriented, as opposed to actor- or text-oriented productions. So I think the future is going to be more grandiose productions, the Disnification of Broadway.

Ben Sprecher, Off-Broadway producer and theatre owner:

I think Broadway will eventually correct itself and there will be two different economic models, one for musicals and one for plays. And when that happens...then Broadway will recapture the plays.... The commitment that the city has made to Times Square, the economics of the tourist dollars...will continue to allow Broadway to be the zenith of the art form.

Michael Feingold, chief theatre critic, *Village Voice*:

Broadway is the largest and most visible segment of the New York theatre, but it doesn't exist. It doesn't have a personality of its own. It only imports.... It serves a geographical and real estate function; there are beautiful theatres there. [I'd like to see] the Shuberts give over the straight play theatres, which are no longer commercial money-making propositions, to the nonprofit theatres that were going to be running plays aimed for a Broadway future anyway. [Similar suggestion from Theodore Mann]

And, for the theatre outside New York, Jon Jory, Producing Director, Actors Theatre of Louisville:

I think the most important thing that will be going on in the next decade is a healthy dialectic between realism and other forms. American realism was king of the mountain, but the new generation of American theatre people, the best of them, are only moderately interested in realism. And unless the institutions prepare themselves and their audiences to absorb and be interested in and be delighted by these new forms, the new wave of young artists are not going to be interested in working in these institutions, and they'll end up being the best 1970s theatres of the new millennium.

Woodie King, Artistic Director, New Federal Theatre:

Because there will be fewer and fewer grants, white theatre in America, especially the nonprofit, will be subsidized by the rich. There will be even less subsidy for black theatre, so black theatre will have to depend very heavily on the audience. That audience will support us, as long as we do not fail them.

Andre Bishop, Artistic Director, Lincoln Center Theatre:

When I went into theatre in the early seventies, our goal and that of most of my friends who ran other Off Off-Broadway theatres was to be an institution, which meant permanence. With the new generation you never hear the word "institution." They tend to come together on a play-by-play basis. The downside is a lack of permanence, a lack of continuity, and I believe any great theatre company has to have permanence.

Suzanne Sato, Vice President, Arts and Culture, AT&T Foundation:

Every time I go to some of the small alternative theatres and see the young audiences they are pulling in that are just never going to go to the major theatres, I'm not sure what their next steps are going to be. Once they've tried their wings and done whatever the Caffe Cino of today is, then what? In the days of the Caffe Cino the next step was the Circle Rep. Today I don't know whether they're going to be able to take the next step. Maybe what happens is that you don't think about organizations as being forever, but of an organization whose moment or trajectory is five years or twenty years, and quite honorably so.

And Robert Falls, Artistic Director, Goodman Theatre:

I think we're going to see a continued breakdown of the lines and definitions of what is a for-profit theatre and a nonprofit theatre, because they're all going to have to be more creative in terms of how they receive money in order to operate. So I think more and more we're going to see nontraditional kinds of funding opportunities, or the creation of different consortiums of how plays get produced.

Some of what Robert Falls foresees is evident already, as the lines between commercial and noncommercial, establishment and alternative, New York City and the rest of the country continue to blur. The New York Shakespeare Festival operates on, Off-, and Off Off-Broadway simultaneously. The Alley Theatre mixes an ongoing resident company with big-name guest stars. The Walt Disney Company chooses avant-garde director Julie Taymor to stage the Broadway version of *The Lion King*. Not-for-profit and commercial theatres come together in the National Alliance of Musical Theatre to share and trade productions, and to create new Broadway musicals away from Broadway.

The Shubert Foundation supports new play development across the country, and the Shubert Organization produces some of those plays on Broadway. The not-for-profit Manhattan Theatre Club sets up a for-profit subsidiary to oversee its transfers to the commercial theatre. The Actors Theatre of Louisville supplements its regular season with festivals of Shakespeare, new plays, and avant-garde performance artists, each with their own audiences.

The Lincoln Center Theatre operates in the commercial arena, filling the gap left by Broadway producers who have abandoned the drama. Theatres at opposite ends of the country co-produce plays that then become part of both subscription seasons. Movie stars who began their careers at Steppenwolf or the Circle in the Square return to act alongside a new generation of actors who, in turn, will be the next decade's stars. Rocco Landesmann, president of Broadway's Jujamcyn theatre chain, got his training at the Yale Rep.

San Diego's Old Globe Theatre, begun as a Shakespeare festival, is home to the first stagings of Neil Simon plays and Stephen Sondheim musicals. Not-for-profit theatres across the country supplement their income by doubling as booking houses, renting their stages to touring commercial productions. Broadway musicals are born in Off Off-Broadway lofts, while important dramatists like August Wilson see their plays staged around the country over a period of years, with New York production almost an afterthought.

Surely the shape of the American theatre has been changed irrevocably. As Ben Cameron and Gigi Bolt predict, individual theatres will come and go, but Arvin Brown is surely wrong. The idea of theatre has taken too strong a hold in too many places in America for it to disappear in the new century. Funding arrangements will change, and the distinction between subsidized and commercial theatre will blur even further. Artists and administrators will face the challenges of attracting new audiences and of creating theatrical experiences that speak to those audiences, so they become the regular theatregoers of the next generation. In some ways, in some shapes, the dream of Margo Jones will continue to live.

Irreversibly, first-class live professional theatre is available to millions more people as the century ends than in 1950. Opportunities for actors, directors, designers, and technicians are greater, as is the possibility of having a fulfilling artistic career outside New York and Hollywood. Opportunities for new dramatists (and, if Jon Jory is right, new creators-of-theatre of other sorts), and for audiences to encounter the work of new dramatists, are and will continue to be far, far greater than they were fifty years ago. This is the big picture, and it is good.

And if reliance on government, foundation, corporate and private funding means that theatres must be aware of the tastes and limits of their sponsors, that is also healthy. Serving the agendas of sponsors, while always trying to educate them and expand their receptivity to the new, is no different from speaking an artistic language an audience is prepared to hear, while challenging and stretching its ability to absorb new languages. The task for artists in the not-for-profit sector is not to escape the real or imagined constraints of their financial dependency, but to do good work within those constraints. Exciting theatre in a form both funders and audiences can handle will prepare both funders and audiences to handle new forms.

No one can predict the exact shape that the next revolution in the American theatre will take, just as no one could have predicted Off-Broadway or regional theatre or not-for-profit theatre. But some things are certain. Whatever it is, it will be born out of the passionate desire of young artists to create exciting, living, relevant theatre in new ways. Some of the work it produces will seem strange and threatening to today's artists and audiences. Much of it will be bad, much will be interesting dead ends, and some will be extraordinary.

It will not bring down or replace the establishment, though that may be the stated aim of some of its practitioners, but will inspire it to learn and evolve. Just as Off-Broadway taught Broadway how to hear the voices of a new generation of playwrights, just as the resident theatre companies taught the commercial theatre a new kind of relationship with the audience and the community, just as the wildest alternative companies of the 1960s left their mark on the most conservative of Broadway musicals, whatever new theatrical revolution the millennium brings will challenge, educate and ultimately feed back into the mainstream. And all of American theatre will be richer for it.

WORKS CITED

Aaron, Jules. "The Mark Taper Forum." *Theater* Summer 1979: 55–63.

"Advance or Retreat?" *American Theatre* April 1991: 43–45.

Atkinson, Brooks. *Broadway*. New York: Macmillan, 1974.

Baldinger, Scott. "Marketing Broadway as a Cool Spot." *The New York Times* 14 April 1996, sec 2: 5+.

Baumol, William J., and William G. Bowen. *Performing Arts — The Economic Dilemma*. New York: Twentieth Century Fund, 1966.

Beck, Julian. "Why Vanguard?" *The New York Times* 22 March 1959, sec. 2: 1+.

Beck, Julian, and Judith Malina. Typescript in Billy Rose Theatre Collection, New York Public Library.

Bentley, Eric. "I Reject the Living Theater." *The New York Times* 20 Oct 1968, sec 2: 1.

Berkvist, Robert. "Lanford Wilson — Can He Score on Broadway?" *The New York Times* 17 Feb 1980, sec 2: 1+.

Berson, Misha. "Keeping Company." *American Theatre* April 1990: 16+.

Biner, Pierre. *The Living Theatre*. New York: Avon, 1972.

Bishop, Andre. Interview with author, 4 Jan 1996.

Bolt, Gigi. Telephone interview with author, 24 May 1996.

Boyd, Gregory. Telephone interview with author, 12 Dec 1995.

Brown, Arvin. Telephone interview with author, 30 Nov 1995.

Brustein, Robert. *Seasons of Discontent*. New York: Simon and Schuster, 1967.

———. *The Third Theatre*. New York: Knopf, 1969.

———. "Arts Wars." *American Theatre* Oct 1989: 18+.

Bushnell, Bill. Telephone interview with author, 24 October 1996.

Cameron, Ben. Telephone interview with author, 29 May 1996.

Carmines, Al. "The Judson Poets' Theatre." *Eight Plays from Off-Off Broadway*. Ed. Nick Orzel and Michael Smith. Indianapolis: Bobbs-Merrill, 1966.

Chapman, John. *The Best Plays of 1950–1951*. New York: Dodd, Mead, 1951.

———. *The Best Plays of 1951–1952*. New York: Dodd, Mead, 1952.

Clurman, Harold. Introduction. *The Playwrights Speak*. Ed. Walter Wager. New York: Dell, 1967. xi–xxvi.

Cohen, Alexander H. Telephone interview with author, 11 October 1996.

Coleman, Janet. *The Compass*. New York: Knopf, 1990.

Cook, Ralph. "Theatre Genesis." *Eight Plays from Off-Off Broadway*. Ed. Nick Orzel and Michael Smith. Indianapolis: Bobbs-Merrill, 1966

Engel, Lehman. *The American Musical Theater*. New York: Macmillan, 1967.

Epstein, Helen. *Joe Papp: An American Life*. Boston: Little, Brown, 1994.

Evans, Greg. "Shubert's New Prexy Vows Firm Foundation." *Variety* 28 Oct 1996: 73+.

Falls, Robert. Telephone interview with author, 5 Dec 1995.

Feingold, Michael. Telephone interview with author, 23 October 1996.

Fichandler, Zelda. Introduction. *The Arena Adventure* by Laurence Maslon. Washington: Arena Stage, 1990.

Funke, Lewis. "Williams Revival? Ask the Playwright." *The New York Times* 8 Jan 1970: 45.

Garfield, David. *A Player's Place*. New York: Macmillan, 1980.

Gelb, Arthur. Telephone interview with author, 23 October 1996.

Gelber, Jack. "Julian Beck, Businessman." *TDR* Summer 1986: 6–29.

Gerard, Jeremy. "A Circle Broken." *Variety* 14 Oct 1996: 69.

Gersten, Bernard. Telephone interview with author, 28 October 1996.

Gilman, Richard. "It's a Show." *New Republic* 9 Nov 1968: 29–32.

Glore, John. "The Empty Space and the Seattle Rep." *Theater Summer* 1979: 64–74.

Gottfried, Martin. *A Theater Divided*. Boston: Little, Brown, 1967.

———. "What Shall It Profit A Theatre If...?" *The New York Times* 23 Aug 1970, sec 2: 1+.

Gregory, Andre. "The Theatre of the Living Arts." *Tulane Drama Review* Summer 1967: 18–21.

Grimes, William. "$10 Seats, for a Broadway Theater's Freedom and Survival." *The New York Times* 11 December 1996: B1+.

Grove, Barry. Telephone interview with author, 4 June 1996.

Guernsey, Otis L. *Curtain Times*. New York: Applause, 1987.

Gussow, Mel. "An Informal Troop of Playwrights and Its Den Mother." *The New York Times* 16 June 1994: c11+.

Hambleton, T. Edward, and Norris Houghton. "Phoenix on the Wing." *Theatre Arts* Nov 1954: 29+.

Hewes, Henry. *The Best Plays of 1962–1963*. New York: Dodd, Mead, 1963.

Horn, Barbara Lee. *Ellen Stewart and LaMama: A Bio-Bibliography*. Westport: Greenwood, 1993.

Hornby, Richard. *The End of Acting*. New York: Applause, 1992.

Houghton, Norris. *Entrances & Exits*. New York: Limelight, 1991.

Janowitz, Barbara. "Theatre Facts 89." *American Theatre* April 1990: 32–43.

———. "Theatre Facts 90." *American Theatre* April 1991: 30–42.

———. "Theatre Facts 92." *American Theatre* April 1993: 1–15.

Jeffri, Joan. *Arts Money*. Minneapolis: University of Minnesota Press, 1989.

Jones, Margo. *Theatre-in-the-Round*. New York: Rinehart, 1951.

Jory, Jon. Telephone interview with author, 19 Dec 1995.

Kauffmann, Stanley. *Persons of the Drama*. New York: Harper & Row, 1976.

Kazan, Elia. *A Life*. New York: Knopf, 1988.

Kennedy, Harold J. *No Pickle, No Performance*. Garden City: Doubleday, 1978.

Kerr, Walter. *God on the Gymnasium Floor*. New York: Dell, 1973.

King, Woodie. Telephone interview with author, 23 October 1996.

Kissel, Howard. *David Merrick: The Abominable Showman*. New York: Applause, 1993.

Kliewer, Warren. "Whose Theatre Is It Anyway?" *American Theatre* April 1990: 66–68.

Krebs, Eric. Telephone interview with author, 25 October 1996.

Kronenberger, Louis. *The Best Plays of 1956–1957*. New York: Dodd, Mead, 1957.

Langley, Stephen. *Theatre Management in America*. New York: Drama, 1974.

———, ed. *Producers on Producing*. New York: Drama, 1976.

———. *Theatre Management and Production in America*. New York: Drama, 1990.

Little, Stuart W. *Off-Broadway*. New York: Dell, 1974.

———. *After the FACT*. New York: Arno, 1975.

London, Todd. "What's Past Is Prologue." *American Theatre* July 1992: 20+.

Lowry, W. McNeil. "The University and the Creative Arts." *Educational Theatre Journal* May 1962: 99–112.

Magat, Richard. *The Ford Foundation at Work*. New York: Plenum, 1979.

Mahard, Martha. "1750–1810." *Theatre in the United States: A Documentary History*. Ed. Barry B. Witham. Vol. I. Cambridge: Cambridge University Press, 1996.

Malina, Judith. Telephone interview with author, 18 October 1996.

Mann, Theodore. Telephone interviews with author, 21 October and 8 November 1996.

Mantle, Burns. *The Best Plays of 1927–1928*. New York: Dodd, Mead, 1928.

Marks, Peter. "Broadway's Producers: A Struggling, Changing Breed." *The New York Times* 7 April 1996. Sec 2, 1+.

——. "It's a Success, but is that Enough?" *The New York Times* 27 October 1996. Sec 2, 1+.

Marlin-Jones, Davey. "The Washington Theatre Club." *Players* Aug 1970: 290+.

Mason, Marshall W. Interview with author, 27 December 1975; published in *Players* April 1976: 108+.

Mayleas, Ruth. *Ford Foundation Support for the Arts in the United States.* New York: Ford, 1986.

——. Telephone interview with author, 22 May 1996.

Miles, Julia. Telephone interview with author, 18 October 1996.

Mintz, S. L. "A Marriage of Convenience." *American Theatre* Nov 1994: 26–29.

Molotsky, Irvin. "Staying Over? This Theater Has a Bunk Stage," *The New York Times* 15 March 1997,

Moore, Thomas Gale. *The Economics of the American Theater.* Durham: Duke UP, 1968.

Mordecai, Benjamin. "Permanence for Permanence's Sake?" *American Theatre* Sept 1984: 28–29.

Morison, Bradley G., and Kay Fliehr. *In Search of an Audience.* New York: Pitman, 1968.

Mosher, Gregory. Telephone interviews with author, 21 October and 15 November 1996.

Pankratz, David B. *Multiculturalism and Public Arts Policy.* Westport: Bergin & Garvey, 1993.

Papp, Joseph. Qtd in "Brooklyn's Gift to the Bard." *Theatre Arts* Jan 1958: 11–12.

Pasolli, Robert. *A Book on the Open Theatre.* New York: Avon, 1970.

Pereira, John W. *Opening Nights: 25 Years of the Manhattan Theatre Club.* New York: Peter Lang, 1996.

Quintero, Jose. *If You Don't Dance They Beat You.* Boston: Little, Brown, 1974.

Reiss, Alvin H. "The Arts Look Ahead." *Fund Raising Management* March 1994: 27–31.

———. *Don't Just Applaud — Send Money!* New York: Theatre Communications Group: 1995.

Richards, Lloyd. Telephone interview with author, 21 May 1996.

Richenthal, David. Interview with author. 5 Jan 1996.

Rinear, David. "1810–1865." *Theatre in the United States: A Documentary History.* Ed. Barry B. Witham. Vol I. Cambridge: Cambridge University Press, 1996.

Sainer, Arthur. *The Radical Theatre Notebook.* New York: Avon, 1975.

Samuels, Steven and Alisha Tonsic. "Theatre Facts 1995." *American Theatre* April 1996, 1–15.

Samuels, Steven, ed. *Theatre Profiles 11.* New York: Theatre Communications Group, 1994.

Sanford, Tim. Telephone interview with author, 3 Jan 1996.

Sato, Suzanne. Telephone interview with author, 23 May 1996.

Shirley, Don. "He Subscribes to Intrepid Audiences." *Los Angeles Times* 14 July 1996. Cal: 42+.

Smith, Cecil. *Musical Comedy in America.* New York: Theatre Arts, 1950.

Smith, Dinitia. "Curtain Calls With No Help From Uncle Sam." *The New York Times* 3 March 1996, sec 2: 5.

Smith, Michael, ed. *The Best of Off Off-Broadway.* New York: Dutton, 1969.

Smith, Sid. "New York or Bust." *Chicago Tribune* 28 Jan 1996, sec 7: 1+.

Sorgenfrei, Carol Fisher. "Intercultural Directing: Revitalizing Force or Spiritual Rape?" in *Staging Difference: Cultural Pluralism in American Theatre and Drama.* Ed. Marc Maufort. New York: Peter Lang, 1995.

Sponberg, Arvid F. *Broadway Talks.* New York: Greenwood, 1991.

Sprecher, Ben. Telephone interview with author, 28 October 1996.

Steele, Scott L. Telephone interview with author, 25 October 1996.

Stein, Howard. Telephone interview with author, 17 October 1996.

Stevens, Gary and Alan George. *The Longest Line.* New York: Applause, 1995.

Sullivan, John. Telephone interview with author, 27 September 1996.

"The Theatre Takes Stock," *Theatre Arts* May 1940, 327–389.

Trachtenberg, Jeffrey A. "The Producers: How to Turn $4,000 Into Many Millions," *Wall Street Journal* 23 May 1996, A1+

Twentieth Century Fund. *Bricks, Mortar and the Performing Arts.* New York: Twentieth Century Fund, 1966.

Tytell, John. *The Living Theatre: Art, Exile, and Outrage.* New York: Grove, 1995.

Weber, Bruce. "Make Money on Broadway? Break a Leg," *The New York Times* 3 June 1993, A1+.

———. "Birth of a Salesman," *The New York Times* 27 February 1997, C13+.

"What It Costs To Produce A Play, And Why." *The New York Times* 15 Feb 1925, sec 7: 1.

White, George. Telephone interview with author, 3 June 1996.

Wilson, August. "The Ground on Which I Stand." *American Theatre* September 1996, 14+.

Witham, Barry B. "General Introduction." *Theatre in the United States: A Documentary History.* Vol I. Cambridge: Cambridge University Press, 1996.

Zadan, Craig. *Sondheim & Co.* New York: Macmillan, 1974.

Zeigler, Joseph Wesley. *Regional Theatre.* Minneapolis: U Minnesota Press, 1973.

———. *Arts in Crisis.* Chicago: a capella, 1994.

Zeisler, Peter. "Mountains Are For Climbing." *American Theatre* Sept 1985: 3.

FOR FURTHER READING

Those wishing to explore the subject further are encouraged to seek out all the sources cited in the notes, and these books and publications in particular:

American Theatre: Monthly magazine published by the Theatre Communication Group since 1984. Essentially the house organ of the not-for-profit theatre community, it features news, articles, play texts and the results of TCG's annual economic surveys.

Atkinson, Brooks. *Broadway* **(1974):** A readable and authoritative history of New York's commercial theatre center.

Berkowitz, Gerald M. *American Drama of the Twentieth Century* **(1992):** Analysis of individual plays and playwrights, and of the dominant movements and styles of drama.

Langley, Stephen. *Theatre Management and Production in America* **(1990):** A combination history, analysis and how-to guide in organizing and running a theatre of any size or financial structure.

Little, Stuart W. *Off-Broadway: The Prophetic Theater* **(1972):** History of the first twenty years of the alternative theatre in New York.

Mantle, Burns (and subsequent editors). *The Best Plays of 1919–1920* **[and subsequent years]:** Annual volume with abridged texts of ten plays, essays summarizing the New York season, and production details (casts, etc.) of Broadway and, in later volumes, Off-Broadway and regional theatre shows. Edited in turn by Mantle (1919–46), John Chapman (1947–51), Louis Kronenberger (1952–60), Henry Hewes (1961–3), Otis L. Guernsey Jr. (1964–84), Guernsey and Jeffrey Sweet (1985–).

Zeigler, Joseph Wesley. *Arts in Crisis* **(1994):** A history of the not-for-profit arts community's uneasy relationship with funding sources, particularly the National Endowment for the Arts.

Zeigler, Joseph Wesley. *Regional Theatre* **(1973):** A history of the beginnings and growth of not-for-profit theatre across America after 1947.

INDEX

New York Times, 7, 24, 36, 90, 108, 152, 194, 196, 212, 218, 226, 230, 238, 243-245, 247-249

Newley, Anthony, 207

Newman, Danny, 104-105, 109, 220, 224

Nichols, Mike, 121, 134, 180, 215

Night of the Iguana, The, 181, 188

Night Thoreau Spent in Jail, The, 97

No Place to Be Somebody, 59, 61

No, No, Nanette, 199

Nolte, Nick, 127

Norman, Marcia, 97

North Light Repertory Company, 135

Nunn, Trevor, 209

Nunsense, 56-57

O'Brien, Connor Cruise, 81

O'Horgan, Tom, 127, 130, 141, 144-145, 148, 206, 208

O'Neill, Eugene, 9, 11, 14, 28, 31-32, 37-39, 81, 83, 136, 177, 184

O'Neill, James, 3-5

Octagon Theatre, 131

Odd Couple, The, 201

Odets, Clifford, 11, 15, 32

Odyssey Theatre Ensemble, 135

Off Off-Broadway Alliance, 156

Off-Broadway Incorporated, 34

Oh Dad Poor Dad..., 55

Oklahoma!, 19-20, 27, 30, 73, 100, 111, 218, 235

Old Glory, The, 56

Oleanna, 169

Oliver!, 27, 75, 81, 97, 179, 207

Olympia Theatre, 7

Omaha Magic Theatre, 136

On Golden Pond, 154

Once Upon a Mattress, 56

Open Theatre, 130-131, 134, 141-142, 159, 247

Operation Sidewinder, 162

Oregon Shakespeare Festival, 122

Organic Theatre Company, 135

Orpheus Descending, 188

Osborne, John, 49, 180

Our Town, 10, 86

Ouspenskaya, Maria, 21

Owens, Rochelle, 78, 145, 160

Pacific Overtures, 205

Pacino, Al, 23, 49, 64, 127, 133, 193

Page, Geraldine, 23, 36, 38

Pageant Players, 142, 144

Pajama Game, 179

Pal Joey, 19

Palace Theatre, 212

Palance, Jack, 49

Papp, Joseph, 46-49, 58-60, 86, 106, 129, 231, 247

Paradise Now, 137-139, 143-144

Pasadena Playhouse, 28, 69

Patinkin, Mandy, 152

Patrick, John, 183

Patrick, Robert, 81, 125, 171

Paul Kauver, 4

Paulding, J. K., 4

Pendleton, Austin, 174

People's Drama, 34

People's Theatre, 133

Perelman, S. J., 193

THE MUSICAL
A LOOK AT THE AMERICAN MUSICAL THEATER
by Richard Kislan
New, Revised, Expanded Edition

Richard Kislan examines the history, the creators, and the vital components that make up a musical and demonstrates as never before how musicals are made.

From its beginnings in colonial America, the musical theater has matured into an impressive art and business, one that has brought millions the experience that director-choreographer Bob Fosse describes as when "everybody has a good time even in the crying scenes."

Kislan traces the musical's evolution through the colorful eras of minstrels, vaudeville, burlesque, revue, and comic opera up to the present day. You'll learn about the lives, techniques, and contributions of such great 20th- century composers and lyricists as Jerome Kern, Rodgers an d Hammerstein, Stephen Sondheim and others. Kislan explains all the basic principles, materials and techniques that go into the major elements of a musical production—the book, lyrics, score, dance and set design.

Richard Kislan's acclaimed study of America's musical theatre has been updated to bring it up to the cutting edge of today's musicals. A new section entitled: Recent Musical Theater: Issues and Problems includes chapters on **The British Invasion** • **Competition from the Electronic Media** • **Escalating Costs** • **The Power of the Critics** • **The Depletion of Creative Forces** • **Multiculturalism** • **The Decline of the Broadway Neighborhood*** **Stephen Sondheim** and his influence on the present day musical theater.

Paper $16.95 • ISBN 1-55783-217-X

THE LONGEST LINE

BROADWAY'S MOST SINGULAR SENSATION: A CHORUS LINE

BY GARY STEVENS AND ALAN GEORGE

Relive the glory of A Chorus Line from behind the scenes, as told by one hundred twenty five artists and professionals who made it happen — cast and management; costume, lighting and sound designers; musicians, carpenters, box office and crew; advertising execs and press agents.

Here is the final authoritative record and celebration of Broadway's "Most Singular Sensation." But it is also the most detailed, in-depth portrait of any musical in Broadway history.

More than 300 photos
Cloth $45.00 ISBN: 1-55783-221-8

A CHORUS LINE

THE BOOK OF THE MUSICAL

The Complete Book and Lyrics of the Longest Running Show in Broadway History

"*A Chorus Line* is purely and simply **MAGNIFICENT, CAPTURING THE VERY SOUL OF OUR MUSICAL THEATER.**"   Martin Gottfried

Photos from the original production
Cloth $24.95 ISBN: 1-55783-131-9

ENVIRONMENTAL THEATER

by Richard Schechner

"There is an actual, living relationship between the spaces of the body and spaces the body moves through; human living tissue does not abruptly stop at the skin. Exercises with space are built on the assumption that human beings and space are both alive." **—From the Introduction**

Here are the exercises which began as radical departures from standard actor-training etiquette and which stand now as classic means through which the performer discovers his or her true power of transformation. Available for the first time in fifteen years, the new expanded edition of ENVIRONMENTAL THEATER offers a new generation of theatre artists the gospel according to Richard Schechner, the guru whose principles and influence have survived a quarter-century of reaction and debate.

This new edition features a new introduction about the influence of his work on American and European performance practice, as well as his classic 1968 essay, "Six Axioms for Environmental Theatre." The volume is richly illustrated with many previously unpublished photos of Schechner productions around the world.

1-55783-178-5 • $16.95

THE LIFE OF THE DRAMA
by Eric Bentley

". . . Eric Bentley's radical new look at the grammar of theatre . . . is a work of exceptional virtue, and readers who find more in it to disagree with than I do will still, I think, want to call it central, indispensable . . . The book justifies its title by being precisely about the ways in which life manifests itself in the theatre. If you see any crucial interest in such topics as the death of Cordelia, Godot's non-arrival . . . This is a book to be read and read again."

— Frank Kermode
THE NEW YORK REVIEW OF BOOKS

"*The Life of the Drama* . . . is a remarkable exploration of the roots and bases of dramatic art, the most far reaching and revelatory we have had."

— Richard Gilman
BOOK WEEK

"*The Life of the Drama* is Eric Bentley's magnum opus or the put it more modestly his best book. I might call it an aesthetic of the drama, but this again sounds ponderous; the book is eminently lucid and often helpfully epigrammatic. Everyone genuinely interested in the theatre should read it. It is full of remarkable insights into many of the most important plays ever written."

— Harold Clurman

paper • ISBN: 1-55783-110-6

THE END OF ACTING
by Richard Hornby

Acting in America has staggered to a dead end. Every year, tens of thousands of aspiring actors pursue the Hollywood grail and chant the familiar strains of the Stanislavski "Method" in classrooms and studios across the nation. The initial liberating spirit of Stanislavski's experiments long ago withered into rigid patterns of inhibitions and emotional introspection. Hornby urges the American theatre artist to emulate the average British actor who, he writes, is "more flexible, has a broader range, is more imaginative, and even has more emotional intensity than his American counterpart."

"**Passionate…provocative**…A clear, comprehensive book bound to be read with great interest by anyone concerned with the future of American acting …"

—VARIETY

"**Few theorists are this brave; even fewer are this able.**"
—William Oliver, CRITICISM

"This very important work is **an essential purchase…**"
—LIBRARY JOURNAL

"**Theatre lovers will find much to ponder** in his zingy restatement of a central argument about American acting."
—PUBLISHERS WEEKLY

paper • ISBN: 1-55783-213-7

DIRECTING THE ACTION
by Charles Marowitz

Every actor and director who enters the orbit of this major work will find himself challenged to a deeper understanding of his art and propelled into further realms of exploration. Marowitz mediates on all the sacred precepts of theater practice including auditions, casting, design, rehearsal, actor psychology, dramaturgy and the text.

Directing the Action yields a revised liturgy for all those who would celebrate a theatrical passion on today's stage. But in order to be a disciple in this order, the theater artist must be poised toward piety and heresy at once. Not since Peter Brook's The Empty Space has a major director of such international stature confronted the ancient dilemmas of the stage with such a determined sense of opportunity and discovery.

*"An energizing, uplifting work ... **reading Marowitz on theater is like reading heroic fiction in an age without heroes.**"*
—LOS ANGELES WEEKLY

*"A cogent and incisive collection of ideas, well formulated and clearly set forth; **an important contribution** on directing in postmodern theatre."*
—CHOICE

*"**Consistently thought-provoking** ... sure to be controversial."*
—LIBRARY JOURNAL

paper • ISBN: 1-55783-072-X

THE COLLECTED WORKS OF HAROLD CLURMAN

Six Decades of Commentary on Theatre, Dance, Music, Film, Arts, Letters and Politics

edited by Marjorie Loggia and Glenn Young

"...RUSH OUT AND BUY *THE COLLECTED WORKS OF HAROLD CLURMAN*...Editors Marjorie Loggia and Glenn Young have assembled a monumental helping of his work...**THIS IS A BOOK TO LIVE WITH;** picking it up at random is like going to the theater with Clurman and then sitting down with him in a good bistro for some exhilarating talk. This is a very big book, but Clurman was a very big figure."

JACK KROLL, *Newsweek*

"**THE BOOK SWEEPS ACROSS THE 20TH CENTURY,** offering a panoply of theater in Clurman's time... **IT RESONATES WITH PASSION.**"

MEL GUSSOW, *The New York Times*

CLOTH •ISBN 1-55783-132-7 PAPER • ISBN 1-55783-264-1

 APPLAUSE

Michael Caine • **William Goldman**
John Cleese • **Eric Bentley**
Oliver Stone • **John Patrick Shanley**
Cicely Berry • **John Russell Brown**
Paddy Chayefsky • **Steve Tesich**
Harold Clurman • **Sonia Moore**
Bruce Joel Rubin • **Janet Suzman**
Josef Svoboda • **Jerry Sterner**
Stephen Sondheim • **Larry Gelbart**

These Applause authors have their work available
in discerning bookshops across the country.

If you're having trouble tracking down an Applause title in your area,
we'll ship it to you direct! Write or call toll-free for our free catalog of
cinema and theatre titles.

When ordering an Applause title, include the price of the
book, $2.95 for the first book and $1.90 thereafter to cover shipping
(New York and Pennsylvania residents:
please include applicable sales tax).
Check/Mastercard/Visa/Amex

Send your orders to: **Applause Direct**
211 West 71st St
New York, NY 10023

Fax: 212-721-2856

Or order toll-free: 1-800-798-7787